Approaches to learning

Approaches to Learning
A Guide For Teachers

Anne Jordan
Orison Carlile
and Annetta Stack

 Open University Press

Open University Press
McGraw-Hill Education
McGraw-Hill House
Shoppenhangers Road
Maidenhead
Berkshire
England
SL6 2QL

email: enquiries@openup.co.uk
world wide web: www.openup.co.uk

and Two Penn Plaza, New York, NY 10121—2289, USA

First published 2008

A catalogue record of this book is available from the British Library

ISBN-10: 0-33-522670-1 (pb) 0-33-522671-X (hb)
ISBN-13: 978-0-33-522670-2 (pb) 978-0-33-522671-9 (hb)

Library of Congress Cataloging-in-Publication Data
CIP data applied for

Typeset by Kerrypress Ltd, Luton, Bedfordshire
Printed in the UK by Bell & Bain Ltd, Glasgow

Fictitious names of companies, products, people, characters and/or data that may be used herein (in case studies or in examples) are not intended to represent any real individual, company, product or event.

The McGraw·Hill Companies

We dedicate this book to our families.

Contents

List of figures   viii
List of tables   viii
Acknowledgements   xi

Introduction   1

1   Philosophy of education   6
2   Behaviourism   21
3   Cognitivism   36
4   Constructivism   55
5   Social learning   68
6   Cultural learning   82
7   Intelligence   97
8   Life course development   113
9   Adult learning   128
10 Values   142
11 Motivation   154
12 The learning body   169
13 Language and learning   184
14 Experiential and competency-based learning   199
15 Inclusivity   216
16 Blended learning   227
17 The future   242

Glossary   252

Figures

1.1	Philosophy and its educational implications	7
1.2	Aristotle's animating principles	16
2.1	Unconditional and conditional responses	22
2.2	A comparison of classical conditioning and Hull's theory	24
2.3	Reinforcement and punishment	25
2.4	An example of a learning outcome	32
3.1	Input-process-output model of brain processes	37
3.2	Perceptual categorization	39
3.3	Rabbit or duck?	40
3.4	Theories of selective attention	42
3.5	How experience is encoded	44
3.6	Modal model of memory	45
3.7	Working memory model	46
3.8	Associative network	48
5.1	Peer group effects on children	70
5.2	Reciprocal determinism	75
6.1	Culture as iceberg	83
7.1	The bell curve of normal distribution	102
7.2	IQ variance of men and women	106
8.1	Biological/maturational model of development	114
8.2	Bronfenbrenner's ecological model of development	115
9.1	Evolving terminology in adult education	129
11.1	Maslow's hierarchy of needs	156
12.1	The brain	173
14.1	Kolb's learning cycle	202
14.2	Skill, competence and competency	203
14.3	Role competence model	204
14.4	From potential to role competence	206
14.5	How to reflect	210
16.1	Waterfall model of software development	231
16.2	Hybrid ID model	232
16.3	Linear navigation	236
16.4	Non-linear navigation	236
16.5	Hierarchical navigation	237
16.6	Composite navigation	237

Tables

2.1	Key terms in classical conditioning	24
2.2	Key terms in operant conditioning	26
2.3	Bloom's cognitive domain	28
2.4	Bloom's affective domain	28
2.5	Bloom's psychomotor domain	29
2.6	Internal processes and their corresponding instructional events	30

3.1 Different types of memory systems — 44
4.1 Comparing behaviourism, cognitivism and constructivism — 55
4.2 Bruner's representational modes — 58
6.1 Assessing classroom culture using Hofstede's indices — 88
7.1 Twentieth-century definitions of intelligence — 97
7.2 Sample tasks from Binet and Simon's tests — 101
7.3 WISC subtest — 103
7.4 Factorial models of intelligence — 104
7.5 Gardner's multiple intelligences — 105
7.6 Curricular implications of intelligence theories — 107
7.7 Intelligence theories and classroom strategies — 108
8.1 Erikson's eight stages of psychosocial development — 117
8.2 Peck's stages of middle age — 117
8.3 Peck's stages of old age — 117
8.4 Kohlberg's theory of moral development — 118
8.5 Piaget's theory of cognitive development — 119
8.6 Piaget's and Vygotsky's theories of development: a comparison — 120
8.7 Biological and cognitive aspects of ageing — 121
8.8 Educational implications of Baxter Magolda's theory — 124
8.9 Educational implications of adult thinking — 125
10.1 Educational values and implications in twentieth-century England — 148
11.1 McGregor's X and Y theory — 158
11.2 Examples of motivational orientations — 159
12.1 Brain lobes and related responsibilities — 174
12.2 Left and right hemisphere cognitive mode specialization — 174
12.3 Stages of psychomotor development — 176
12.4 Left and right brain thinking — 180
13.1 Socio-cultural roles of language in relation to the curriculum — 184
13.2 Cognitive roles of language in relation to classroom activities — 185
13.3 Relationship between language and thinking — 189
13.4 Piaget's developmental stages: cognitive and linguistic development — 189
13.5 Phonic and whole-word method of reading — 195
14.1 The importance of experience in definitions of learning — 200
14.2 Theorists and experiential elements — 201
14.3 Bloom's taxonomies of learning — 205
14.4 Criteria for assessing reflective writing — 209
14.5 A constructively aligned approach to learning to drive — 212
14.6 Hard and soft transferable skills — 213
15.1 Simplified typology of disabilities — 216
15.2 Moving to inclusion: form of organization and reorganization — 222
16.1 Synchronous and asynchronous communication tools — 234

Acknowledgements

We would like to acknowledge the help of many people in the writing of this book. First, we are indebted to our editor Catherine Pratt for her thoroughness and acuity.

We would also like to acknowledge the assistance of Claire Marie Fanning who constructed the glossary and Rob Carlile who laboured over permissions and referencing.

Peter Jordan read chapters for us and made many helpful suggestions, and Celia Carlile gave us constant support.

We would like to thank our colleague Mary Fenton for the use of her house as a writing retreat, and our Heads of School and Department – Dolores Gilhooly, Paul Barry and Mícheál Ó hEigeartaigh at the Waterford Institute of Technology – for their support.

Finally, we would like to acknowledge the help of Willie Donnelly, Head of Research in WIT, for funding support.

We are truly grateful for all their help. We wish to acknowledge the following for permission to reproduce material within this book. Every effort has been made to contact copyright holders, but if any have been overlooked, we should be pleased to make the necessary arrangements at the first opportunity.

Figures:
Figure 5.3 BANDURA, ALBERT, SOCIAL FOUNDATIONS OF THOUGHT & ACTION: A SOCIAL COGNITIVE THEORY, 1st Edition, © 1986, Pg.24. Reprinted by permission of Pearson Education, Inc., Upper Saddle River, NJ.
Figure 14.1 Kolb, D. (1984). *Experiential Learning*. Englewood Cliffs, NJ: Prentice Hall.

Tables:
Table 7.3 Wood, C., Littleton, K. and Sheehy, K. (eds) Development Psychology in Action. Oxford: Blackwell Press and Open University Press. Copyright The Open University, Reproduced by kind permission.
Table 12.2 Rosenzweig, M. R., Breedlove, S.M. and Watson, N.V. (2005) Biological Psychology: An Introduction to Behavioural and Cognitive Neuroscience (4th edn.). Sunderland, MA: Sinauer Associates, Inc.

Introduction

This book aims to make life easier for educators by gathering together many of the theoretical approaches that inform the modern principles and practices of western education. Without sacrificing depth or rigour, it attempts to provide a lucid and succinct overview of these theoretical approaches, and considers their implications for policy and practice.

The authors are committed to the view that theory has many practical implications and to its value in supporting, confirming and optimizing best practice. This is expressed in the title *Approaches to Learning: A Guide for Teachers* which is deliberately ambitious.

Underlying the book is the maxim that there is 'nothing as practical as a good theory' (Lewin 1943: 35) and that educators base their professional practices on some aspects of theory, however derived.

Educational theory may be considered as the distilled experiences of others and the purpose of this book is to share the experience and conclusions of theorists who have thought deeply about the educational process.

Consciously or unconsciously, everyone holds theories of learning, since all action is based on assumptions which may or may not have been articulated or tested. We hope that this book will help educators to become aware of alternative views, so that they can clarify their own.

The educator's role as a facilitator of student learning is dependent upon the theory of learning held. The educator's views may form a coherent whole; alternatively they may hold scraps of incompatible theory. It is important not to have principles which clash, so bringing them to light will help in their organization so that they can be used more consciously to engage in ongoing inquiry.

A knowledge of theory gives the educator:

- insight into theoretical positions;
- access to the considered experience of others;
- validation and affirmation of existing practice;
- mind-tools for recognizing, analysing and evaluating issues;
- power to manipulate and develop concepts in a reflective manner;
- terminology to explore epistemological and pedagogical topics;
- shared educational discourse for engagement in the scholarship of teaching;
- justifications for personal teaching practices to colleagues and stakeholders;
- protection from unproven and faddish ideas.

There are many theories of education, drawn from a number of separate disciplines. This book places them side by side in order to make links and comparisons. It allows the educator to see areas of interest that can be pursued in relation to others, adding depth and balance to knowledge. With only a partial knowledge of theory there is a danger of becoming so committed to one theoretical approach that it shuts off consideration of others. For example, an educator may become so enamoured of popular 'discovery' or 'guided' methods of learning that they ignore the insights of theorists who claim that knowledge is appropriated and passed down from one generation to another. This makes it difficult to gain an objective view of the general direction of theory.

The book will be of value in pre-service, in-service teacher education, postgraduate studies, curriculum design and administration. It is an ideal introductory course text for university education and teacher training programmes. It can be read as a series of stand-alone chapters or as an integrated overview of theoretical perspectives drawn from philosophy, psychology, sociology and pedagogy that are useful in guiding educational principles and practice.

Since the text is an overview, it will stress the more important texts and theorists. References therefore will be to established sources rather than to cutting-edge research or findings which have not yet settled into general meta-theories.

Since this is an introductory text that covers a vast area, it is pitched at a level that can be understood easily. There are difficulties with simplifying complex philosophical arguments in some chapters – for example mind-body debates and the problem of consciousness in chapter 12 'The learning body'. However, despite the attempt at reasonably simple explanations, the text is well-referenced, so that interested readers can pursue topics in greater depth if they wish.

A number of key theorists such as Vygotsky have different dimensions to their work, and are viewed from different perspectives in different chapters so the student will obtain a multi-faceted view with the bonus of revision to embed the material in the memory. By the end of the book it is hoped that readers will have a nuanced and balanced understanding of the theories presented.

Education can be construed according to a number of dimensions, and each chapter will tend to emphasize one set of dimensions over others, although the most obvious dimension of learning and teaching will appear in every chapter. Other dimensions are those of:

- behaviour – thinking;
- individual – society;
- adult-centred – child-centred;
- process – outcome;
- institution – learner.

This book originates from a specific context of western education policy and practice, particularly of the English speaking world. Most of our examples and references therefore are to English or North American education.

We use the term 'learner' when referring to individual learners and their cognitive processes. We use the term 'pupils' or 'students' when referring to them in relation to the teacher or the classroom.

Each chapter contains:

- an accessible introduction to relevant theories;
- critical insights drawn from the theories discussed;
- a summary of key ideas;
- examples and illustrations drawn from contemporary research and practice;
- bulleted lists of points made;
- practical implications for educationalists.

Chapter 1, 'Philosophy of education', considers the development of western learning theories in the light of educational philosophy. The major paradigms discussed are those of idealism, empiricism and development. The chapter traces the philosophical underpinnings of teaching strategies such as reflective questioning, problem-solving and critical thinking.

Chapter 2, 'Behaviourism', provides an account of behaviourist learning theory and its influence upon learning and teaching. It presents an overview of behaviourism's main constructs and it considers the role of behaviourism in current learning and teaching strategies.

Chapter 3, 'Cognitivism', presents a succinct account of theories of cognitive information-processing. It discusses the five processes involved in cognition – sensation, perception, attention, encoding and memory and outlines their implications for the learning process. The chapter also offers advice to learners and teachers on how to enhance learning capability.

Chapter 4, 'Constructivism', is not one, but an amalgam of theories which emphasize meaning-making. Three perspectives of constructivism are discussed: trivial constructivism and individual meaning-making; social constructivism, which emphasizes collaborative meaning-making; and critical constructivism, which considers the construction of meaning as empowerment. The chapter concludes with the implications of constructivist theory for educators.

Chapter 5, 'Social learning', considers the role of society in learning. Social learning is examined from two perspectives. The sociological perspective explores ways in which societal structures influence the learning of social roles. The psychological perspective outlines the ways that social identities are formed and considers the relationship between identity, self-esteem and self-efficacy.

Chapter 6, 'Cultural learning', explores the ways in which culture influences learning. This chapter considers theories about the cultural determination and expression of meaning, and outlines the educational implications of these theories.

Chapter 7, 'Intelligence', outlines the concept of intelligence and presents a number of traditional and modern definitions and their justifications. This includes an examination of the use of intelligence testing for educational selection purposes, and concludes by drawing out other learning and teaching implications.

Chapter 8, 'Life course development', deals with changes and development over the life course. Three models are outlined, each of which takes a different perspective on learning and development. A number of developmental theories are examined which contrast holistic, psychosocial and moral theories with cognitive ones. The final section considers the key issues discussed and outlines their teaching and learning implications.

Chapter 9, 'Adult learning', provides an explanation of the terminology associated with adult education and learning. It outlines the history of adult education before analysing some areas of contemporary interest, including access, power and the rise of instrumentalism. Finally it sets out some implications for learning and teaching practices in the education of adults.

Chapter 10, 'Values', explores the value of education as an instrument in achieving the goals of society and the individual. The chapter also discusses the policies and goals of educators and the ways that values shape practice. The values of educators in shaping the curriculum are discussed in the final part of the chapter.

Chapter 11, 'Motivation', outlines how motivation theories affect learning. This chapter traces the evolution of motivation theory and discusses motivation from the perspectives of content and process. This chapter concludes with the practical implications of motivational theories for teaching and learning.

Chapter 12, 'The learning body', presents individuals as embodied learners. The chapter draws on a range of disciplines to argue that learning is not simply a function of the mind, but is inherently physical. The physical environment and physiological needs of learners are explored and the chapter concludes by addressing the teaching and learning implications of the theories presented.

Chapter 13, 'Language and learning', considers the significance of language in thinking and learning. It investigates language development from a number of different perspectives, including its role in reproducing societal advantage. The chapter concludes with suggestions for enhancing linguistic and communicative strategies in the classroom.

Chapter 14, 'Experiential and competency-based learning', examines theories of experiential learning, and skill and competence acquisition. The first section of the chapter presents the ideas of key experiential theorists. The second section outlines a framework for the development of competence-based learning. The chapter concludes with the practical implications of these theories for teaching and learning.

Chapter 15, 'Inclusivity', presents an overview of the historical constructs of disability. The chapter discusses two current discourses of disability, the deficit and the inclusivity models, together with their justifications, and indicates the stance adopted by the authors. It evaluates the educational consequences stemming from both discourses and points to a compromise position.

Chapter 16, 'Blended learning', begins by defining and distinguishing the terms blended learning and computer-based learning. The chapter outlines the development of relevant theories and their current use in online collaborative learning systems.

Chapter 17, 'The future', considers three major transformations occurring in modern society – individualization, the network society and globalization, and identifies significant trends and implications for education, together with some strategies for educators.

References

Lewin, K. (1943) Forces behind food habits and methods of change, *Bulletin of the National Reseach Council,* 108: 35–65.

Chapter 1 Philosophy of education

Introduction

Some people think that the philosophy of education is the most important aspect of teacher training. Others claim it is so far removed from classroom practice that it is a waste of time. This chapter begins by explaining the value of educational philosophy before identifying three major philosophical categories – ideas, experience and development – under which the work of some key theorists is grouped as shown in Figure 1.1. We also outline the educational implications and consequences of these categories and theorists.

The philosophy of education is important because it explains how educational theories arise. By examining the philosophy of education, we are able to see why and how theories complement or oppose each other. An understanding of philosophy is therefore useful in guiding and critiquing the development of educational theory. Philosophical knowledge may provide a justification for teaching methodologies; reveal and challenge assumptions about the nature of teaching; and provide a language for educational debate.

Finally, philosophy is vital for the promotion of teaching as a scholarly and professional activity. Education has only recently been recognized as a subject in its own right. Many educational theories are drawn from other disciplines, and a philosophy of education can provide a pedagogical history of ideas, theories and vocabulary. It helps to place the educational discipline on a similar philosophical footing to other disciplines through the establishment of a distinct discourse and rationale.

Key definitions in educational philosophy

The philosophy of education can be defined as the study of the purposes, processes, nature and ideals of education.

The word 'education' derives from one or both of the following concepts:

- 'Educare' – to draw out and realize potential;
- 'Educere' – to bring up and nurture.

Both of these concepts merge in Kant's famous claim that the purpose of education is to enable humanity to develop and to improve: 'Man can only become man by education' (Kant 1803/1960: 6).

Education attempts to develop personality in a preferred direction. 'Educare' and 'educere' come together here, because 'development' indicates growth and the 'preferred direction' indicates a specific direction for that growth to occur.

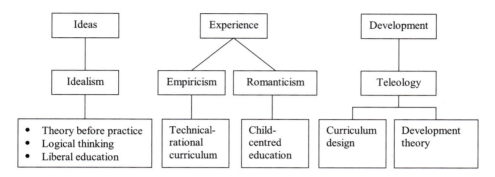

Figure 1.1 Philosophy and its educational implications.

Ideas

This category of western thought claims that ideas are more important than, and take precedence over experiences. Ideas are universal unchanging, and act as the template and organizing framework for experience. From this flows a view of education as the acquisition of the mental training necessary to comprehend ideas. This view is meritocratic – only those capable of abstract thought can benefit from such training.

Idealism

The philosophical doctrine that stems from the category of thought associated with ideas is 'idealism' – the notion that ideas represent reality. Idealism originates with Plato, the third-century BC thinker, who believed that there is an objective truth, expressed through the unchanging world of the 'Forms'. These Forms were originally proposed by Plato's mentor Socrates, who wrote nothing himself, but who featured in a series of dialogues written by Plato. In these, Socrates engages in discussions with Athenian citizens, drawing out their ideas on virtue.

For Socrates, ideas exist prior to experience in two ways: they are more important, and they are already in existence. In the Socratic dialogues, Socrates gives the example of the slave boy who had no knowledge of geometry but was able to understand a theorem drawn in the sand. He claims that the boy already possessed this knowledge in some way, and was 'remembering' it (Weiss 2001). Socrates believed that there were objective mathematical truths and more important still, truths about virtue.

A belief in the objective truth of ideas was a rejection of the Sophists' position that truth was relative. The Sophists were paid teachers of argument who saw two sides (at least) to every argument and believed that individuals simply needed help to present their own sides convincingly. For example, stealing is good for a burglar but bad for a householder. Another reason for Plato's commitment to the world of ideas is the unreliability of the senses. In his dialogue, the *Theaetus*, he shows that the world of experience is misleading, transient and personal, with the same object appearing white at one time and grey at another.

Plato's thinking has significant implications for ideas about education and knowledge. According to Plato, to be morally good is to possess true knowledge. But the process of acquiring true knowledge is painful, because most of us are chained to the world of the senses, unable to look beyond. Clear-sightedness and knowledge involves overcoming prejudice and ignorance after rigorous mental and ideological training (*Republic Bk VII*).

The elevation of mental over physical activity or experience reappears in the writings of the French seventeenth-century philosopher René Descartes. Descartes is famous for the dualism he proposed between the mind and the body – the claim that the mind and body are separate entities, with only the mind in touch with ultimate reality. The body inhabits the gross world of physical sensation and is controlled by the mind, just as the automatons that Descartes saw in the Royal Gardens at St Germaine in Paris were controlled by water.

Descartes' thinking was similar to Plato's. For both, ideas are in the mind and the senses are deceptive. Descartes proposed a method of 'systematic doubt' in which everything in the universe was to be questioned until he came to something he could not doubt. By this means he arrived at his famous principle, 'Cogito ergo sum' – 'I think, therefore I am'. The philosopher cannot doubt that he is thinking; therefore his existence is proven. Having established one certainty, Descartes proceeded, by a sequence of logical deductions, to establish the existence of the universe.

Plato and Descartes illustrate the main characteristics of idealist thought, and their ideas were instrumental in shaping the 'problem of knowledge' – how do we know what we know? What is the role of the senses? Is everything we know in the mind?

Idealism has three main implications for education:

- an emphasis on theory before practice;
- an emphasis on logical thinking;
- a high value attached to liberal education.

Theory before practice

The principle that education should concentrate solely on conceptual and moral development is an educational legacy of idealism. Teaching should deal with abstract subjects such as mathematics and philosophy, with principles expounded before application. The teacher's role is to draw out the knowledge of principles that learners already possess and help learners to organize these coherently. In this view of education, teachers are very important.

Teachers are also needed for the clarification of ideas, because texts alone are insufficient. In the *Phaedrus*, Socrates maintains that the written word is subject to misinterpretation by readers. Dialogue is preferable because the teacher can offer clarification or challenge misinterpretations, guiding learners towards true principles and away from faulty conclusions.

An example of Socratic questioning

In Book I of *The Republic* (37), the Sophist Thrasymachus claims that 'justice is the advantage of the stronger'. Socrates questions him about this. Here is a simplified version of their dialogue.

Socrates:	Do you think it is just to obey all laws?
Thrasymachus:	Yes. Laws are made by the stronger for their advantage so it is just to obey all laws.
Socrates:	Does a ruler sometimes make mistakes when making laws?
Thrasymachus:	Yes. Sometimes he may make a law that is not to his advantage.
Socrates:	Because it is just to obey all laws, is it therefore sometimes just to obey laws that are not to the advantage of the ruler?
Thrasymachus:	Yes.

(Plato *The Republic* 335 a–d)

Here Socrates has led Thrasymachus to contradict himself. Justice both is and is not to the advantage of the stronger.

Socratic or dialogic questioning provides not only a useful classroom technique but a basic justification of the teacher's role. In recent times, there has been a renewed interest in teacher questioning and classroom discussion as an aid to students' acquisition of concepts. For example, the UK 'Thinking Together' programme for primary school children aims to develop critical thinking through appropriate questioning by peers and teachers (Dawes et al. 2000). Even in distance or online learning contexts, it is important to create a learning environment that allows for the possibility of multiple interpretations in order to guide learners towards a better understanding of concepts.

Theory before practice: educational implications

- Theoretical subjects are valued more than practical ones in the curriculum.
- Learners' previous ideas are established.
- Misconceptions are challenged.
- Ideas are organized in a subject outline.
- General theories are extracted from examples.
- Theory is presented and then tested.
- General principles are emphasized over particular examples.
- Learning is guided through dialogue and questioning.

- Understanding ideas is emphasized over their memorization.

Logical thinking

Logical thinking is the second educational legacy of idealism. Dialogical approaches such as those used by Plato led to logical thinking and the rules that were laid down by Plato's successor, Aristotle. Some of Aristotle's most important rules concern concept formation and deductive reasoning. Deductive reasoning progresses from the general case to the particular case by logical inference. Aristotle (1995) offers a well-known example in a three-step argument called a syllogism:

1. Major premise – all men are mortal.
2. Minor premise – Socrates is a man.
3. Conclusion – Socrates is mortal.

These ideas are the bases of mathematical and geometrical theorem construction. They allow us to explain why some arguments are faulty as a result of incorrect relationships between premises and their conclusions. Aristotle's rules have had other applications too. For example, in order to evaluate argument, Aristotle classified different types of false reasoning and fallacies. These include reasoning in which argument is swayed by appeals to emotion or by threats. A public demonstration of the rules of argument still survives in the 'viva voce' or defence of the PhD thesis, which developed in the Middle Ages.

Logical and analytical thinking has regained importance in late twentieth-century education. The 'Thinking Skills' and the associated 'Philosophy for Children' movements attempted to incorporate critical thinking and logic into the school curriculum (Lipman et al. 1980).

Descartes' thinking has also had implications for contemporary education. For example, systematic doubt became a forerunner of empiricism and the western scientific method, and is particularly important in defences of higher education whose role is to develop sceptical, critical and independent thinkers.

Logical thinking: educational implications

- Critical thinking is encouraged in schools.
- Scepticism is a valued academic stance.
- Educators search for a range of analytical tools.
- Convergent and divergent thinking are developed as part of education.
- Intellectual freedom and freedom of speech are prized by academic institutions.
- Thinking is promoted as a generic transferable skill.

Liberal education

Aristotle claimed that the good life can be achieved through an education in the liberal arts, where knowledge is valued for its own sake and is its own reward. This is the third educational legacy of idealism. A liberal education is devoted to the study of first principles, or theoretical ideas, because humanity's goal is to acquire knowledge.

Aristotle's reasons for the promotion of liberal education were not related to the mind alone. A liberal or free education consists of subjects suitable for the free citizen, and includes literature and the arts which develop the whole person. Newman claims that a liberal education promotes the attributes of freedom, equitableness, calmness, moderation and wisdom – in short, a philosophical habit of mind (Heath 1959). On the contrary, 'illiberal subjects' like trades and skills 'absorb and degrade the mind' and are only suitable for slaves and wage-earners. Therefore, no subject should be included in the curriculum simply because of its vocational value.

Cartesian mind–body dualism has also influenced curriculum design in the past; some subjects have been valued above others because of their emphasis on ideas and the mind, at the expense of experience and the body. For example, the curriculum in the English grammar school and the German gymnasium reflected an elitist preference for the theoretical and cerebral above the practical and physical.

The role of the liberal education teacher or curriculum designer is to introduce learners to the finest exemplars of thought from all ages. For Hirst (1965), a British educationalist, the curriculum must initiate the learner into all the major forms of thought. The curriculum should therefore be broad and wide-ranging. Even when the overall concept of a liberal education was under attack from narrow vocationalists in the twentieth century, it survived in a subject called Liberal Studies, taught as part of further and higher education.

Liberal education: educational implications

- Education is valued for its own sake rather than for its usefulness.
- A balanced curriculum is necessary to develop the whole person intellectually and morally.
- Some subjects are more highly valued than others – for example, the arts and humanities are valued over vocational subjects.
- Liberal education introduces learners to a range of disciplines and ways of thinking.
- Teaching is a complex human activity demanding personal characteristics and insight.
- Debate and discussion are encouraged in liberal classrooms.

Experience

The second major category of western thought identified in this chapter claims that experience is more significant than theory. Learning involves either 'doing' or being 'done to'.

This category is split into two philosophical strands: empiricism and romanticism. Empiricists claim that the learner is the passive recipient of experience. What matters is the way this experience is organized. This perspective leads to a technical conception of education, in which teachers and curriculum developers are important arrangers of appropriate experiences.

Diametrically opposed is the romanticist claim that formal education is unnecessary and restrictive. Children learn naturally from their experiences and from contact with key influences.

Empiricism

The view that all knowledge is gained from the senses came to prominence in the seventeenth century, when the English philosopher John Locke in his *Essay Concerning Human Understanding* argued that 'there is nothing in the mind which was not first in the senses' (Smith et al. 2004). In this view, the mind is a blank slate on which experiences are imprinted. According to Locke, all primary and secondary ideas, including abstract ideas, come either from the senses or the mind's reflections on sensory experience.

The eighteenth-century empiricist David Hume in his *Enquiry Concerning Human Understanding* (Hume 1739/2007) developed Locke's argument. In establishing a science of human nature, Hume attempted to rely solely on the evidence of the senses and experience. He denied the existence of any ideas which did not come from experience, including those of God, the self, causation and inductive knowledge. Concerning causation, he said that all we perceive from our experience is a regular association between two events. We cannot prove that one event is the cause of another. Using the same argument, Hume attacked the principle of induction – the process of inferring from particular cases to general rules, the basis of the scientific experimental method.

According to the empiricists, for a statement to be valid it must either be true by definition or it must be open to verification by experience. A.J. Ayer, a twentieth-century empiricist, endorsed this view. He classified valid statements as either analytic or synthetic.

Analytic: Verifiable by analysing the meaning of the words: 'A bachelor is an unmarried man.'

Synthetic: Verifiable by empirical observation: 'The heart contains four chambers.'

He dismissed statements on ethics, aesthetics, and theology as mere value judgements (Ayer 1952).

A compromise between idealism and empiricism is found in the theory of knowledge proposed by the eighteenth-century German philosopher Immanuel Kant. According to this theory, the world consists of:

- *Noumena* – representing ultimate reality and unknowable, but giving rise to mental organizing structures or categories;
- *Phenomena* – things as they appear to us, structured by the mental categories that organize our perceptions.

(Körner 1955: 91)

This solution avoids both mind–body dualism and the problem of causality. Kant's intermediate view suggests that the mind structures experience, as spectacles structure sight. Twentieth-century thinkers such as Noam Chomsky (1975) show their debt to Kantian theory when they claim that the grammatical structures of language are innate, but vocabulary and word usage are learned from experience.

Educational implications of empiricism: the technical-rational model

Empiricism leads to the commonplace view of education as the 'filling of empty vessels' – that is, imparting knowledge to those who lack it. It requires nothing from the learner but passivity and a willingness to learn.

This view emerges in the work of nineteenth-century experimental psychologists such as Pavlov, whose behaviourist argument is presented in Chapter 2, 'Behaviourism'. The emphasis on the careful structuring of stimuli and the observation of learners' responses led to the behaviourist concept of a 'technology of education'. Behaviourism was highly influential in education in the first part of the twentieth century, especially in the area of training and competencies. Its curricular approach was 'technical–rational' or 'means–end' because it prioritized technical questions about the correct approach to methods over a consideration of the ends of education. Behaviourist learning theory was most strongly endorsed in the former USSR and the US– countries with strong traditions of experimental psychology.

The American educationalist Benjamin Bloom expanded on the technical–rational model (Bloom and Krathnohl 1956). His Cognitive Taxonomy of Learning specifies different levels of knowledge (from knowledge, the lowest, to evaluation, the highest) and shows how they can be demonstrated in observable and verifiable behaviours, rather than in mental acts:

1. knowledge – demonstrated in outlining, recounting, defining and enumerating ideas;
2. comprehension – demonstrated in paraphrasing, recognizing, illustrating and explaining ideas;
3. application – demonstrated in transferring, employing and organizing ideas;
4. analysis – demonstrated in breaking down, categorizing, comparing and contrasting ideas;
5. synthesis – demonstrated in summarizing, generalizing about, integrating and constructing ideas and arguments;
6. evaluation – demonstrated in appraising, discriminating between and assessing ideas or resolving problems and arguments.

Educational implications of the technical–rational model

*   Learning is a science and has general principles.
*   The teacher or designer determines what is learned and how, according to scientific principles.

- The purposes or ends of education are not discussed; values are taken for granted.
- The learner will respond to learning stimuli in a predictable way.
- The technical–rational model works best in the training of skills and competencies, where behaviour can be observed.

Romanticism

Romanticism emerged in the eighteenth century to provide an alternative perspective on the role of experience in learning. Jean-Jacques Rousseau was romanticism's strongest proponent in what is often called its first didactic text. *Émile,* published in 1762(/2007) deals with the proper education for a boy. For Rousseau gender was biologically determined, and he thought that a different education process was necessary for girls, as shown in *Émile et Sophie ou les Solitaires* (1780/1994), the sequel to *Émile.*

According to Rousseau, humans are naturally good but corrupted by civilization. Therefore, the child should be kept away from society and learn through exposure to natural influences – for example, if the child breaks a window, they should suffer the consequences of the cold wind that will rush through. Rousseau thought that formal learning, such as that acquired through reading or mathematics, should be delayed until the moral and psychological foundations of personality had been laid down through interaction with the natural world. Girls should learn to be the primary educators of children in the private and moral sphere, whereas boys should learn to carry out their public responsibilities in the wider world.

Romanticism also attached importance to the emotions and therefore to the education of the whole person. This included the cultivation of feeling and an emphasis on the individual, as opposed to the group. It encouraged self-expression and self-actualization. 'Senses and feeling were primary; thought and abstraction were to be at their service' (Noddings 2007: 15).

Educational implications of romanticism: child-centred education

Unlike the technical–rational model, which places the teacher at the centre of the educational process, romanticism is child-centred. Rousseau's text *Émile* was the foundation for many current theories of child-centred education. For example:

- Steiner teaching methods emphasize an education that balances head, heart and hands (Easton 1997).
- Montessori methods of infant teaching emphasize learning through natural materials and natural environments (Montessori 1912).
- A. S. Neill's experiment with progressive education in his famous school, Summerhill, emphasized the natural goodness of the child and the rejection of all compulsory tuition in favour of the child's right to choose what and what not to learn (Neill 1992).

The modern western emphasis on recognizing and encouraging differences in individuals can be seen as originating in Rousseau's theory.

Educational implications of child-centred education

- The purpose of education is the development of the whole person.
- The child's experiences are the central elements of education.
- Children should be free to choose what to learn and how to learn.
- Individual experiences, expression and creativity are encouraged as part of the curriculum.
- Individual learning plans can be used to recognize the unique characteristics of every child.
- All learners are different, and their individuality is unconditionally prized.
- Teachers exert minimal control but act as facilitators of learning experiences.
- The teacher provides an appropriate and rich environment.

Development

Before the twentieth century, development, the third category of western thought, was attached to philosophy rather than psychology, the discipline with which it is more commonly associated. Development is shaped by the idea that human growth involves the unfolding of some innate human, cognitive or biological potential towards a final destination. Education consists of providing the conditions favourable to the full expression of this development.

To understand the relationship between development and education, think of the metaphor of the seed, which will grow to its full potential in an enriched environment or fail to thrive because of a lack of proper nutrients. This idea is common to many school mission statements, which often state 'We will help every child to achieve his or her potential'. How that potential is identified is another matter.

Teleology

The philosophical strand that emerges from the development category is teleology, the study of purposes, which has its origins in Aristotelian thinking. Aristotle was the first major thinker to consider the development of natural organisms. He was a materialist, interested in studying natural and biological processes. In particular, he wanted to know what things were for and their function or 'goodness' – he was interested in their teleology.

Aristotle was conscious of the development of living things as a process, characterized by stages from seed or embryo to plant or animal. He identified three types of animating principles, or 'souls', in living things. These are cumulative, with higher souls incorporating the characteristics of lower ones (see Figure 1.2).

Living things develop according to their animating principles and natures. For example, Aristotle saw human nature as made up of:

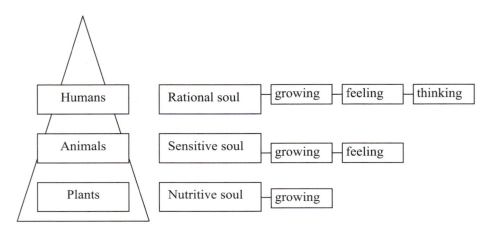

Figure 1.2 Aristotle's animating principles.

- an 'irrational' element, shared with the animal kingdom and concerned with bodily appetites and passions;
- a rational, cognitive element, unique to humans and capable of governing the irrational elements.

In humanity, the highest and most fulfilling form of human activity is directed towards the acquisition of knowledge and rationality: 'All human beings by nature desire to know' (Aristotle 1995). There is another aspect of rationality, however – moral goodness. Humans seek happiness as their ultimate goal, and happiness is achieved only through the rational pursuit of the virtuous life. For Aristotle, the acquisition of knowledge and the achievement of happiness are two sides of the same coin.

The ends or purposes of human development are determined, but the methods of achieving these purposes are not. Rather, they involve activities that need to be controlled and learned. Nature, habit and reason are three equally important forces that need to be cultivated through education, according to Aristotle (*Politics*). One of the primary tasks of the educator is to train the young to control the irrational part of their natures and achieve self-discipline. Aristotle considered repetition very important as part of this aspect of learning. For example, the essence of moral behaviour is in following the right rule, and the ability to do so depends on forming the right habit. Similarly, intellectual qualities such as rationality are produced through teaching that develops the facility to recognize the right scientific or ethical principle in any given situation. Aristotle also thought it was important to balance the theoretical, practical and imaginative parts of nature so, unlike Plato, he endorsed play and leisure as part of liberal education: 'There are branches of learning and education which we must study merely with a view to leisure spent in intellectual activity, and these are to be valued for their own sake' (*Politics*).

Educational implications of teleological thinking: curriculum design

Aristotelian thinking has been influential in curriculum design. Because people are driven by the desire to achieve various ends, it is important for the curriculum (in Latin, the course for a chariot race) to set clear aims and objectives. The technical–rational model of curriculum planning focuses on teaching objectives or outcomes and on appropriate instructional techniques to achieve them. This is in accord with Aristotle's interest in aims or ends and their achievement.

Implications for curriculum design

- Students need to know why they are learning a topic.
- Students are motivated by goals.
- Goals or learning outcomes should be used to indicate what students will be able to do on completion of the learning.
- Goals may need to be manufactured through assessment.
- Goal-matching, where student goals are aligned to teaching goals, is an efficient motivator.

Educational implications of teleological thinking: development theory

In the modern era, developmental theories have become attached to the modern discipline of psychology. One of the most significant thinkers in this area was the Swiss developmental theorist Jean Piaget who, like Aristotle, was highly influenced by biology. According to his theory of cognitive development discussed in Chapter 4, 'Constructivism' and Chapter 8, 'Life course development', children progress through several identifiable, pre-determined stages in their intellectual growth. Piaget's contemporary, the Russian psychologist Lev Vygotsky, while agreeing that there are identifiable stages, disagreed about their determined nature. This is discussed in Chapter 8, 'Life course development'.

Key ideas

- The philosophy of education studies the purposes, processes, nature and ideals of education.
- The philosophy of education explains how educational theories arise, and how they complement or oppose each other.

- Idealism holds that ideas represent ultimate reality so theory precedes practice and conceptual organization is paramount
- Empiricism and romanticism stress the significance of experience so learning is natural – but requiring the provision of experiences.
- Development philosophies emphasize the purpose of human activity and the nature of such development.
- The purposes of education are articulated and expressed at a practical level through the curriculum.

Conclusions

In considering the value of the philosophy of education, you might find it helpful to consider the benefits that educational philosophy offers to the field of education generally, as well as to the educational profession and the individual educator.

In the educational field, the philosophy of education:

- shows that opposing positions such as idealism and empiricism are defensible;
- enables us to consider the origin and provenance of educational practices;
- provides a language for educational discourse and debate;
- presents well thought-out arguments for different theoretical stances;
- challenges faulty argument, superficial debate and educational fads;
- provides a source of alternative ideas to challenge prevailing orthodoxies;
- analyses education's aims, roles and methods.

For the education profession, the philosophy of education:

- justifies educational practices;
- contributes to the scholarship of teaching;
- provides education with deep intellectual roots;
- links educators with a tradition of educational discourse;
- facilitates argument and debate;
- helps develop evaluative and critical thinking.

For the individual educator, the philosophy of education:

- enriches and deepens personal experience;
- gives intellectual credence to instinctive or intuitive practice;
- provides pleasure in the exploration of educational ideas;
- provides intellectual backing for educational views;
- facilitates open-mindedness by presenting alternative perspectives.

Therefore, philosophy forms an important part of every educator's education.

References

Aristotle (1981) *The Politics* (Rev ed. T.J. Saunders), London: Penguin Classics.

Aristotle (1995) *Selections* (trans. T. Irwin and G. Fine 1955). Indianapolis: Hackett Publishing Company, Inc.

Ayer, A. J. (1952) *Language, Truth and Logic*. New York: Dover Publications.

Bloom, B. and Krathnohl, D. (1956) *Taxonomy of Educational Objectives: The Classification of Educational Goals By a Committee of College and University Examiners. Handbooks 1 to 3*. New York: Longmans Green.

Chomsky, N. (1975) *The Logic Structure of Linguistic Theory*. New York: Plenum.

Dawes, L., Mercer, N. and Wegerif, R. (2000) *Thinking Together: A Programme of Activities for Developing Thinking Skills at KS2*. Birmingham: The Questions Publishing Company Ltd.

Easton, F. (1997) Educating the whole child, 'head, heart and hands': Learning from the Waldorf Experience, *Theory into Practice*, 36(2): 87–94.

Heath, D. (1959) Liberal education: John Henry Newman's conception, *Educational Theory*, 9(3): 152–5.

Hirst, P. (1965) Liberal education and the nature of knowledge, in R.D. Archambault (ed.) *Philosophical Analysis and Education*. London: Routledge.

Hume, D. (1739/2007) *A Treatise of Human Nature*. Sioux Falls: NuVision Publications.

Kant, I. (1803/1960) *Education* (trans. A. Churston). Arbor, MA: The University of Michigan Press.

Körner, S. (1955) *Kant*. London: Penguin Books.

Lipman, M., Sharp, A. and Oscanyan, F. (1980) *Philosophy in the Classroom*. Princeton, NJ: Temple University Press.

Miller, J. (1984) *Rousseau: Dreamer of Democracy*. London: Yale University Press.

Montessori, M. (1912) The Montessori Method, *Scientific Pedagogy as Applied to Child Education in 'the Children's Houses'* trans. Anne E. George New York: Frederick Stokes Company MCMXII.

Mulcahy, D. (1972) Cardinal Newman's Concept of a Liberal Education, *Educational Theory*, 22(1): 87–98.

Neill, A.S. (1992) *Summerhill School: A New View of Childhood*, A. Lamb (ed.). New York: St Martin's Press.

Noddings, N. (2007) *Philosophy of Education* (2nd edn). Colorado, CA: Westview Press.

Plato (1968) *The Republic* (trans. B. Jowett). Massachusetts: Airmont Publishing.

Rousseau, J. (1762/1991), *Émile* or *On Education*. Allan Bloome ed. London: Penguin.

Rousseau, J. J. (1780/1994) *Émile et Sophie ou Les Solitaires*. Paris: Rivages.

Russell, B. (1912/1959) *The Problems of Philosophy*. Home University Library: Oxford University Press.

Smith, J., Clark, K., and Lints, R. (2004) *101 Key Terms in Philosophy and their Importance for Theology*. Westminster: John Knox Press.

Stewart, D. (1993) Teaching or facilitating: a false dichotomy, *Canadian Journal of Education,* 18(1): 1–13.

Weiss, R. (2001) Virtue in the Cave, Moral Inquiry in Plato's Meno. Oxford: Oxford University Press.

Chapter 2   Behaviourism

Introduction

Whenever a mobile phone rings on any bus or train, people scramble to check whether it's theirs. This is a clear example of a near-automatic response to a stimulus. It illustrates perfectly one of the fundamental laws underlying behaviourism – the crucial bond between stimulus and response.

Behaviourism is the most influential and generalizable theory of learning that claims a scientific basis. This is because, like the most useful theories in any field, it is universal and underpinned by only a few principles. As its name suggests, it concentrates on behavioural changes in organisms. Thus, behaviourists define learning as a relatively permanent change in behaviour as the result of experience. This change in behaviour is always observable, with some behaviourists proposing that if no observable change happens, no learning has occurred. Although behaviourists do not deny that learners think, they mainly choose to ignore inaccessible mental processes and focus on observable behaviour. The use of animals in early behaviourist experiments, which confined observations to external behaviour, may have reinforced the behaviourist exclusion of cognitive activity.

Although there are problems with the behaviourist avoidance of any discussion of mental activity, the theory has nevertheless led to a more critical interest in what learners can be seen to do in order to learn. Moreover, some later behaviourists have acknowledged cognitive activity by stressing the importance of expectation and motivation within the learning process.

The development of behaviourism

Classical conditioning

Behaviourism had its origins in the last years of the nineteenth century, when physiologists such as Ivan Pavlov investigated animals' automatic and involuntary responses to stimuli (Pavlov 1927). Classical behaviourists believe that all learning conforms to observable scientific laws governing behavioural associations and patterns; the learner simply responds to external stimuli in a deterministic manner.

Figure 2.1 illustrates Pavlov's classic experiments with dogs which are well known. Pavlov noted that the smell of food caused dogs to salivate. This is an 'unconditional response' because the dogs reacted naturally to the food (the 'unconditional stimulus'). Pavlov began ringing a bell (a 'conditional stimulus') immediately prior to providing the food, and discovered that after a certain number of repetitions,

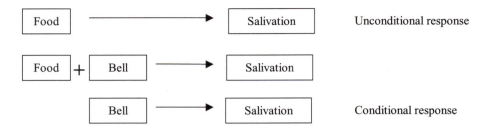

Figure 2.1 Unconditional and conditional responses.

the bell alone was sufficient to cause salivation. This is a 'conditional' or trained response and needs to occur contiguously, or close in time, to the unconditional.

When the conditional stimulus (the bell) is repeatedly presented without the associated unconditional stimulus (the food), the conditional response (salivation) declines until it is non-existent. This is called 'extinction'. The principle of conditional response underpins the behaviour modification called 'classical conditioning', which is at the heart of behaviourism. Behaviourists tend to use the term 'conditioning' instead of 'learning' to indicate that the subject is changed by external rather than cognitive events.

The theory of classical conditioning can be used to explain how people learn a variety of involuntary responses, especially those associated with physiological functioning or the emotions. For example, most people experience darkness as an unconditional stimulus for going to sleep; therefore, in particular environmental settings, darkness may elicit a 'go-to-sleep' response. Classical conditioning is also useful for explaining the development of fears and phobias. For example, a person who is bitten by a dog may become afraid of that breed of dog, or even of all dogs.

Reinforcement

Shortly after Pavlov, the American psychologist Edward Thorndike introduced a theory of learning that emphasized the role of experience in strengthening or weakening a stimulus–response bond (Thorndike 1911). Thorndike created puzzle boxes from which animals learned to escape through trial and error. Thorndike believed that rewarding correct responses strengthened a particular behaviour, whereas ignoring incorrect responses gradually weakened it. This is the principle of reinforcement, which is defined as any event that increases the probability that an associated behaviour will be repeated. Thorndike's idea that rewards promote learning is a key component of behaviourist theory to the present day. His experiments provide information about the nature of voluntary or self-directed behaviour, in contrast to the simple responses emphasized in classical conditioning. Although Thorndike does not refer directly to cognition, his studies on trial and error suggest that subjects undertake some level of mental information-processing.

Generalization

American psychologist John Watson extended the role of classical conditioning beyond reflexes to include emotional responses and, in so doing, demonstrated the principle of generalization. His best-known experiment, the case of 'Little Albert', demonstrated how fears may be conditioned. This experiment involved an 11-month-old infant who learned to fear white rats through a conditioned association with loud noises. Little Albert was subsequently conditioned to fear similar objects or animals such as white rabbits, white furry toys and cotton wool; in other words, his fear became generalized (Watson and Rayner 1920).

Watson also called for the use of scientific objectivity in learning and coined the term 'Behaviourism' (Watson 1913). He was the most radical of the early behaviourists:

> Give me a dozen healthy infants, well-formed, and my own specified world to bring them up in, and I'll guarantee to take any one at random and train him to be any type of specialist I might select – doctor, lawyer, artist, merchant-chief and, yes, even beggar-man and thief, regardless of his talents, penchants, tendencies, abilities, vocations and the race of his ancestors.

> (Watson 1930: 82)

Drives

Clark Hull attempted to describe behaviour in terms of a series of scientific laws with many variables and complex equations (Hull 1943). His theory typified the scientific approach to psychology that was prevalent in his time. He was influenced by Darwinian evolutionary theory and maintained that behaviour functions as a survival mechanism. For him, behaviour is directed towards maximizing the chances of survival. His theory revolves around the satisfaction of biological needs, including hunger, thirst and sleep, which are essential to survival.

According to Hull, organisms possess two key characteristics – drive and habit strength. Drive is an internal state of arousal, which motivates behaviour; 'habit strength measures the association between a particular stimulus and response. An organism will usually choose the response connected to the strongest habit. For example, rats in a maze that offers a choice of routes will generally choose the route to which they are most accustomed.

The classical behaviourist view has the stimulus leading directly to the response. In comparison, between the stimulus and response, Hull interposes the organism whose drive and habit strength may vary, so that the response depends not only on the stimulus but also on the characteristics of the intervening organism. Figure 2.2 shows the organism itself as an intervening variable between stimulus and response and a summary of the key terms used in classical conditioning is given in Table 2.1.

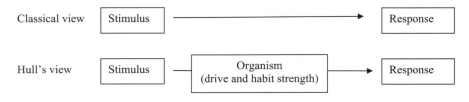

Figure 2.2 A comparison of classical conditioning and Hull's theory.

Table 2.1 Key terms in classical conditioning

Classical conditioning	Learning in which a subject comes to respond to a conditional stimulus repeatedly presented along with an unconditional stimulus
Unconditional stimulus	Any stimulus that elicits an automatic reaction in an organism
Neutral stimulus	A stimulus that does not cause the organism to respond
Conditional stimulus	A neutral stimulus that elicits a particular reaction by association with an unconditional stimulus
Unconditional response	An automatic reaction elicited by a stimulus
Conditional response	The behaviour that occurs when the conditional stimulus is presented
Contiguity	The close association in time of conditional and unconditional stimuli
Extinction	The elimination of behaviour by removing the unconditional stimulus
Variation	The process of varying the stimuli in order to produce a more generalized response
Generalization	The behaviour that occurs when organisms respond in the same way to stimuli that are similar to an original conditional stimulus
Drive stimuli	Needs such as hunger, thirst and sleep
Repetition	The pattern in which frequent and contiguous presentation of the stimulus and response is designed to produce an association between them
Habit strength	The frequency of association between a particular stimulus and response, which usually leads an organism to choose the response connected to the strongest habit

Operant conditioning

Burhaus Frederic Skinner is the best-known psychologist in the US behaviourist tradition. In the 1930s, he adopted a carefully structured approach called 'operant conditioning' in which the behaviour of the subject determines the response to the subject's own actions (Skinner 1938).

For example, in his 'Skinner Box', Skinner used positive reinforcement to train rats to press a lever to obtain food pellets. The positive reinforcement provided by the food increases the probability that the rats will press the lever again. Negative reinforcement removes an aversive stimulus after the correct response – for example, rats press a lever to remove an electric shock. The relief from painful experience also increases the probability that the lever will be pressed again.

Skinner uses the term 'reinforcer' rather than 'reward' because 'reinforcer' has an association with behaviour whereas 'reward' does not. A response followed by a reinforcing stimulus is strengthened and is therefore more likely to occur again. The larger and more appealing the reinforcer, the faster a response will be learned. A response that is not followed by a reinforcing stimulus is weakened, and is therefore less likely to occur again. The link between stimulus and response gradually becomes weaker and subsequently dies – for example, rats repeatedly pressing a lever without receiving food pellets will eventually abandon that behaviour. This results in extinction. Therefore:

- desired behaviours are rewarded causing their frequency to increase;
- undesired behaviours are punished causing their frequency to decrease.

Although Skinner did not consider punishment as effective as reinforcement in modifying behaviour it is still commonly used as a deterrent. Types of reward and punishment are shown in Figure 2.3.

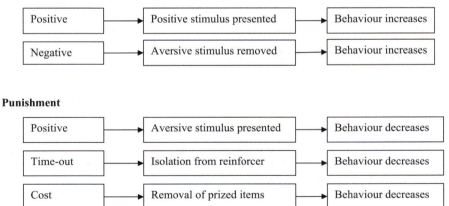

Figure 2.3 Reinforcement and punishment.
Source: based on Oates et al. (2005: 55).

Skinner experimented with what he called continuous and variable reinforcement schedules. In continuous reinforcement, every correct response is reinforced; in variable reinforcement, only some are. Skinner found that variable reinforcement schedules lead to steadier response rates because of the possibility that the next response will pay off.

In other experiments, Skinner (1958a) trained pigeons to play a type of table tennis by a process called 'shaping'. At first pigeons were rewarded when they performed an action that vaguely approximated to the target behaviour. Then the reward was restricted to actions that more closely matched the target behaviour. Gradually their behaviour was 'shaped' until it was satisfactory. A summary of the key terms used in operant coniditoning is given in Table 2.2.

Table 2.2 Key terms in operant conditioning

Operant conditioning	The process of shaping behaviour by following it with reinforcement that increases in frequency
Reinforcement	An event that increases the probability that the event preceding it will be repeated
Continuous reinforcement	A pattern in which every desirable response is followed by reinforcement
Variable reinforcement	A pattern in which only some desirable responses are followed by reinforcement
Magnitude	A term that describes the scale of a large and appealing reinforcer that is likely to produce faster learning of responses
Repetition	The frequency of reinforced operant behaviour that strengthens association between stimulus and response
Extinction	The elimination of behaviour by removing reinforcement
Shaping	The process of reinforcing behaviour as it becomes more like the target behaviour

Later developments in behaviourism

Although Thorndike had described animal learning in terms of trial and error, Gestalt theorists such as Wolfgang Köhler (1925) presented apes with problems involving out-of-reach food. They appeared to solve the problem through a process of sudden cognitive insight rather than by simple trial and error (Davey 2004: 264).

By the mid-twentieth century, there was a growing recognition that conditioning involves a cognitive element. Neo-behaviourists acknowledge that operant and classical conditioning together do not completely determine behaviours. For example, the American psychologist Edwin Chace Tolman demonstrated that rats could go beyond simple stimulus–response behaviour and could learn, remember and use facts about a maze (Tolman et al. 1946). Tolman later described such mental coding, storing and accessing of spatial and other information as a 'cognitive map' (Tolman 1948). At the time, however, this research failed to make much impact because behaviourists such as Skinner argued that studying behaviour was more useful than investigating mental states (Skinner 1950).

Behaviourism and its focus on external behaviour dominated the field of psychology until the 1960s when cognitive approaches brought a renewed interest in internal mental processes.

Educational implications of behaviourism

Education has always had the modification of behaviour as one of its main purposes, and behaviourist principles operate at all educational levels – from the smile and approval of the infant's teacher to the award of credits and degrees at the highest levels. Although different educational sectors use behaviourist principles to different extents and in different ways – adults need less behavioural control than children, for example – we can see that behaviourism has influenced ideas about learner behaviour, curriculum planning, and the teacher's role in the classroom.

Learner behaviour

Neo-behaviourists recognized the importance of learners' internal characteristics, such as personality, motivation and habit. Hull (1943) factored in motivation and habits as variables in his scientific 'laws'. Skinner (1953) talks about students developing self-control and self-monitoring programmes where they identify their own reinforcers and apply behaviourist principles to themselves. For example, a student might identify tendencies towards lateness, monitor performance, decide which stimuli are effective, set goals, and consider reinforcers.

In the 1960s, the investigations of cognitive science into processes like memory and perception (see Chapter 3, 'Cognitivism') provided new perspectives on learning. Whereas classical behaviourism focused only on the external manipulation of the organism, the development of cognitive science led to a stronger awareness of the importance of internal as well as external behaviours.

Bloom's taxonomy of learning

In the 1950s, the neo-behaviourist Benjamin Bloom attempted to develop a model that linked external and internal behaviours (Bloom and Krathwohl 1956). In his influential taxonomy of learning, he proposed three domains or spheres of learning – the cognitive, affective and psychomotor – which translate learning into overt observable behaviours. Each domain presents a set of behaviours, which are hierarchical according to complexity and sophistication.

The cognitive domain is the best-known and most educationally applicable of Bloom's domains and deals with the ways that internal knowledge may be revealed by external behaviour. Behaviours progress from those demonstrating basic subject knowledge up to an ability to evaluate or judge the worth of knowledge. For example, learning a language moves from knowing simple vocabulary at the lowest level to the ability to evaluate literary texts at the highest level (see Table 2.3).

It is important to remember that the levels in the cognitive domain may not be sequential or fixed. For example, young children's learning activities need not be confined to the lower levels of the cognitive taxonomy, and people may operate concurrently at different levels such as knowledge and analysis. Moreover, advanced learners may use higher-order evaluation skills to identify the need for new knowledge, a lower-order skill.

Table 2.3 Bloom's cognitive domain

Levels	Behaviours
Evaluation	Appraising, discriminating, assessing, resolving
Synthesis	Summarizing, generalizing, integrating, constructing
Analysis	Breaking down, categorizing, comparing, contrasting
Application	Applying, transferring, employing, organizing
Comprehension	Paraphrasing, recognizing, illustrating, explaining
Knowledge	Outlining, recounting, defining, enumerating

Source: based on Bloom and Krathwohl (1956).

The affective domain is less well known because it deals with attitudes and values in relation to particular subject areas. It is useful in categorizing values and levels of professionalism. Behaviours progress from simple attentiveness up to an integration of values and their transfer to other appropriate situations (see Table 2.4). For example, trainee teachers may attend only to events inside the classroom. However, at the highest level they may see that teaching also affects what happens outside the classroom.

Table 2.4 Bloom's affective domain

Levels	Behaviours
Generalization	Transferring exemplified norms to wider-related contexts
Value system	Exemplifying social or professional norms revealing integration of values
Value	Acting respectfully, acting responsibly, taking care, principled action
Response	Responding, reacting, answering, signalling
Attention	Being present, attending to, noticing, heeding

Source: based on Bloom and Krathwohl (1956).

The simplest and most obviously behavioural domain is the psychomotor. It is useful in indicating levels of skilled performance. Behaviours move from the ability to give an overview of a task up to mastery of a skill through practice, integration and automatization (see Table 2.5). For example, a woodwork student progresses from following a set of worksheet instructions through to making individual joints up to designing, constructing and evaluating a complete piece of furniture for a woodwork project.

Table 2.5 Bloom's psychomotor domain

Level	Behaviours
Mastery	Acting automatically with smooth and effortless expertise
Conscious control	Displaying competence with concentrated effort
Coordinated performance	Combining individual elements of a psychomotor skill
Partial performance	Performing individual elements of a psychomotor skill
Procedural task knowledge	Stating procedures, listing sequence of actions, following instructions

Source: based on Bloom and Krathwohl (1956).

Curriculum planning and models of instruction

Bloom's taxonomies, particularly in the cognitive domain, have been used to guide curriculum planning; his concept of 'mastery learning' (1968) has been particularly influential. 'Mastery learning' involves the statement of educational objectives and their translation into learner behaviours so as to generate criteria for assessment grades at various levels in the domain. For example, in English literature, behaviours that demonstrate an understanding of the concept of alliteration might include:

- providing a definition (knowledge);
- giving an example (comprehension);
- recognizing alliteration in context (application);
- looking closely at examples (analysis);
- appraising the effectiveness of alliteration in a given context (evaluation).

The explicit linking of cognitive developments and behaviours helps teachers both to devise learning activities that allow learners to practise the behaviours, and to look for these behaviours when assessing learners' performance.

The 1950s saw the scientific interest in behaviour modification merge with the scientific interest in management. In the United States, this produced a general application of management principles and systems theory in industry and education. An example of this is the 'technical rational' model of curriculum developed for the US school system by Ralph Tyler (1949) after the Second World War. This model was based on an analysis of the ways in which educational material could be broken down into discrete elements and sequenced in the appropriate order for presentation to learners.

Skinner thought that this systematic delivery of material could be performed reliably by teaching machines that could take on the task of drill and repetition, important in forming behavioural habits (Skinner 1958b). This would allow the teacher to engage in more social interaction with learners. These machines, initially mechanical and later computer-based, presented materials – usually text or numbers – in carefully sequenced, small, incremental steps. This emphasis on correct sequencing led to the development of instructional design (see Chapter 16, 'Blended learning'), which is an approach to instruction that attempts to incorporate systematically all the events affecting learning (Gagné et al. 1992). Instructional design principles have been used to guide curriculum planning in the training and vocational world and in the field of computer-based learning.

The teacher's role in the classroom

The sequencing of curricular events led to an interest in the correct sequencing of classroom events and the teacher's role in stimulating learners' behavioural responses. Gagné focused on the importance of arranging stimuli to produce the most appropriate and desirable behavioural sequences. He specified nine 'internal processes and their corresponding instructional events' (Gagné and Medsker 1996: 140; see Table 2.6). These events can be used to structure lesson plans, sessions or learning materials.

Table 2.6 Internal processes and their corresponding instructional events

Teacher action	Learner response
1 Gaining learner's attention	1 Reception and attentiveness
2 Stating session objectives	2 Knowing what to expect
3 Reminding what was done before	3 Stimulation of long-term memory
4 Highlighting key features	4 Perceiving what is important
5 Structuring learning	5 Creating links and associations
6 Encouraging activity	6 Performing
7 Providing feedback	7 Learning awareness and satisfaction
8 Evaluating progress	8 Strengthening learning
9 Enhancing attention and signalling future learning	9 Gaining learning overview

Source: based on Gagné and Medsker (1996: 140).

Practical implications of behaviourism

Although current educational practice is perhaps most influenced by contemporary theories of constructivist meaning-making (see Chapter 4, 'Constructivism'), four aspects of it also display behaviourist features: curriculum planning, learning outcomes, assessment and behaviour management.

Curriculum planning

The following list outlines curriculum-planning steps commonly undertaken by teachers at different educational levels.

1. identify the need for the programme;
2. determine the aims and instructional objectives of the programme;
3. define the characteristics of the target group;
4. list the precise learning outcomes;
5. categorize learning outcomes according to Bloom's taxonomies;
6. break the material down into small units;
7. carefully sequence these units;
8. provide frequent practice to strengthen the stimulus–response bond;
9. ensure that the learner responds (does things);
10. observe and assess any behavioural changes;
11. provide opportunities for frequent learner feedback;
12. reinforce 'correct' behaviour with immediate rewards;
13. evaluate the effectiveness of the programme;
14. modify and improve the programme.

Learning outcomes

Learning outcomes, which have developed from the behavioural educational objectives described above, are increasingly used at all levels of education, although their application is more straightforward when the behaviours are easily observed. Their use is more difficult when applied to complex and internal thought processes.

A learning outcome is an explicit statement of what a learner will be able to do as a result of completing a course of study. A learning outcome statement includes:

- action, expressed using precise behavioural verbs;
- context, which requires reference to the conditions of performance;
- threshold, which is an indication of acceptable performance – that is, a statement about the performance threshold required.

Learning outcomes help learners at all levels to understand exactly what is expected of them and to tailor their learning activities accordingly. Figure 2.4 identifies the elements of a typical learning outcome. One of the major contributions of behaviourism to contemporary educational practice has been to remove the mystique and vagueness that has frequently characterized the discourse of educational aims and objectives.

Assessment

It is commonly held that effective assessment tasks should test the performance of behaviours stated in learning outcomes under the same conditions as those under which they were learnt. For example, if the learning outcome states that apprentice carpenters will be able to hang a door, the assessment should require them to hang a door rather than describe the technique in a written examination, which is what often happens.

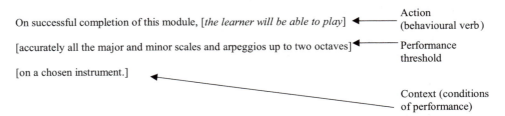

Figure 2.4 An example of a learning outcome.

Behaviourist principles may also be seen in the move towards criterion-referenced assessment. The extent to which a learner has achieved stated learning outcomes is judged according to behavioural criteria specified in those outcomes. This replaces older concepts of norm-referenced assessment, which are based on rating learner performance in relation to average or 'normal' group performance. In norm-referenced assessment, the pattern of distribution around the norm means a certain portion of learners must be rated as performing at a below-average level. When learners are assessed according to criteria, however, it is possible that all could meet the criteria and be judged as performing at a satisfactory level. This shift in assessment practices is therefore clearly of benefit to learners.

Behaviourist principles are useful as part of formative assessment, which is a kind of assessment designed to provide feedback for the learner and teacher, rather than to record or certify achievement. Formative assessment may be seen as a form of reinforcement, designed to motivate and encourage learners. To be effective, the reinforcement of desired behaviour must be provided consistently and in a timely manner so that the correct response is reinforced. When it comes to assessment, therefore, learners should receive feedback as quickly as possible after the assessment task.

Behaviour management

Changing or strengthening learners' behaviours is the aim of most elementary learning programmes, with this strengthening of specific behaviours acting as a precursor to the development of cognitive skills.

As part of the process of behaviour management, teachers can use operant conditioning techniques, which Skinner claims work best in providing motivation for learning (Skinner 1969). Indeed, positive reinforcement or the use of praise as a motivator lies behind practices that seek to reward learners when they demonstrate the behaviour the teacher has set out to inculcate. Reinforcers may be:

- material, such as prizes and awards;
- social, such as teacher attention, approval or praise;
- activity-related, such as an opportunity to engage in a favourite activity;

- intrinsic, such as feelings of self-actualization or pride.

The use of punishment to deter undesired behaviours is not recommended because learners may simply try to avoid being caught behaving in an inappropriate way, rather than discontinuing the behaviour in question. The use of sanctions or agreed consequences of behaviour is preferable to punishment because this strategy draws on the principles of operant conditioning, such that learners are instrumental in determining outcomes and hence appropriate reinforcement.

Behaviour modification in the form of Applied Behavioural Analysis (ABA) is an effective teaching method for autistic children and those with learning and behavioural difficulties. In this method, teachers identify appropriate target behaviours, which are broken down into small steps that require the child to exhibit the desired behaviours, which are carefully reinforced. Applied Behavioural Analysis is an expensive method requiring one-on-one tuition, but has been shown to be more effective than mainstream teaching. Parents are often taught the techniques (Oates et al. 2005: 57–8). It should be noted that ABA has been criticized for its behaviourist approach, which includes a view of the learner as deficient, with education providing a remedy determined by experts.

Key ideas

- Behaviourism focuses on observable learning events as demonstrated by stimulus and response relationships.
- Learning always involves a change in behaviour.
- Mental processes should be excluded from the scientific study of learning.
- The laws governing learning apply equally to all organisms, including human organisms.
- Organisms begin life as blank slates: there are no innate laws of behaviour.
- Learning results from external events in the environment.
- Behaviourism is a deterministic theory: the subject has no choice but to respond to appropriate stimuli.

Conclusions

In drawing conclusions about behaviourism, you may find it useful to assess the negative, positive and interesting aspects of the theory.

On the negative side, behaviourism is popularly linked to power and control and has connotations of animal training. It is also associated with an outmoded industrial training model that fails to take account of people's ability to take action for themselves. It can be considered anti-humanistic in its refusal to acknowledge human freedom and choice. Behaviourism gives insufficient weight to contextual factors such as the social, economic and political conditions and forces that promote or constrain action. It also fails to consider other determinants in learning, such as inherited intelligence and personality.

In higher learning, behaviourist techniques may not be effective in promoting deep learning, which is related to personal understanding and meaning-making. In adult, further, and higher education, it is also difficult to apply behaviourist principles, because they often fail to take account of creative processes and of incidental, unexpected and self-initiated learning. In general, behaviourism is often seen as anti-intellectual.

On the other hand, behaviourism is efficient in promoting rapid learning, because of its precise specification of actions and learning outcomes. Behaviourist principles are also useful – they offer practical and specific advice to the teacher or curriculum planner about what to do.

Behaviourism is not totally antagonistic to other theories of learning; rather, it can co-exist with later learning theories that focus on cognition or the social acquisition of meaning. It may serve as a foundational element on the basis of which more complex cognitive processes are developed. For example, some Asian cultures see repetitive skill acquisition as a necessary prerequisite to the development of creativity.

Behaviourism is still of interest to students and educators because many human behaviours can be related to or explained by the theory. Many behaviourist practices have recently been incorporated into the educational world – these include the use of learning outcomes in standardized systems that promote lifelong learning and progression. It is possible to take a more sophisticated view of what behaviourist theory can offer, particularly when it is considered as a complement to cognitivist and constructivist theories of learning, which are considered in the following chapters.

References

Bloom, B. (1968) Learning for mastery, *Evaluation Comment*, 1(2): 1–5.

Bloom, B. and Krathwohl, D. (1956) *Taxonomy of Educational Objectives: The Classification of Educational Goals, by a Committee of College and University Examiners. Handbooks 1 to 3: The Cognitive, Affective and Psychomotor Domain.* New York: Longmans Green.

Davey, G. (ed.) (2004) *Complete Psychology*. London: Hodder, Arnold.

Gagné, R.M., Briggs, L.J. and Wager, W.W. (1992) *Principles of Instructional Design* (4th edn). Forth Worth: Harcourt Brace College Publishers.

Gagné, R.M. and Medsker, K.L. (1996) *The Conditions of Learning: Training Applications.* Fort Worth: Harcourt Brace College Publishers.

Hull, C.L. (1943) *Principles of Behavior: An Introduction to Behavior Theory.* New York: Appleton Century Crofts.

Köhler, W. (1925) *The Mentality of Apes* (trans. E. Winter). London and New York: K. Paul, Trench, Trubner and Co. Ltd.

Milgram, S. (1963) Behavioral study of obedience, *Journal of Abnormal and Social Psychology*, 67: 371–8.

Oates, J., Sheehy, K. and Wood, C. (2005) Theories of development, in J. Oates, C. Wood and A.Grayson (eds) *Psychological Development and Early Childhood*. Oxford: Blackwell Publishing.

Oates, J., Wood, C. and Grayson, A. (2005) *Psychological Development and Early Childhood*. Oxford: Blackwell Publishing.

Pavlov, I.P. (1927) *Conditioned Reflexes: An Investigation of the Physiological Activity of the Cerebral Cortex* (trans. and ed. G.V. Anrep). Oxford: Oxford University Press.

Skinner, B.F. (1938) *The Behavior of Organisms*. New York: Appleton-Century-Crofts.

Skinner, B.F. (1950) Are theories of learning necessary? *Psychological Review*, 57(4): 193–216.

Skinner, B.F. (1953) *Science and Human Behavior*. New York: Macmillan.

Skinner, B.F. (1958a) Reinforcement today, *American Psychologist*, 13: 94–9.

Skinner, B.F. (1958b) Teaching machines, *Science,* 128: 969–77.

Skinner, B.F. (1969) *Contingencies of Reinforcement: A Theoretical Analysis*. Englewood Cliffs, NJ: Prentice-Hall.

Thorndike, E.L. (1911) *Animal Intelligence*. New York: Macmillan.

Tolman, E.C. (1948) Cognitive maps in rats and man, *Psychological Review*, 55: 189–208.

Tolman, E.C., Ritchie, B.F. and Kalish, D. (1946) Studies in spatial learning: II. Place learning versus response learning, *Journal of Experimental Psychology*, 36: 221–9.

Tyler, R. (1949) *Basic Principles of Curriculum and Instruction*. University of Chicago Press.

Watson, J.B. (1913) Psychology as the behaviorist views it, *Psychological Review*, 20: 158–77.

Watson, J.B. (1930) *Behaviorism* (revised edn). University of Chicago Press.

Watson, J.B. and Rayner, R. (1920) Conditioned emotional reactions, *Journal of Experimental Psychology*, 3(1): 1–14.

Chapter 3 Cognitivism

Introduction

How is it that if someone speaks your name, you immediately hear it even though you are not consciously attending to it? Certain automatic brain processes have taken place for this to occur, and these processes are studied by cognitive psychologists.

Cognitivism involves the study of mental processes such as sensation, perception, attention, encoding and memory that behaviourists were reluctant to study, because cognition occurs inside the 'black box' of the brain.

Cognitivists believe that learning results from organizing and processing information effectively. If educators understand how learners process information, they can design learning experiences that optimize this activity. For example, an awareness of how learners transfer short-term memories into meaningful knowledge is likely to be useful in the classroom.

The development of cognitivism

Four factors influenced the development of cognitivism as a separate discipline in psychology:

- the development of experimental psychology;
- the move from an interest in external behaviours to internal brain processes;
- the inadequacy of behaviourism to explain language acquisition;
- the development of computers and an interest in artificial intelligence.

Experimental psychology

There is a long tradition of experimental memory research by psychologists beginning in the 1880s with Hermann Ebbinghaus, who used nonsense syllables and words to investigate how memory is laid down (Davey 2004: 235).

The British psychologist Frederic Bartlett, who wrote a book called *Remembering* in 1932, is best known for his development of the concept of 'schema'. G.A. Miller wrote a classic article, 'The magical number seven, plus or minus two', which investigated short-term memory as a separate cognitive entity (Miller 1956). This early work on memory paved the way for more sustained research, such as that by Atkinson and Shiffrin (1968) or Baddeley and Hitch (1974) discussed later in the chapter.

The shift from behaviourism to cognitivism

Behaviourists came to realize that not all learning could be explained by Pavlov's and Watson's theories of simple stimulus–response and reinforcement. In 1927 Köhler demonstrated that apes solved problems through a form of thinking he termed 'insightful behaviourism' (Köhler 1925).

Neo-behaviourists such as Tolman expanded this mental focus to a consideration of purposive behaviour in animals and people. He demonstrated that rats build up a mental representation or cognitive map of their environment and develop expectations rather than a set of inflexible links between stimuli and response (Tolman 1948).

Language acquisition

Evidence of human cognition came from contested theories of language acquisition. Skinner's book *Verbal Behavior* (1957) claimed that language was an activity shaped by the stimulus–response mechanism. The structural linguist Naom Chomsky challenged this by arguing that stimulus–response does not explain how children can generate sentences they have not heard before.

Computers and artificial intelligence

Computer scientists in the 1950s were interested in mental processes that could be reproduced by machines. The computer came to be used as a metaphor for cognitive function, and the brain came to be seen as a computing device. For example, cognitive theory employs an information-processing, input-process-output model, similar to that used in the computer industry (see Figure 3.1).

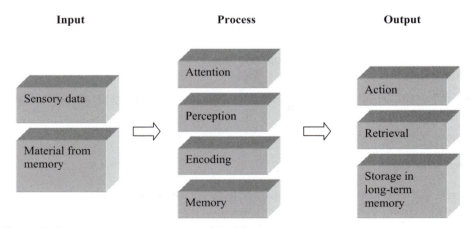

Figure 3.1 Input-process-output model of brain processes.

Principles of cognition

In this section, we consider the five basic processes involved in cognition – sensation, perception, attention, encoding and memory – all of which have implications for the learning process.

Sensation

By sensation, we mean the process through which stimuli from the external environment are held very briefly in sensory registers before being transferred for further processing. For example, visual information is available for only about half a second, and fewer than ten items can be held at any one time. Auditory information is retained long enough for language processing to occur (Massaro 1993).

Perception

Perception is the process by which we interpret and make sense of the things that are presented to our senses. This involves:

- pattern recognition;
- object recognition;
- bottom-up or top-down processing;
- unconscious perception.

Pattern recognition

Early in the twentieth century, Gestalt theorists, who studied holistic aspects of cognition, identified strategies by which people group perceptions of pattern. Patterns are perceived according to the four laws of perception (see Figure 3.2):

Proximity – we have a tendency to perceive closed figures rather than fragmented or unconnected objects.

Similarity – we tend to perceive smooth continuous lines rather than sudden changes in direction.

Continuity – similar information, objects, elements and so on are generally categorized and grouped together.

Closure – objects close to each other may be grouped together.

Object recognition

Whereas patterns are two-dimensional, objects are three-dimensional. Marr (1982) proposed a theory of how we recognize three-dimensional objects, from an increasing range of visual cues as an artist might build up a picture, starting with an outline and adding detail:

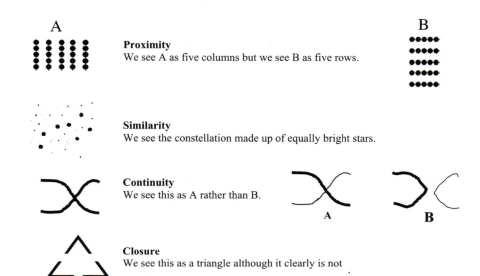

Figure 3.2 Perceptual categorization.
Source: based on Andrade and May (2004:30).

2-D (*Primal sketch*)	We see patterns, lines, corners and some black and white shading.
2.5-D	We see some depth information, texture gradients and binocular cues.
3-D	We see 3-D nature and spatial relationships between objects and the scene.

Bottom-up or top-down processing

A key debate in cognition relates to whether it is:

- bottom-up – all the information needed for perception is provided by the sensory stimulus; or
- top-down – contextual knowledge and reasoning processes are used to make sense of sensory input.

The American psychologist James Gibson (1950) argued for the bottom-up theory, developing his ideas while making training films for pilots. He claimed that pilots use environmental cues to gauge distance and depth, arguing that all the information the pilots needed came not from their prior knowledge but from the following invariant cues:

Interposition	closer objects obscure more distant ones;
Texture gradient	closer objects appear more textured than distant ones;

Linear perspective	parallel lines converge as they recede;
Relative retinal size	distant objects appear smaller;
Motion cues	objects appear to move if the observer is moving (motion parallax);
Optical flow pattern	images such as the ground or sky flow as the observer approaches a point.

The English psychologist Richard Gregory (1980) argues against this bottom-up model and claims that higher-order processes such as inference, deduction and knowledge of context are necessary for perception. He cites letter and word recognition from incomplete information as an example of top-down processing. Some of his evidence is based on visual illusions and ambiguous images that need to be interpreted on the basis of previous experience and expectation. For example, in a

Figure 3.3 Rabbit or duck?
Source: based on Andrade and May (2004:3).

book about small furry animals, the image in Figure 3.3 would be perceived as a rabbit, whereas it would be seen as a duck in a book about birds.

A common-sense compromise suggests that bottom-up and top-down approaches are both involved in perception. At the initial stage, the bottom-up approach is needed to establish the sensory data and the invariants. This is followed by a top-down interpretation that adds contextual and higher-order inferences and deductions. Learning often requires this mixed approach.

Unconscious perception

This aspect of cognition is the ability to perceive phenomena to which we are not consciously attending, such as being aware that one's name has been spoken. Unconscious perception is thought to be involved in subliminal learning, which has been the focus of a thriving industry in motivational tapes and CDs that aims to activate the process (Andrade 2005: 556).

Attention

As we have seen, cognition begins with the perception of sensory inputs. This is followed by attention – the cognitive process of selectively concentrating on one thing while ignoring others. 'Attention acts as a means of focusing limited mental resources on the information and cognitive processes that are most salient at a given moment' (Sternberg 1999: 69). It determines what reaches conscious awareness. So, how are we able to focus on one stimulus and avoid being overloaded with information? We do this first with controlled and automatic processes and then through focus.

Controlled and automatic processes

Controlled processes require intentional effort and conscious awareness. Automatic processes, on the other hand, require little intention or effort and are usually outside conscious awareness and control. They can be performed rapidly and at the same time as other processes. A learner driver finds that driving is a highly controlled process that demands full attention, but for an experienced driver the process is automatic.

Automatic processes often develop as a result of skilled practice. Errors may occur when automatic processes are carried out inappropriately – for example, driving to work when you meant to drive to the bank.

Focus

How do we focus attention on one piece of information to the exclusion of others? This is a topic of obvious interest to the educator.

Three types of theory have been used to explain the processes of selective attention (see Figure 3.4). The first was proposed by Broadbent (1958), who thought that a filter or bottleneck operated immediately after incoming information was registered by the senses; this prevents us being overwhelmed by sensory data. Alternatively, Treisman (1964) argued that all sensory information is processed beyond the sensory stage, but unattended messages are not filtered but weakened (or 'attenuated'). This explains how you might hear your own name spoken in a crowded room – stimuli such as names are so strong that they reach awareness, even if faintly. Finally, Kahneman (1973) suggested that instead of filters or weakened messages, only a limited number of messages can be processed. That is, only a certain amount of attention is available at any one time so the amount of attention a message receives depends on its importance. If attention is divided, it will be directed to where it is needed most.

A later theory (Navon and Gopher 1979) suggested that there might be separate banks for different types of processing – visual and auditory. Two tasks will interfere if only both are drawing on the same bank.

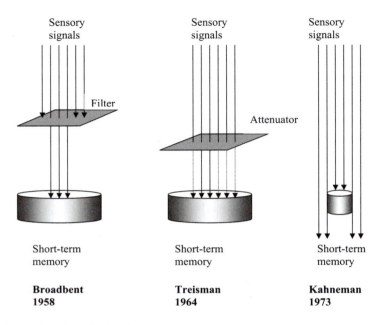

Figure 3.4 Theories of selective attention.
Source: based on Naish (2005).

Encoding

Having perceived and then attended to stimuli, we need to encode information by organizing it in the form of a mental representation, or schema. It could be argued that learning involves the process of encoding experience. For example, research has shown that instructions to organize material can be as effective as instructions to learn it. In one study, three groups of participants were given packs of cards containing words.

- Group 1 was asked to organize the pack in a meaningful way (recall was not mentioned).
- Group 2 was asked to learn the words for recall.
- Group 3 was asked to organize the pack and learn the words.

When the groups were asked to recall the words, there was no difference in their performance. For group 1, the very act of organizing the pack precipitated learning (Mandler 1967).

Schemata

A schema is 'a mental framework or organized pattern of thought about some aspect of the world such as class of people, events, situations or objects' (Bartlett 1932, quoted in Davey 2004: 231).

Schemata are like templates developed from previous experience, into which information can be organized. They mean that people do not have to reinterpret the world every time they encounter it. Schemata have 'slots' that can contain either fixed or variable values. Schemata can be:

Cultural	knowledge of a familiar culture;
Person-related	expectations about a familiar person;
Self-related	beliefs we hold about ourselves;
Role-related	knowledge of roles played;
Scenes	descriptions of layouts or contents of a location;
Scripts	representations of a typical sequence of events.

(Schank and Abelson 1977)

An example of schema for dining in a restaurant could be as follows:

Schema:	Type of restaurant, location, style, cuisine and clientele;
Scenes:	The layout of the restaurant, tables, chairs, décor, waiters;
Script:	Travelling to the restaurant, being allocated a space, having the food cooked, being served and paying for the meal;
Slots:	Type of restaurant, type of décor, type of food.

The idea of schemata was neatly demonstrated in a study in which participants were asked to look around a house from a burglar's perspective or from an estate agent's perspective (Anderson and Pichert 1978). The two groups' recall was very different, with the 'burglars' noting open windows and broken locks, and the estate agents noting decorative problems and room sizes. Different schemata had been applied to the same information to achieve different goals.

The encoding of experience and the generation of schemata involve two components:

- The *bottom-up* inflow of information from the external world, mediated through attention and perception;
- the *top-down* action of prior knowledge that helps to interpret the bottom-up input. In this component, repeated experience is generalized as schemata (or 'accreted'), and new experience causes old schemata to be improved ('tuned'). Inconsistent experience can cause old schemata to be replaced by new ('reconstructed').

Schemata construction involves structuring material so that tuning or reconstruction is facilitated (see Figure 3.5). These processes offer some insight into learners' interpretations.

Memory

Memory is our ability to retain and recall information. Although we may think of memory as one particular faculty, it involves different kinds of inter-related systems: sensory, short-term (STM) and long-term (LTM). Each of these has a different purpose (see Table 3.1).

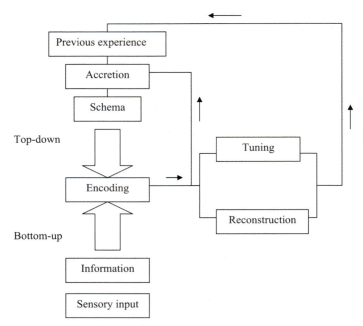

Figure 3.5 How experience is encoded.

Table 3.1 Different types of memory systems

Memory type	Amount of data	Duration
Sensory	Very large	Very short
STM	Limited	Short
LTM	Very large	Very long

In addition, Tulving (1985) subdivides LTM into:

Episodic   memories of things that have happened;

Semantic   memories of facts, concepts and principles;

Procedural   knowledge of how to do things.

For example, when asked by a teacher about the events of a field trip, a learner makes conscious use of episodic memory. Semantic memory is used to recall a complex scientific equation, and procedural memory is used to carry out a familiar experimental technique in the laboratory.

People suffering from amnesia may have badly damaged episodic memories of past life yet their semantic memory (of language, say) and their procedural memory may be perfect (Baddeley and Wilson 1988). A particularly striking example of evidence of separate short-term and long-term memories is seen in the comparison between two amnesiacs, referred to as H.M. and K.F. The short-term memory of H.M. was normal in that he could recall sequences of letters and numbers given to him, but his long-term memory was practically non-existent. He could not remember where he lived or recognize a photograph of himself, nor could he recall the name of the Prime Minister (Postle and Corkin 1998). K.F. was the exact opposite: she could remember only one item in short-term memory tests, but her long-term memory was normal (Shallice and Warrington 1970).

The way memory operates has been described according to three major theoretical models: modal, working memory and deep and surface processing. There is also the neural network model, which tries to encompass memory, knowledge acquisition and cognition as a whole.

The modal model

Atkinson and Shiffrin (1968) proposed a modal model containing two separate

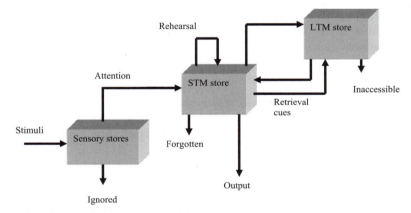

Figure 3.6 Modal model of memory.
Source: based on Atkinson and Shiffrin (1968)

storage systems, STM and LTM, which code information differently (see Figure 3.6).

In this model, external data goes into the sensory stores before entering the STM store. Selected information is transferred from the sensory memory stores to STM. Residual information is ignored and lost.

STM is a store of limited capacity and duration. It is sometimes known as 'working memory' because it has several functions such as rehearsal, coding, decision-making and retrieval. It has a capacity of approximately 5 to 9 bits of information. Some information may be chunked in larger bits, however, and therefore more can be stored and manipulated. The life of material in STM can be prolonged briefly by repetition (rehearsal) as in the repetition of a new telephone number until it is dialled. If the information is encoded (related to prior knowledge and placed in a schema) it can be transferred to LTM stores. Otherwise it will be forgotten.

The LTM is a store of enormous capacity and indefinite duration. Information held in LTM is encoded in schemata. The strength of a particular memory will depend upon the number of associations with similar schemata and the intensity of the memory as determined by vividness and emotional impact. If material has been weakly encoded or infrequently recalled, it may be in LTM but inaccessible.

Retrieval

A process of cueing enables memories to be retrieved from LTM. A memory may be triggered by many different cues such as mnemonics and the 'method of loci' where items in a list are recalled by associating them with particular places. This method is attributed to the ancient Greek poet Simonides, who remembered the names of those killed in a fire in a banqueting hall by memorizing where they had been sitting at dinner (Bruning et al. 2004: 70–4).

Although there are certain controlling processes such as encoding and rehearsal, the modal model is essentially passive with memory stores acting merely as storage locations. It is also sequential; information must first go through STM before being transferred to LTM. This cannot explain how, for example, the amnesiac K.F. (see above) was able to lay down new long-term memories despite the absence of short-term memory capability.

Working memory

Baddeley and Hitch (1974) proposed this more dynamic model of memory, which was further developed by Baddeley (1986, 2001). The working memory model consists of three parts: the central executive, the phonological loop and the visuo-spatial scratchpad (see Figure 3.7).

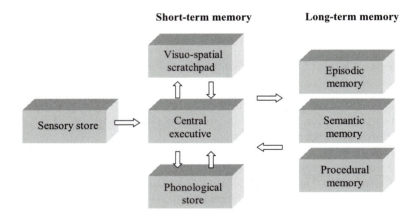

Figure 3.7 Working memory model.
Sourse: Based on Baddeley (1983).

The central executive controls what enters into STM and decides what processes will be undertaken (transfer to LTM, for example). The central executive also controls the other two components – the phonological or articulatory loop and the visuo-spatial scratchpad. Although under the overall control of the central executive, these two also have their own resources of attention and processing.

The phonological or articulatory loop is an auditory memory store that holds a limited amount of acoustic data for a brief period of a few seconds by means of rehearsal. Similarly, the visual-spatial scratchpad is a short-term store in which visual images can be examined and manipulated (for example, by rotation).

In terms of learning, this model suggests that it is important for learners to look back on what they have already done. In this way, associations can be made between new material arriving bottom-up from the environment and top-down material already stored in memory. For example, people sometimes experience a 'learning plateau' when they feel unable to learn new material. One explanation is that previous material has not yet become organized and encoded in memory so the new material has no suitable synaptic connections available to it. Consistent work to embed previous learning will help new learning.

Deep and surface processing model

Developed by Craik and Lockhart (1972), this is a qualitatively different approach from the models above. It is less interested in interacting subsystems than in the depth of information-processing and its implications for memory and recall. The model proposes that incoming information is processed at different levels. The strength of encoding will determine the duration of the memory. Mere repetition, for example, leads to shallow encoding resulting in short-lived memory. Deep encoding involves the generation of connections to previous knowledge and existing schemata and results in more permanent memories.

Although this is a plausible hypothesis, there is no clear description of the processes that enable shallow encoding to lay down short-term memories and deep encoding to lay down long-term memory. The definitions appear to be circular. Nevertheless, the notion of deep and surface processing has influenced areas of learning theory, and underpins the idea of deep and surface learning developed by Ferenc Marton and Roger Säljö (1976). According to Marton and Säljö, deep learners try to understand material by linking it to already known concepts; surface learners simply remember facts, which promotes neither understanding nor retention.

Associative network models

All three models above are to some extent based on an outdated computer model that emphasizes sequential steps and central control in information-processing. But brains are not computers. Brains are much slower than computers in processing individual signals. On the other hand, brains are very good at parallel processing, with many activities going on at once. In fact, contemporary supercomputers try to be brain-like by having parallel processors linked together.

The associative network model attempts to address the deficiencies of these earlier, computer-based models by representing knowledge as a web within which memory processes operate. The networks consist of:

- nodes – individual concepts;
- links – relations between the nodes;
- activation of the links.

This model claims that knowledge is not stored as separate units. Rather, what is stored is connection strength between different ideas in the network. When people search their memories, they stimulate particular nodes. This activates the links connected to those nodes, which activate other links and so on. Thus activation spreads from node to node. Memory strength in particular areas of knowledge means strong links between nodes. When a particular node is activated, it 'lights up' a whole array of associated nodes. Figure 3.8 is an example of an associative network of ideas.

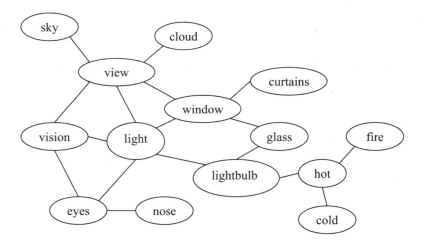

Figure 3.8 Associative network.

Practical implications of cognitivism for educators

Cognitivists maintain that learning involves developing effective ways of building schemata and processing information. Knowing how learners process information should be helpful in designing appropriate learning experiences. For cognitivists, the teacher is in control of the learning, although they also hold that people learn best when encouraged to discover information pertinent to their own needs. Thus, teachers should design material that stimulates learners' cognitive processes and encourages learners to make mental connections for themselves.

In this section, we outline some of the practical educational implications of cognitivism as they correspond to key stages in the cognitivist model of learning: sensation, perception, attention, encoding and memory.

Sensation

Teachers and instructional designers need to consider carefully the amount and type of information they present and the speed at which it is presented. Paivio (1986) argues that the mind processes visual and auditory material along different channels and in different ways for encoding, storage and later retrieval. In order to take account of processes of sensation teachers should:

- limit competing and distracting sensory impressions;
- use materials and draw on experiences that involve all the senses;
- present information in more than one sensory mode to facilitate dual encoding;
- direct the processing of sensory information.

Perception

Information-processing is both 'bottom up' and 'top down'. Top-down processing is perhaps the more important. In order to take account of processes of perception teachers should:

- arouse perceptual interest with strongly defined material;
- emphasize the distinctiveness of material in processing;
- point out patterns in materials;
- present material in a structured form – e.g. diagrams or stories;
- place learning in context and take contextual factors into account;
- review knowledge and assist learners to see relationships between old and new;
- explore attitudes and emotional responses to a topic and deal with any negativity.

Attention

A key concern for teachers is how to direct learners' attention when there are competing sensory impressions and memory.

One way that teachers can address the issue of engaging learners' attention is by means of Howard Gardner's work on multiple intelligences (MI) theory discussed in Chapter 7, 'Intelligence'. He suggested that 'any rich, nourishing topic – any concept worth teaching – can be approached in at least five different ways that will map onto the multiple intelligences' (Gardner 1991: 245). Gardner thinks of a topic as a room with several entry points that will engage the attention of different types of learners. These entry points and the means that teachers can use to access them include the:

Narrational	by means of a story;
Logical-quantitative	by deductive reasoning;
Foundational	by discussing underlying concepts;

Aesthetic   by appeal to artistic sensitivity;
Experiential   by some direct experience.

Attention is linked to learner motivation. Keller's ARCS motivational model proposes that motivation includes four categories – attention, relevance, confidence and satisfaction (Keller 1983; Keller and Kopp 1987).

In order to gain and maintain attention teachers should:

- arouse initial interest by novelty and departure from the expected;
- present the subject in an interesting way – e.g. presenting a problem;
- vary teaching methods with exercises and activities that maintain interest;
- promote active listening in lectures or presentations.

Short-term memory

Short-term memory (STM) is limited both in capacity and duration. In order to take account of these limitations on STM teachers should:

- limit the number of lists or items to be committed to memory at one time;
- be aware that learners remember first and last items on a list better than central ones;
- group items into 'chunks' with less than ten items to be memorized at one time;
- be conscious of interference between different types of information to be learnt;
- use repetition or maintenance rehearsal to retain information for a short period.

Working memory

The concept of working memory has replaced STM as a model for more active and non-serial processing of information. Encoding is the process of organizing material and making it meaningful so that it can eventually be placed in long-term memory.

In order to activate working memory teachers should:

- tell learners which information is most important;
- begin with an overview or outline of the material to be learnt;
- state the objectives or learning outcomes of a learning session;
- develop automaticity and speed of response in learners through regular practice;
- encourage learners to use the knowledge they already possess;
- encourage reflection and meta-cognition;
- link difficult-to-remember items to more meaningful ones;
- encourage visualization – use image representations;

- use verbal memory aids such as mnemonics;
- use mind-mapping techniques;
- use guided questioning to activate existing schemata and concepts;
- match encoding strategies with material to be learned;
- understand that learners may need to make schemata explicit and challenge their own assumptions;
- present content in increasing order of complexity;
- revisit topics to strengthen retention.

Long-term memory

Long-term memory (LTM) is the permanent repository of accumulated information. Retrieval requires cues that may be sensory, cognitive or emotional. Cues create associations that activate (LTM). For example, particular songs often arouse powerful memories. In order to promote recall teachers should:

- link materials to cues that can be used to recall them;
- remind learners that cues are sufficient to recall the material;
- encourage learners to create their own cues;
- teach revision techniques;
- encourage learners to discover and use their strengths and styles.

Key ideas

- Learning does not always involve a change in behaviour.
- Cognitivism focuses on internal mental learning processes.
- The key metaphor in cognitivism is the computer model.
- This model assumes discrete stages through which information is processed.
- Learners actively process, store and retrieve information for use.
- Learners organize and interpret information to create knowledge.

Conclusions

Cognitivism presents a scientific approach to learning and offers a coherent understanding of the processes involved. It presents theoretical support for teaching practices and suggests a range of useful teaching strategies that encourage learning.

However, it could be argued that its focus on learning as an individual mental event ignores social processes and embodiment. Its treatment of teaching as a technical-rational activity ignores the element of reflective practice and artistry involved.

Cognitivism can be seen as a progressive step towards an approach that combines cognitive processes with the element of individual and shared meaning-making that is constructivism. This is explored in the next chapter.

References

Anderson, R.C. and Pichert, J.W. (1978) Recall of previously unrecallable information following a shift in perspective, *Journal of Verbal Learning and Verbal Behaviour*, 17: 1–12.

Andrade, J. (2005) Consciousness, in N. Braisby and A. Gellatly (eds) *Cognitive Psychology*. Oxford: Oxford University Press.

Andrade, J. and May, J. (2004) *Instant Notes on Cognitive Psychology*. London: BIOS Scientific Publishers, Taylor & Francis Group.

Atkinson, R.C. and Shiffrin, R.M. (1968) Human memory: a proposed system and its control processes, in K.W. Spence (ed.) *The Psychology of Learning and Motivation: Advances in Research and Theory*, Vol. 2. New York: Academic Press, 89–195.

Baddeley, A.D. (1983) Working memory, *Philosophical Transactions of the Royal Society*. London: B302, 311–24.

Baddeley, A.D. (1986) *Working Memory*. London: Oxford University Press.

Baddeley, A.D. (2001) Is working memory still working? *American Psychologist,* 56(11): 851–64.

Baddeley, A.D. and Hitch, G. (1974) Working memory, in G. Bower, (ed.) *The Psychology of Learning and Motivation: Advances in Research and Theory*. New York: Academic Press, 742–75.

Baddeley, A.D. and Wilson, B.A. (1988) Frontal amnesia and the dysexecutive syndrome, *Brain and Cognition,* 7: 212–30.

Bartlett, F.C. (1932) *Remembering: A Study in Experimental and Social Psychology*. Cambridge: Cambridge University Press.

Broadbent, D. (1958) *Perception and Communication*. Oxford: Pergamon Press.

Bruning, R.H., Schraw, G.J., Norby, M. and Ronning, R.R. (2004) *Cognitive Psychology and Instruction*, (4th edn). New Jersey: Pearson, Merrill Prentice Hall.

Craik, F.I.M. and Lockhart, R.S. (1972) Levels of processing: a framework for memory research, *Journal of Verbal Learning and Verbal Behaviour*, 11: 671–84.

Davey, G. (ed.) (2004) *Complete Psychology*. London: Hodder, Arnold.

Gardner, H. (1991) *The Unschooled Mind: How Children Think and How School Should Teach*. New York: Basic Books.

Gibson, J.J. (1950) *The Perception of the Visual World*. Boston: Houghton Mifflin.

Gregory, R.L. (1980) Perceptions as hypotheses, *Philosophical Transactions of the Royal Society of London B*, 290: 181–97.

Kahneman, D. (1973) *Attention and Effort*. Englewood Cliffs, NJ: Prentice-Hall.

Keller, J.M. (1983) Motivational design of instruction, in E.D. Reigeluth (ed.) *Instructional Design Theories and Models: An Overview of their Current Status*. Hillsdale, NJ: Erlbaum.

Keller, J.M. and Kopp, T.W. (1987) An application of the ARCS model of motivational design, in E.D. Reigeluth (ed.) *Instructional Theories in Action*. Hillsdale, NJ: Erlbaum Associates, Inc.

Köhler, W. (1925) *The Mentality of Apes* (trans. E. Winter). London and New York: K. Paul, Trench, Trubner and Co. Ltd.

Mandler, G. (1967) Organisation in memory, in K.W. Spence and J.T. Spence (eds) *The Psychology of Learning and Motivation Vol I*. New York: Academic Press, 327–72.

Marr, D. (1982) *Vision: A Computational Investigation into the Human Representation and Processing of Visual Information*. San Francisco, CA: W.H. Freeman.

Marton, F. and Säljö, R. (1976) On qualitative differences in learning 1– outcome and process, *British Journal of Educational Psychology*, 46: 4–11.

Massaro, D. (1993) Information processing models: microscopes of the mind, *Annual Reviews*, 44: 383–425.

Miller, G.A. (1956) The magical number seven, plus or minus two: some limits on our capacity for information processing, *Psychological Review*, 63: 81–97.

Naish (2005) in N. Brainsby and A. Gellathy (eds) *Cognitive Psychology*. Milton Keynes: Open University Press.

Navon, D. and Gopher, D. (1979) On the economy of the human information processing system, *Psychological Review*, 210(6): 94–102.

Paivio, A. (1986) *Mental Representations: A Dual Coding Approach*. Oxford: Oxford University Press.

Postle, B.R. and Corkin, S. (1998) Impaired word-stem completion priming but intact perceptual identification priming with novel words: evidence from amnesic patient H.M., *Neuropsychologia*, 39(12): 421–40.

Schank, R. and Abelson, R. (1977) *Scripts, Plans, Goals, and Understanding: An Inquiry into Human Knowledge Structures*. Hillsdale, NJ: Lawrence Erlbraum.

Shallice, T. and Warrington, E.K. (1970) Independent functioning of verbal memory stores: a neuropsychological study, *The Quarterly Journal of Experimental Psychology*, 22: 261–73.

Skinner, B.F. (1957) *Verbal Behavior*. New York: Applegon Century Crofts.

Sternberg, R.J. (1999) *Cognitive Psychology* (2nd edn). Orlando, CA: Harcourt Brace College Publishers.

Tolman, E.C. (1948) Cognitive maps in rats and man, *Psychological Review*, 55: 189.

Treisman, A.M. (1964) Verbal cues, language and meaning in selective attention, *American Journal of Psychology*, 77(2): 206–19.

Tulving, E. (1985) How many memory systems are there? *American Psychologist*, 40: 385–98.

Chapter 4 Constructivism

Introduction

Some teachers take a great interest when their pupils offer an incorrect answer to a question. In such a situation, these teachers proceed by asking pupils to explain how they arrived at that answer. It is likely that these teachers are operating from a constructivist perspective, which sees learners as constructors of meaning. By investigating the origins of a wrong answer, the teacher can uncover the learner's thinking processes, subsequently challenging and refining faulty mental constructs.

It is difficult to draw a clear distinction between constructivism and cognitivism (see Chapter 3, 'Cognitivism') because constructivism is a natural progression from cognitivism and both are interested in cognitive processes. But whereas cognitivism focuses on how information is processed, constructivism focuses on what people do with information to develop knowledge. In particular, constructivism holds that people actively build knowledge and understanding by synthesizing the knowledge they already possess with new information. For constructivists, learning is an active process through which learners 'construct' new meaning. See Table 4.1 for a comparison of behaviourism, cognitivism and constructivism.

Table 4.1 Comparing behaviourism, cognitivism and constructivism

Theory	Mental activity	Learning process	Role of teacher
Behaviourism	Irrelevant	Stimulus–response Reinforcement External event	Controls environment and stimuli
Cognitivism	Perception attention processing	Memory Surface and deep learning Encoding Internal event	Applies cognitive principles to facilitate cognitive processes
Constructivism	Meaning-making	Retuning schemata and mental constructs Internal event	Supports meaning-making Challenges existing ideas

The distinction between cognitivism and constructivism becomes clearer if we consider an example such as reading. This activity requires the cognitive processes of perception and recognition of the shapes of letters, as well as the recall of their sounds from memory. But if a book is to be understood, the reader must construct an understanding of the meaning of the text and what it means to the reader. In this chapter, we outline the background to constructivist theory, before tracing its development through the major ideas of several key proponents: Piaget, Bruner, Vygotsky, Bandura, Freire and Habermas. The chapter also provides an overview of constructivism's chief implications for the educator.

Main categories of constructivist theory

Rather than one unified theory, constructivism is a broad group of theories that explains knowledge acquisition and learning. It has links to other fields including social science, philosophy, politics and history, each of which recognizes that learners interpret and make their own sense of experience and the information they receive.

The different types of constructivist thinking are generally classified according to their main emphases. At one extreme, there is a common-sense belief that individuals build and refine their personal understandings of the world based on what they already know; at the other, is a type of radical constructivism such as that championed by the US academic Ernst von Glasersfeld. He claims that knowledge is a process and product of the human brain, and that the extent to which knowledge reflects external reality cannot therefore be determined: 'we are responsible for the world we are experiencing' (von Glasersfeld 2007).

Here we will discuss the categories of constructivism that are most relevant to learning and education – trivial constructivism, social constructivism and critical constructivism.

Trivial constructivism

When used to describe this category of constructivist thought, 'trivial' means 'obvious' rather than 'insignificant' or 'unimportant'. It indicates the common-sense view that knowledge is not acquired through a process of transmission from an external source to an individual; rather, people actively construct knowledge in an effort to make sense of the world.

According to trivial constructivism, people construct mental models of the way things are. These mental models – or 'constructs' – form personal understandings. When new information is received, the new mental constructs have to be accommodated within previously existing constructs. The new knowledge is adapted rather than adopted. A particularly important process occurs when new constructs conflict with old. Learners are likely to become puzzled, causing them to reconsider and reconfigure mental constructs. This iterative and active process leads to richer understanding and improved learning.

Within certain limits, different learners receive different impressions of any new information because this information is being accommodated within the learners' different and previously existing constructs. This has significant implications for the learning and teaching process because teachers must be aware that learners bring different mental frameworks to that process. For example, if a teacher refers to the word 'home', pupils from different family and home environments will interpret the concept differently.

It is important to sound a note of caution here. Constructivism says that learning is a personal act, but not to the extent that learning is completely different for every individual, rendering shared meaning impossible. Constructivism is underpinned by the belief that we and our mental constructs are more alike than unlike – how else could we survive as social beings?

The thinkers most often associated with trivial constructivism are Jean Piaget and Jerome Bruner.

Piaget

Jean Piaget (1896–1980) is commonly considered the pioneer and parent of constructivist thought. His theory of cognitive development, also discussed in Chapter 8 'Life course development', is based on the idea that children's active engagement with their environment leads them to the construction of meaning and to learning. Play is particularly important for cognitive development, because this is when children actively explore the world. Piaget (1969) argued that cognitive development and conceptual change occur as a result of interactions between existing cognitive structures and new experience. For example, a child may think that a plant gets its nourishment from the ground through its roots. Classroom experiments, however, will show that the plant makes its food in its leaves through photosynthesis.

Another form of learning occurs through cognitive conflict, when children's views are opposed by those of others. This leads to disequilibrium or destabilization of existing constructs; learners must therefore search for new constructs, which can synthesize the different viewpoints and restore equilibrium. This process occurs internally and is later manifested externally by talk and actions. It has been called an 'inside-out' theory (Garton 2004).

According to Piaget, children must go through the process of reconfiguration of their own mental schema for themselves. Teachers must not interfere with this process by imposing their ready-made solutions because children will accept their authority without making the knowledge their own (Piaget 1972). These views led to the 'discovery learning' school movement of the 1960s in which children were encouraged to discover the principles of subjects such as mathematics and science through processes of exploration.

Although Piaget's theory has been criticized for its emphasis on the individual at the expense of social or cultural learning, his contribution to developmental and educational theory has been significant.

Bruner

According to the American psychologist Jerome Bruner, learning is goal-directed and driven by curiosity. Bruner adopted Piaget's ideas about active learning to form the basis of his principles of instruction and discovery learning (Bruner 1960). Over his long career, Bruner moved from a cognitivist investigation of the principles underlying concept-formation (Bruner et al. 1956) to a more sophisticated constructivist position in *The Culture of Education* (Bruner 1996), which examines the social importance of language and culture in meaning-making.

Bruner believed that learning involves three processes:

- knowledge acquisition, in which the learner asks, 'Does this confirm or refine my previous knowledge?' or 'Does this challenge my previous knowledge?';
- knowledge transformation, in which the learner asks, 'What other things can this knowledge now do?';
- knowledge review, in which the learner asks, 'Is the knowledge relevant?' and 'Is this knowledge adequate for the job in hand?'

He also considered that, to become mature thinkers, people must acquire three major intellectual skills for representing the world (Bruner 1966). In children, these usually appear in the sequence shown in Table 4.2.

Table 4.2 Bruner's representational modes

Mode	Representation	Example
Enactive	This is direct knowledge of how to do something.	A child sees herself in a mirror.
Iconic	Knowledge is represented by internal images that stand for an idea.	An older child (5 to 7 years) may draw a mirror including a reflection.
Symbolic	More abstract and flexible thought occurs. Language is the main tool for reflective thinking.	An adolescent may describe the physics of reflection for a plane mirror.

Bruner (1966) proposed a theory of instruction, which is based on structuring and sequencing material in accordance with cognitivist ideas of mental processing. He also developed a curriculum model, which is based on a spiral in which topics are revisited at increasingly advanced levels, with each new iteration building on previous ones. This model is cognitivist insofar as it draws on top-down and bottom-up processes described in 'Chapter 3, Cognitivism' but it also incorporates constructivist thinking in its emphasis on new material being accommodated within old to form new understanding.

In his later work, Bruner (1996) recognized that individual meaning-making occurs within a broader context and culture. Culture provides a framework and an environment, enabling learners to make predictions about what will happen in the future. This leads to the claim that knowledge is socially constructed.

Social constructivism

Trivial constructivism assumes that the acquisition of knowledge is an individual process with individual outcomes, which depends on personal mental frameworks and processes. But, although constructivism may emphasize individual difference, our experience in everyday life is not of difference but of similarity. We participate in the construction of a shared world. Therefore, social constructivism emphasizes the role played by society and culture in learning. In this category of constructivist thought, culture and social communities shape the manner in which individuals perceive, interpret and attach meanings to their experiences; society forms how and what people think. Knowledge is constructed in the context of the environment in which it is encountered. In particular, social constructivists argue that knowledge is the result of social interaction and language use.

As a result, social constructivism maintains that it is possible for people to have shared meanings and understandings that are negotiated through discussion. At the same time, it acknowledges that no two people will have exactly the same discussions with exactly the same people. To this extent it allows that multiple realities exist, and it has this view in common with von Glasersfeld's radical constructivism.

Social constructivism is most closely associated with the work of Lev Vygotsky and Albert Bandura.

Vygotsky

The Russian psychologist Lev Vygotsky wrote in the 1930s but his work was not consistent with Soviet ideology, so his theories only began to receive wide recognition in the 1960s and 1970s. In essence, he emphasized social processes as the means by which all reasoning and understanding arises. In particular, interactions with parents and other important adults lead to the creation of knowledge, which is internalized by children. Unlike Piaget's 'inside-out' approach, Vygotsky's is an 'outside-in' theory (Garton 2004).

For Vygotsky, human activity is distinguished by the extensive use of tools. Language is the most important 'tool' for social interaction and knowledge construction. Vygotsky argued that language is an external tool that children use first to communicate – for example, with their parents – and next to 'think out loud'. Eventually, children begin to carry on discussions internally, developing concepts or 'self-talk'. In this way, language becomes a tool for and of self-regulation. This is what Vygotsky (1978) meant when he argued that all higher mental functions are internalized social relations: 'Schools are another cultural tool with a function of providing theoretical or scientific knowledge as opposed to the empirical and unstructured knowledge that people acquire naturally. This scientific knowledge has been fashioned over centuries and does not have to be reinvented by every child unaided' (Vygotsky 1986: 171). Unlike Piaget, Vygotsky affirms the role of teachers and experts in guiding learning.

As well as passing on theoretical knowledge, teachers support learners in the learning process. The concept for which Vygotsky is best known is the Zone of

Proximal Development (ZPD). This is an intellectual space where learner and teacher interact. The teacher can gauge intellectual development of the learner and provide the appropriate support to advance the learner's thinking. With teacher support, learners can achieve more than they would unaided. More knowledgeable peers can perform the same function as teachers (Vygotsky 1978: 86).

Vygotsky's ideas were ahead of their time and have generated much later research into the way that experts support learners. Barbara Rogoff, for example, describes 'apprenticeship in thinking' in which novices, under the guidance of experts, engage in more advanced thinking than they could perform on their own. She suggests that cognitive development is a result of 'the internalization by the novice of the shared cognitive processes, appropriating what was carried out in collaboration to extend existing knowledge and skills' (Rogoff 1990: 141).

Bandura

Whereas Vygotsky argued that people learn by means of language – that is, by discussing concepts – the Canadian psychologist Albert Bandura went further and proposed that imitation of others is a cognitively efficient means of learning.

In a series of famous experiments in the 1960s Bandura showed kindergarten children a film of a woman playing with a Bobo doll – an inflatable clown weighted at the bottom so that it righted itself when knocked down. In the film, the woman punched and kicked the Bobo doll, and struck it with a toy hammer, while shouting 'sockaroo!' After viewing the film, the children were allowed into a room containing Bobo-dolls and toy hammers. The children proceeded to attack the dolls in precisely the same way as the woman in the film, even shouting 'sockaroo!' Bandura had come from a behaviourist tradition, which sees learning or training as the product of rewarding approximations of a target behaviour. In contrast, the Bobo doll experiment demonstrated what Bandura called 'observational learning' or 'modelling' (Bandura et al. 1961). In everyday life, modelling is evident in the way children like to play with toy versions of machines and domestic appliances that they see their parents using.

Modelling involves imitative rather than original behaviour, but it can be seen in a constructivist light – that is, people adapt modelled behaviour as a mental framework for their own purposes. From an educational point of view, it is clear that much learning occurs by observation. Modelling is part of all learning – for example, in most subjects teachers will present examples of good work that they would like students to use.

Critical constructivism

Critical constructivism, also known as 'critical pedagogy', is particularly applicable to the adult and community education context. This view of learning gives primary importance to raising people's consciousness of the social and cultural conditions in which they find themselves – particularly when their circumstances are characterized by domination and disempowerment. It emphasizes the importance of people being self-reflective, of their being able to challenge dominant social views and articulate counter views.

The background to critical constructivism's concern with power relations may be understood in relation to the thinking of Michel Foucault. His analysis of power relations informs the work of two important critical constructivists considered here, Paulo Freire and Jürgen Habermas.

Foucault

According to the French philosopher Michel Foucault, knowledge is inextricably linked with power. Foucault saw fields of knowledge – that is, disciplines – as types of 'discourse', which consist of theories, practices, attitudes and habits. People internalize these discourses, which means that they generally do not have to be coerced into thinking and behaving in socially acceptable ways. In the classic text *Discipline and Punish* (1977), he shows how nineteenth-century discourses of deviancy led to the creation of specific forms of social control, such as the 'panopticon', a general viewing platform for the mass surveillance of prisoners. For Foucault, the key feature of the panopticon was that prisoners could never know when they were being watched, so they were more likely to behave according to the rules and then to internalize those rules. He also argued that psychiatry developed as a means of containment and control of the mentally abnormal, and that the nineteenth-century development of statistics contributed to governmental knowledge and control of populations. For Foucault, social knowledge is always politically charged, a claim with which Freire would have concurred.

Freire

The most well-known proponent of critical pedagogy was Paulo Freire. He was a Christian socialist who worked with poor illiterate peasants in Brazil in the late 1940s, when people had to be literate to vote in presidential elections. His educational ideas were influenced by liberation theology, Marxism and anti-colonialism. In *Pedagogy of the Oppressed* (1970), he stressed the need for a new kind of education for oppressed peoples, which would not be merely an imposition of the colonizer's culture but which would allow people to see how their individual circumstances were in fact a product of that culture. This could lead to a form of 'praxis', in which people's knowledge of their situation develops in tandem with their action within it and upon it, as they seek to change it (Hamilton 2002: 18).

Freire was also opposed to what he referred to as the 'banking' model of education – that is, a model of education in which teachers deposit knowledge into students' accounts. He disliked the way this model positions learners as passive, because this reinforces dominant ideologies and social structures. Similarly, he objected to the separation of teacher and student roles, which he felt reinforced conventional power relations, and he argued that the relationship should be more democratic and reciprocal. For this reason, the teachers in his literacy schemes were the peasants themselves.

Habermas

Jürgen Habermas claimed that reason and knowledge are constructed through the act of communication between people (McGuigan 2002). He calls this use of reason 'pragmatic' because it is practical and directed towards action. Reason is specific to the context in which it is used; what counts as reasonable in a particular case may need to be revised in the light of usefulness and experience (Habermas 1992). Habermas calls this construction of reason and knowledge by means of the social practice of communication 'communicative rationality' (Cooke 1994).

Like other forms of social action, communication relies on a set of rules. It can proceed only on the basis of agreement on principles and on adherence to truth and honesty, and disagreement can be resolved only through explicit and rational procedures. In reasoned argument, speakers claim that what they say is right, true and honest, and they offer to justify these claims if challenged. When challenged, speakers must be able to offer reasons that are acceptable to both parties. If not, the communication is unacceptable because it is irrational.

Our implicit knowledge of the rules of communication needs to be translated into explicit knowledge so all parties understand them. Communication therefore is an instrument through which knowledge is constructed and shared and through which moral values are expressed. The act of mutual understanding achieved through communication is a basis for coordinating action. Nowhere is this more important than in the social and political sphere, where democratic 'communicative rationality' or debate can relate sociological and other knowledges to the problems of society (Morrison 2001: 220). Indeed, it is through communication that people can begin to understand and question their social and political circumstances.

Educational implications of constructivism

Because constructivism is principally a theory about how people learn, we can draw many educational implications from the work of the key constructivist theorists, and those who have used constructivist principles. Some constructivist practices in education include:

- the diagnosis of learners' individual learning styles;
- the identification of learners' strengths or intelligences;
- curricular practices such as Individual Learning Plans (ILPs);
- attention to cultural inclusivity;
- innovative learning and teaching strategies such as problem-based learning;
- links between community-based learning and formal education;
- authentic assessment practices, which incorporate learners' views.

Trivial constructivism: Piaget and education

As a scientist, Piaget was particularly interested in the development of scientific and mathematical thinking, and these fields have often seen the application of his theories. For example, the Nuffield Mathematics Project of the 1960s encouraged children to discover the principles of mathematics for themselves by exploring ideas and using mathematical games and toys rather than by simply learning conventional methods. This kind of discovery learning is based on the idea that children learn effectively when guided to discover principles or causes through their own investigations. Subsequent research has shown that primary school children left to work out their own methods of addition fare no worse than those taught the standard adult rules (Littleton and Wood 2006: 202–4).

An important aspect of discovery learning may be peer interaction and talk among children in the classroom. Discussion with peers is likely to occur on more equal terms than discussion with a teacher, so it can be more effective in engendering the socio-cognitive conflict important in children's reconsideration of existing ideas and formulation of new ones. This can be seen in an important experiment by Doise and Mugny in which 6-year-old children were shown a model village and asked to recreate how it would look if rotated. To complete the task, children were variously matched with their classmates, some with peers performing at a level above their own and some with the best performers in the class. When children were matched with those at the next level up, they made progress, but when the weakest performers were matched with the best, they did not. This suggests that the introduction of socio-cognitive conflict between the children enabled the weaker performers to take on their peers' points of view and arrive at a solution. But if the partners were too expert, there was no discussion, a solution was imposed and the children did not advance (Littleton and Wood 2006: 206–7).

Despite Piaget's reservations about formal teaching and learning activities, his principles suggest that teachers should:

- nurture pupils' playfulness and natural curiosity about the world;
- use raw data and primary sources;
- provide physical, interactive and manipulative materials for pupils to work on;
- use cognitive terminology such as 'classify', 'analyse', 'predict' and 'create';
- encourage and accept learner autonomy and initiative;
- create opportunities for exploratory classroom discussion;
- engage pupils in experiences likely to engender cognitive conflict.

Trivial constructivism: Bruner and education

For Bruner, the teacher's task is to develop children's skills at particular ages, in different modes of representation. Bruner claims that any subject can be taught in some form to anybody at any age (Bruner 1960). The skill, of course, is to present knowledge in forms that are appropriate to the various ages of child learners. Thus, Bruner suggests that the following activities may be appropriate to his three representational modes:

Mode	Activity
Enactive	children should handle things, actually or virtually.
Iconic	children should see and imagine things.
Symbolic	children should perform symbolic operations.

Social constructivism: Vygotsky and education

Vygotskian thinkers have developed his theories to include guided learning and scaffolding.

Guided learning: joint knowledge construction aided by skilful teacher-managed discussion.

Scaffolding: supports which help learners to construct new knowledge.

Scaffolding may consist of resources, challenging activities and mentoring provided by teachers or more experienced peers. Scaffolding is a powerful metaphor as it suggests supports that are gradually withdrawn when learners have constructed their understanding and can act independently.

The level of scaffolding required is also affected by how far into the ZPD learners have progressed. Four stages have been identified in learners' progression through the ZPD:

1 Scaffolding is provided by others.
2 Scaffolding is provided by learners themselves – for example, by self-talk.
3 Scaffolding becomes redundant as learners act automatically.
4 Scaffolding is required again if there are changes in the task or context.

(Tharp and Gallimore 1988)

Scaffolding strategies for the classroom

In order to scaffold learning, teachers should:

- provide time for pupils to construct relationships with each other;
- allow pupils' responses to drive lessons, determining the teaching methodology and content;
- inquire about pupils' understanding of concepts, including false understandings, before sharing their own understanding of these concepts;
- encourage pupils to engage in dialogue with the teacher and with each other;
- encourage inquiry by asking open-ended questions and encouraging peer questioning;
- seek elaboration of pupils' responses to questions;
- wait for a response after asking questions;

- create metaphors and use different teaching styles to aid mental representation;
- model the behaviour or the techniques to be acquired.

Critical constructivism and education

The claims of critical constructivism that knowledge is situated and contextual mean that generalizations for practice are not appropriate. Critical constructivism suggests that educators need to be aware of the unequal power relationships between educational providers, teachers and pupils. This is especially true of adult and community education where the ownership of knowledge may be contested or where learners may be disempowered through a lack of choice or autonomy.

Key ideas

- Knowledge is situated and constructed in social contexts.
- The learner is an active agent in the interpretation of the world.
- Constructivism focuses on meaning-making and the understanding of knowledge.
- Learning involves the interpretation of experience to construct meaning.
- Mental constructs may be modified as a result of confirmation or challenge.
- Other people are important in the formation and modification of mental constructs.

Conclusions

In drawing conclusions about constructivism, you may find it useful to assess the drawbacks as well as the benefits of the theory.

Although a constructivist approach to teaching, learning and curricula has been recommended in schools since the 1960s, some critics argue that it is still difficult to see constructivist principles acted out in the classroom. Indeed, we can identify several reasons why teachers might resist constructivist practices.

- Schools must generally follow imposed curricula, the rigidity of which often makes it difficult for teachers to respond to pupils' constructions of knowledge.
- Teachers are inadequately trained in constructivist teaching and learning, as well as scaffolding strategies.
- Class size can make individual appraisals of pupils' progression through the ZPD difficult.
- Teachers may feel or find that classroom discussion is inefficient in facilitating learning.
- Teachers attempting to apply constructivist principles may have concerns about classroom control and pupil behaviour.

- It may be difficult to assess and evaluate the extent of pupils' learning in a constructivist classroom.

On the other hand, it is clear that many effective educational practices are directly influenced by constructivism, so it should still be of interest and use to all educators because it underpins much of what they do, even if they are not aware of it. For example, the current interest in group and project work at educational levels ranging from the primary school to university level suggests that shared meaning-making is important for reasons ranging from increased motivation to enhanced task perform-ance.

References

Bandura, A., Ross, D. and Ross, S.A. (1961) Transmission of aggressions through imitation of aggressive models, *Journal of Abnormal and Social Psychology*, 63: 575–82.

Bruner, J. (1960) *The Process of Education.* Cambridge, MA: Harvard University Press.

Bruner, J. (1966) *Toward a Theory of Instruction.* Cambridge, MA: Harvard University Press.

Bruner, J. (1996) *The Culture of Education.* Cambridge, MA: Harvard University Press.

Bruner, J., Goodnow, J. and Austin, A. (1956) *A Study of Thinking.* New York: Wiley.

Cooke, M. (1994) *Language and Reason: A Study of Habermas's Pragmatics.* Cambridge MA: MIT.

Foucault, M. (1977) *Discipline and Punish: The Birth of the Prison.* London: Penguin Books Ltd.

Freire, P. (1970) *Pedagogy of the Oppressed.* New York: Continuum.

Garton, A.F. (2004) *Exploring Cognitive Development: The Child as Problem Solver.* Oxford: Blackwell Publishing.

Habermas, J. (1992) Further reflections on the public sphere, in C. Calhoun (ed.) *Habermas and the Public Sphere.* Cambridge, MA: MIT, 421–61.

Hamilton, P. (2002) Mapping the field, in P. Hamilton and K. Thompson (eds) *The Uses of Sociology.* Milton Keynes: The Open University and Blackwell Publishing, 1–40.

Littleton, K. and Wood, C. (2006) Psychology and education: understanding teaching and learning, in C. Wood, K. Littleton and K. Sheehy (eds) *Developmental Psychology in Action.* Oxford: Blackwell Press and Open University Press, 193–229.

McGuigan, J. (2002) The public sphere, in P. Hamilton and K. Thompson (eds) *The Uses of Sociology.* Milton Keynes: The Open University and Blackwell Publishing, 81–114.

Morrison, K. (2001) Jürgen Habermas, 1929–, in J.A. Palmer (ed.) *Fifty Modern Thinkers on Education: From Piaget to the Present*. London: Routledge.

Piaget, J. (1969) *Mechanisms of Perception* (trans. G.N. Seagrim). New York: Basic Books.

Piaget, J. (1972) *To Understand Is To Invent*. New York: The Viking Press.

Rogoff, B. (1990) *Apprenticeship in Thinking*. New York: Oxford University Press.

Tharp, R. and Gallimore, R. (1988) *Rousing Minds to Life: Teaching, Learning and Schooling in Social Context*. New York: Cambridge University Press.

von Glasersfeld, E. (2007) *An Exposition of Constructivism: Why Some Like it Radical*. Italy: Associazione Oikos. http://www.oikos.org/constructivism.htm (accessed 23 August 2007).

Vygotsky, L.S. (1978) *Mind in Society*. M. Cole, V. John-Steiner, S. Scribner and E. Souberman (eds) Cambridge, MA: Harvard University Press.

Vygotsky, L.S. (1986) *Thought and Language*. Cambridge, MA: MIT Press.

Chapter 5   Social learning

Introduction

One of a mother's greatest concerns when her child goes to school for the first time is that the child will make friends there. Children learn essential social skills by interacting with their classmates and with adults. Although learning is a personal process, it usually occurs in a social setting.

In defining what is meant by social learning we need to consider two aspects.

Sociological aspect: the learning of the skills of social interactions and social roles within a specific society.

Psychological aspect: the way that learning as a cognitive activity is influenced by social factors.

This chapter looks at learning in the light of the sociological and psychological theories that combine to form the field of social learning.

Theories of social learning

Here we present theories and findings that shape social learning. We first discuss the most important sociological theories that influence learning and education. This is followed by an exploration of psychological theories of social identity and individualization. The final part of the chapter will discuss their educational implications.

Sociological theories

The major sociological theorist to be discussed is Émile Durkheim, one of the nineteenth-century founders of the discipline of sociology. For Durkheim, society is more important than the individual (Alpert 1959). Society regulates all social life through its institutions and systems. The totality of beliefs and sentiments of society's members forms the basis of the moral and legal codes that integrate society and the individual. This is of great importance to education because it suggests that the business of education is to mould children in accordance with the norms and needs of society.

There are three elements in Durkheim's model of any society:

- system – the totality of organizations and groups in society;

- structure – the links between these organizations and groups;
- function – the role of these social bodies in realizing the values and expectations of the society.

Rather than the modern child-centred idea of education which adapts itself to the varying needs and talents of each student, Durkheim believed that the function of education is to maintain and transmit integrative social values through the socialization of individuals (Meighan and Siraj-Blatchford 2003: 253). It is the child who needs to adapt to society. According to Durkheim:

- the curriculum should reflect the collective culture and aims of the society rather than developing individual talents;
- teachers should enable pupils to become useful members of society, conforming to social values;
- the pupil should be receptive to the values of school and society.

(Durkheim 1956)

Social institutions and groups

Learning occurs within social spheres and contexts, which inform, develop, deepen and influence individual identity, thinking, learning and meaning-making processes. Of particular interest here is the influence of social groups and institutions, as well as class structure and inequality.

The US sociologist Charles Cooley (1909) identified three influential primary groups, or social institutions – family, peers and community – that play a vital role in shaping human behaviour and functioning, including learning.

Family

Experiences and initial social relationships are first developed in the family. The values expressed in this social group are most important in shaping children's early behaviour and thinking because children model their behaviour and attitudes on family members.

In the eighteenth century, Rousseau saw parents as the natural educators of their children. From the beginning of the nineteenth century, however, education was increasingly taken over by the state with an educational discourse that downplayed the role of the family.

More recently, this discourse has changed again because of perceived failures within formal systems of education, particularly for socially disadvantaged groups. For example, home schooling is popular with families who wish to preserve their own particular values, particularly if they feel that these values may be undermined by mainstream public schooling. Similarly, home–school liaison programmes now seek to involve parents in the education of their children and intergenerational learning is promoted, with the aim of integrating children's home and school experiences (Conaty 2002). It is ironic that schools are now seeking the help of the family to solve problems created partly by changes in family structures.

Peer groups

In peer groups, individuals learn to interact, behave and conform in socially acceptable ways. They acquire social roles, responsibilities and identities, which are developed through relationships and group participation. Group members develop strong emotional ties that unite them in meaningful and affective ways and learn emotional control. Individuals who do not belong to, or participate meaningfully in social groups, run a greater risk of developing mental and emotional problems (Goffman 1961; Laing and Easterson 1970). Some types and characteristics of peer group interactions are shown below.

Social play

The US psychologist and philosopher George Herbert Mead highlighted the importance of play in the social development of the child. During play, children rehearse and act out the social norms and behaviours they witness (Mead 1913; 1934/1970).

Friendship and peer groups

As shown in Figure 5.1, the influence of peers becomes more important than that of the family group as children move into their teenage years. Although parental influence is still important in career and money matters, the peer group is more important in establishing social status and identity (Sebald 1986). At this stage of development, belonging to the peer group may be more important than adopting educational values (Hargreaves 1967).

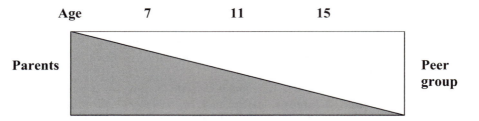

Figure 5.1 Peer group effects on children.
Source: based on Sacker et al. (2002).

Group allegiance

Group socialization may also lead to group stereotyping. For example, the famous Boys' Camp experiments of the 1950s showed that group members ascribe positive qualities to the group to which they have an allegiance – the 'in group' – and negative qualities to other groups – the 'out groups' (Manheim 1960).

Groupthink

Group socialization can also lead to 'groupthink', in which group consensus and conformity override objective analysis. In groupthink, the importance of group unity can sometimes prevent group members from voicing opinions or misgivings for fear of being disconnected from the group. Individual objections may even be overridden in order to sustain group cohesion. Esser and Lindoerfer claim that 'Groupthink was tragically evident in the decision process by which NASA decided to launch the space shuttle *Challenger* in January 1986' (Myers 2005: 316).

Community groups

According to Cooley (1909), the third primary group is the community. Although not mutually exclusive, community groups may be categorized into different types:

- *Normative groups* These include all varieties of religious and other belief groups that maintain codes of conduct and social control through shared world views and values;
- *Civil groups* These include political parties, community associations, lobby groups such as environmental, and charitable organizations that socialize members into shared responsibilities, rights and obligations;
- *Interest groups* These vary with the nature of the cultural environment. They range from pigeon fanciers to music appreciation societies to Buddhist meditation groups. These share and support cultural interests;
- *Vocational groups* These include professional bodies and trades unions whose purpose is to support members in the construction of identity and in promoting and protecting their interests.

Communities such as the above offer members:

- shared history and values;
- a collective identity;
- reciprocal obligations and rights;
- a shared discourse.

(Mercer 2000: 106)

There is much recent interest in communities of learners and communities of practice where learning is acquired through social group interactions and participation. The more experienced members exercise control and power. 'Situated learning' occurs in these 'communities of practice'. Learners progress from novice to expert through a form of cognitive apprenticeship (Lave and Wenger 1991).

Social groups and advantage

Since Marx's work on class struggle and capitalism in the mid-nineteenth century, we have understood that there is a relationship between class and social advantage. Although the extent and nature of this relationship has been hotly debated, the issue of class and class structure is central in sociological thinking, and influences various strands of social learning theory.

According to Marxist theories, the class in society which controls the means of production also controls cultural life. This dominant class disseminates a particular set of cultural and ideological values which serve to perpetrate the interests and advantages of the dominant class and has an impact on other classes. In education, the dominant class invests its social and cultural capital in order to reproduce and maintain its advantage. For example, Wilcox (1988) found that children from upper-class and middle-class backgrounds received numerous forms of remediation when faced with potential learning problems but children from lower socio-economic backgrounds received little or no remediation because their problems were 'to be expected' (Wilcox 1988: 295).

The work of Bourdieu and Bernstein discussed in Chapter 6, 'Cultural learning', and Chapter 13 'Language and learning' demonstrates ways in which this class advantage operates. Any actions or expectations that privilege or reinforce the status of one class over another may be seen as forms of 'symbolic violence' (Bourdieu and Passeron 1977:5). Several studies have revealed examples of such symbolic violence in the classroom. Rist (1970/2000) showed that teachers had preconceived notions about pupils' intellectual ability based on socio-economic background, social environment and sibling(s) ability.

The American educationalist Michael Apple challenges the rhetoric claiming that schools offer advantages to all irrespective of social class. However, an examination of the outcomes shows that success is highly related to the class to which one belongs (Apple 1990). Educators need to consider the ways that their own class background influences their perceptions of learners from different social class backgrounds and how their own practices and expectations may be perpetuating injustice.

The extent to which individuals are in charge of their educational destinies is addressed by the fundamental dichotomy of structure versus agency (Abercrombie et al. 2000: 9).

Structure: the organization of social life in accordance with societal structures.

It suggests that social structures completely shape individuals.

Agency: the extent to which individuals have freedom to take control of their actions.

It suggests that individuals have the power to shape social structures.

Many educational debates can be conceptualized in terms of structure and agency. Sociological theorists tend to hold that class is a major determinant of educational success. Educational rhetoric however, often proclaims the view that a learner can use education to overcome class disadvantage.

Psychological theories

This section deals with theories drawn from social psychology which emphasize ways in which social interactions and experiences affect individuals, their sense of identity and their self-esteem. It explains how social groups shape behaviours, attitudes and self-esteem.

Social identity

The social groups to which we belong have profound effects on how we act and on how we perceive ourselves. This is more than a socialization process; it is also psychological because it involves socio-cognitive strategies such as perception. In his work on inter-group relationships, the psychologist Henri Tajfel found that groups define themselves according to minimal criteria. For example, it may be enough to be placed in a team or simply labelled as a group. The members of the group consider themselves to be the 'in group' and other groups to be the 'out groups'. In the 'in group', similarities are enhanced, as are the differences from the 'out groups'. For group members, self-identity is also enhanced as is social status (Tajfel and Turner 1986). This group stereotyping is a socio-cognitive perceptual strategy. Cognitively, it simplifies thinking (inside is good; outside is bad) and socially it increases group solidarity and facilitates a united response to outsiders.

Schools have long realized the importance of group membership and belonging. In the English school system, for example, there is long tradition of 'house' groupings to create a sense of belonging and to enhance performance by generating competition – the houses of Gryffindor, Hufflepuff, Ravenclaw and Slytherin in J.K. Rowling's *Harry Potter* books exemplify this strategy. The simple act of segregating people by means of the 'sorting hat' is sufficient to create the group and generate feelings of group affiliation and animosity towards other groups.

Animosity towards the 'out group' can cause inter-group conflict and discrimination. In a school setting, differences between groups of high and low achievers will tend to be accentuated as will differences between groups from different ethnic or social backgrounds unless measures are taken to reduce this potential conflict. The classic boy's summer camp studies conducted by Sherif in 1966 demonstrated that inter-group competition encourages group conflict. These studies also suggest that group membership is sufficient to instil 'in-group' favouritism along with justifying exploitation of 'out groups'. In his studies, Sherif arbitrarily divided previously unacquainted boys into two groups which were separated from each other for a period of a week. The studies showed that by the mere act of dividing them into two groups, the boys consistently favoured and formed alliances with members of their own in group. Only when the boys were reunited in common tasks did hostility levels drop.

Reciprocal determinism

Individuals, their behaviours and their social environment are dynamically bound together in a process of 'reciprocal determinism' (Bandura 1986).

Individual characteristics

- Self-identity – self-conception as distinctive.
- Self-esteem – feelings of personal worth.
- Self-efficacy – individual ability within particular areas.
- Expectancy – individual expectations of attainment with respect to goals.

Overt behaviour

- Actions – things that an individual does.
- Performance – how well things are done.

Social environment

- Group identity – group conception as distinctive.
- Social status – position in a group hierarchy.
- Social interactions – activities between group members.

The dynamic relationship between these is illustrated in Figure 5.2. Self-identity is created both by actions in the world and our interactions with groups. Overt behaviour is determined by our identity and our group status. Our group identity is determined by our overt behaviour and our individual identity.

For example, the identity a pupil in the lowest stream of a school is formed by past and present academic performance and the group with whom they most closely interact. The relationship is a dynamic one. If a pupil begins to identify with other groups of peers who are performing at a higher level, then self-identity will change and create expectancies that will affect overt behaviour in the classroom (harder work). This in turn will have an effect on the relationship between that student and the class group.

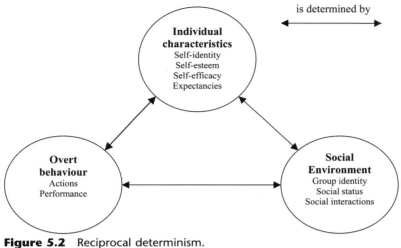

Figure 5.2 Reciprocal determinism.
Source: Bandura (1986:24).

Educational implications of social learning theory

Social learning theory proposes that social life and psychological life interact as part of learning, so that learning cannot be considered a purely individual activity. Rather, it is situated in social institutions, social groups and social class. Personality, cognitive and social factors interact dynamically to create identity, expectancy, self-esteem, efficacy and ultimately, performance. This section of the chapter will consider the educational implications of social learning under its sociological and psychological aspects.

Sociological aspects

- Identify societal norms by:
    o looking for examples in literature, art and history that embody norms;
    o explaining the role of social institutions;
    o devising a curriculum to reflect knowledge valued by society;

- Transmit societal norms by:
    o embedding civil values in the curriculum;
    o raising consciousness to energy saving and environmental issues;
    o modelling respectful and committed behaviour;
    o grounding discussion on mutual social values;
    o assigning social responsibilities to learners;

- Recognize learners' social and community action such as:
    o service in the community;

   o research on local issues;
   o participation in political action;

  • Celebrate social norms by:
   o presenting historical and contemporary exemplars as role models;
   o celebrating social and civic rituals as part of the curriculum.

Teachers can enhance the learning experience if they are mindful of the ways in which family, peers, community and class affect learning.

The family

In order to promote the role of families as partners in education, teachers should:

- establish communication links with families;
- appoint school liaison personnel to visit homes;
- make parents welcome in school;
- give parents an active role in the running of the school;
- consult parents and involve them in school life;
- explain the terms of educational discourse to parents;
- ask parents for help and advice;
- involve parents as educators and role models;
- promote intergenerational family learning;
- train parents to help their child to learn (e.g. paired reading technique);
- set homework projects that require family help (e.g. genealogy or history).

Peer groups

Peer groups protect against social isolation. Learners who are meaningfully integrated with their peers are increasingly protected against early drop-out and bullying (Lubell and Vetter 2006). Also, peer groups engaged in learning tasks achieve a wider range of information and deeper meaning-making than individuals can achieve on their own (Gabriel and Montecinos 2001). Peer groups can challenge individual views by providing alternative perspectives, and they can also generate the drive to resolve differences so that social relationships are maintained. The influence of peer groups can be negative if the values of the group run counter to those of education – for example, where belonging to the group is more highly valued than academic achievement.
  In order to promote peer group integration and cohesion, teachers should:

- use small-group learning that encourages shy pupils to participate;
- develop strategies to engender healthy group competition in learning;
- vary the composition of groups in terms of friendship, gender or/and ability;
- assign specific roles to group members;
- organize field trips and visits to foster group cohesion;

- arrange extra-curricular activities that increase social cohesion;
- encourage students to join social clubs and societies;
- employ class debates to explore alternative perspectives;
- create virtual groups through synchronous (electronic conferencing) and asynchronous (email, bulletin boards, blogging) methods.

The community

While communities play a vital role in supporting social cohesion, learning communities have an intellectual function. Such communities create groups of learners who share a common intellectual or professional interest. This is expressed through their role in the creation, interrogation and sharing of knowledge. This is undertaken in a form of discourse that is inclusive in allowing members to share ideas and exclusive in keeping others out. Communities of knowledge and of practice may range from small study groups within a school to communities of researchers dispersed throughout the world.

In order to develop communities of learning, teachers should:

- behave as partners rather than the sole possessors of knowledge;
- create a culture of collaboration;
- let expert learners share their knowledge;
- share community history, traditions and rituals;
- look for collaborative possibilities outside school (virtual links);
- encourage inquiry within the classroom;
- create an atmosphere where ideas are challenged;
- introduce novice members to the language and practices of the community;
- use more experienced learners to mentor novices;
- engage groups in collective learning activity;
- promote reasoned debate;
- emphasize the rights and responsibilities of membership.

Equity and equality

Educators need to be aware that the achievement of equality involves more than increased access to educational opportunities. After all, students are acutely aware of their social and intellectual status in class. Learners must be supported in positive ways that allow them to achieve equality of outcomes.

In order to promote equity and equality, teachers should:

- have high expectations of all learners;
- handle streaming or banding with great care and sensitivity;
- show respect for differences of opinions, beliefs, values and attitudes;
- provide additional support for vulnerable learners as an entitlement;
- vary the social and intellectual composition of groups in learning projects;
- celebrate learners' strengths and multiple intelligences;
- be aware of differences of language codes from different social groups;

- encourage elaborated language (see page 187);
- recognize effort as well as achievement.

Psychological aspects

Identity

The individual identity of learners is formed by their perception of the groups with which they identify and the way they themselves are perceived by the group. In order to promote positive self-identity in a learning context, teachers should:

- encourage different types of group formation based on friendship, team activity or interest;
- use mixed ability groupings to prevent stratification;
- vary the composition of groups so that learners can establish themselves within different groups;
- encourage group loyalty;
- permit friendly competition between groups;
- encourage people to take up roles within a group to promote self-esteem;
- encourage groups to recognize members' contributions;
- look out for isolated learners and integrate;
- be alert to bullying and stereotyping.

Self-esteem

Although Bandura's theory of reciprocal determinism suggests that self-esteem is influenced by past and present action and the learner's social environment, the teacher can play a significant part in enhancing or maintaining the self-esteem of learners. Learners often identify good teachers as those who boost self-esteem and bad ones those who diminish it. In order to maintain or improve learners' self-esteem, the teacher should:

- relate to learners as people rather than merely learners;
- refer to learners by name;
- be particularly conscious of adult learners' sensitivity and self-esteem;
- protect learners from public failure;
- give learners an opportunity to act as teachers;
- build guaranteed success into learning activities;
- recognize effort as well as achievement;
- celebrate individual success;
- praise learners' contributions to classroom activities;
- treat mistakes as opportunities to learn;
- provide regular and constructive feedback;
- avoid sarcasm, ridicule and criticism;
- avoid comparisons or criticism;
- praise in public, criticize in private.

Key ideas

- Learning does not occur in isolation; it is socially constructed.
- Learning has both sociological and psychological implications.
- Society regulates social life through institutions and systems.
- According to Durkheim the business of education is to mould children in accordance with societal needs.
- Learning is a process of socialization mediated through membership of various groups.
- Education reproduces class and structural inequalities in society (Bandura).
- Intra- and inter-group processes are important in forming individual identity.
- There is a dynamic relationship between individual self-esteem, the social environment and the learner's action.
- There is a tension between *structure* (the extent to which societal structures shapes individuals) and *agency* (the extent to which individuals determine their own destiny).

Conclusions

For behaviourists, learning is a conditioned individual response to stimuli; for cognitivists, it is the individual application of mental processes; for constructivists, it revolves around the construction of meaning. For social learning theorists however, learning is the product of shared experiences in a range of social settings.

This chapter outlines some aspects of social learning. Drawing on the work of Durkheim and his successors, it explores learning as a process of socialization and the way societal structures and class influence learning. The chapter also shows how social processes are involved in establishing learner self-esteem. It shows that social influences on individual psychology are not simply in one direction; there is a dynamic and reciprocal relationship in which social environment, action and individual interact. It reminds the educator that learning is not just an individual activity; it is embedded in the social fabric of society and both reflects and influences social processes.

However, it also invites reflection on the limitations of the educator's influence over learning. The teacher and the classroom form only minor parts of the learner's world. There a tension between structure and agency both for the learner and the teacher. The learner's own agency in engaging in learning is constrained by class and social structures. Similarly, the teacher's own agency in teaching is constrained by the educational system and an inability to change many features of the learner's experience.

Nevertheless, for many oppressed or socially disadvantaged people, education is a major tool for combating oppression and disadvantage and offers an avenue for advancement and social progress.

References

Abercrombie, N., Hill, S. and Turner, B.S. (2000) *The Penguin Dictionary of Sociology*, (4th edn). London: Penguin Books.

Alpert, H. (1959) Émile Durkheim: a perspective and appreciation, *American Sociological Review*, 24(4): 462–5.

Apple, M.W. (1990) *Ideology and Curriculum* (2nd edn). New York: Routledge.

Bandura, A. (1986) *Social Foundations of Thought and Action: Social Cognitive Theory*. Upper Sadle River, NJ: Pearson Education.

Bourdieu, P. and Passeron, J.P. (1977) *Reproduction in Education, Society and Culture*. London: Sage.

Conaty, C. (2002) *Including All: Home, School and Community United in Education*. Dublin: Veritas.

Cooley, C.H. (1909) *Social Organisation: A Study of the Larger Mind*. New York: Charles Scribner's Sons.

Durkheim, E. (1956) *Education and Sociology*. New York: Free Press.

Gabriel, A.J. and Montecinos, C. (2001) Collaborating with a skilled peer: the influence of achievement goals and perceptions of partner's competence on the participation and learning of low-achieving students, *The Journal of Experimental Education*, 69(2): 152–79.

Goffman, E. (1961) *Asylums: Essays on the Social Situation of Mental Patients and Other Inmates*. New York: Doubleday and Co.

Hargreaves, D. (1967) *Social Relations in a Secondary School*. London: Routledge and Kegan Paul.

Jordan, A. and Carlile, O. (2005) Learning Societies: Global Trends towards National Qualification Frameworks, *International Chinese Conference on the Development Models of the Modernization Process in the Eastern and Western Countries – China and the World*. Liuzhou, Guanxi. China.

Laing, R.D. and Easterson, A. (1970) *Sanity, Madness and the Family*. London: Penguin Books.

Lave, J. and Wenger, E. (1991) *Situated Learning: Legitimate Peripheral Participation*. Cambridge: Cambridge University Press.

Lubell, K. and Vetter, J. (2006) Suicide and Youth Violence prevention: The promise of an integrated approach, *Aggression and Violent Behaviour*, 11(2):167–75.

Manheim, H.L. (1960) Intergroup interaction as related to status and leadership differences between groups, *Sociometry*, 23(4): 415–27.

Mead, G.H. (1934/1970) *Mind, Self, and Society from the Standpoint of a Social Behaviorist* (17th edn). C.W. Morris (ed.) Chicago and London: The University of Chicago Press.

Mead, G.H. (1913) The social self, *Journal of Philosophy*, 10: 374–80.

Meighan, R. and Siraj-Blatchford, R. (2003) *A Sociology of Education* (4th edn.). New York: Continuum.

Mercer, N. (2000) *Words and Minds*. London: Routledge.

Myers, D.G. (2005) *Social Psychology* (8th edn). New York: McGraw-Hill.

Rist, R. (1970/2000) Student social class and teacher expectations: the self-fulfilling prophecy in ghetto education, *Harvard Educational Review*, 70(3): 257–301.

Sacker, A., Schoon, I. and Bartley, M. (2002) Social inequality in educational achievement and psychosocial adjustment throughout childhood: magnitude and mechanisms, *Social Science and Medicine*, 55(5): 863–80.

Sebald, H. (1986) Adolescent's shifting orientation toward parents and peers: a curvilinear trend over recent decades, *Journal of Marriage and the Family*, 48(1): 5–13.

Sherif, M. (1966) *Group Conflict and Co-operation: Their Social Psychology*. London: Routledge and Kegan Paul.

Tajfel, H. and Turner, J. (1986) The social identity of intergroup behaviour, in S. Worchel and W.G. Austin (eds) *Psychology of Intergroup Relations*. Chicago: Nelson-Hall.

Wilcox, K. (1988) Differential socialisation in the classroom: implications for equal opportunity, in G. Spindler (ed.) *Doing the Ethnography of Schooling*. Prospect Heights, IL: Waveland Press.

Chapter 6   Cultural learning

Introduction

In many countries and periods of history, the education of girls has differed from that of boys. Cultural norms have often dictated that women are designed and destined for different activities from men, and should be educated accordingly. This is just one example of the influence of culture on learning. This chapter will explore other such cultural influences and implications, bearing in mind that 'cultural learning' can mean 'learning *about* a culture' and also 'learning *within* a culture'. As authors, we come from a specific western cultural perspective and we are aware of the dangers of commenting on other cultures. It is impossible to stand outside our own cultural framework but we will nevertheless attempt to be self-aware and self-reflexive in our analyses.

According to Bronfenbrenner (1979), human development occurs in an environment consisting of four interrelated and nested structures:

- settings where the person is present – home, school, workplace;
- places where these settings interconnect – interaction between home and school;
- settings where the person is not present – government, business, technology;
- the overarching cultural context – economic, social and intellectual climate.

Every human structure and meaning – from race, nationality, ethnic grouping, religion, social class and gender to the family, school and workplace – is culturally determined. Learning occurs within culture because culture encompasses every aspect of human experience. But culture is also the content of learning, insofar as all learning is induction into a culture (Bruner 1996). The word 'culture' comes from the Latin 'colere', meaning 'to cultivate' or 'to care for'. Culture is something cultivated. To learn is to be introduced into:

- the values, beliefs and norms of a culture;
- the experiences and products valued by a culture;
- the ways of thinking and acting that are prevalent in that culture.

This chapter outlines theories of how human meaning-making is culturally determined, and considers the implications for pedagogy, cognitive style and learning. It suggests a range of practical ways that teachers can respond to, and make the most of, culturally diverse classrooms.

Principles of cultural studies and learning theory

Culture can be defined as 'a fuzzy set of attitudes, beliefs, behavioural norms, and basic assumptions and values that are shared by a group of people, and that influence each member's behaviour and his/her interpretations of the "meaning" of other people's behaviour' (Spencer-Oatey 2000: 4). A popular metaphor for culture is the iceberg with observable behaviours above the waterline. Below lie several layers usually outside conscious awareness but nevertheless determining human behaviour. Figure 6.1 illustrates this metaphor, using the culture of the family as an example.

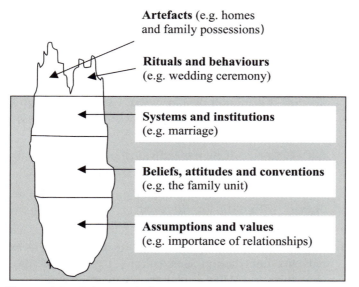

Artefacts (e.g. homes and family possessions)

Rituals and behaviours (e.g. wedding ceremony)

Systems and institutions (e.g. marriage)

Beliefs, attitudes and conventions (e.g. the family unit)

Assumptions and values (e.g. importance of relationships)

Figure 6.1 Culture as iceberg.

Like education, cultural studies draws its theory from a variety of disciplines in the social sciences, the humanities and the arts. Sources include psychology, philosophy, history, literary criticism, anthropology, linguistics and semiotics. Also like educational research, the study of culture cannot be said to have a methodology of its own but draws its methodology from a wide variety of fields. In the past, there was a tendency to view culture as large scale and homogenous. Modern perspectives display a growing awareness of greater varieties of culture, of subcultures within cultures, and of the complexity of cultural identities. Cultural studies therefore encompasses a very broad field. This chapter is focused on aspects that have an obvious impact on education – for example, diversity.

Modern western perspectives recognize cultural diversity. People are born into a particular gender, ethnic group and race, live in a particular region in a particular country, belong to a particular social class and have a particular religious orientation or not.

Modern educational practice tries to accommodate the resulting cultural diversity. In the following discussion, we outline some of the ideas that are of importance to cultural learning theory and are likely to be of use to the educator attempting to nurture a culturally diverse and inclusive learning environment:

- cultural dimensions;
- habitus;
- cultural reproduction;
- cultural capital.

Hofstede's cultural dimensions

The Dutch organizational anthropologist, Geert Hofstede, developed the idea of cultural dimensions, an indexing system that can be used to describe, categorize and compare cultures. Hofstede's (1991, 2001) cultural dimensions are:

Power distance index (PDI)   the extent to which people without power accept the unequal distribution of that power. China scores highly on this index, for example, because subordinates accept the formal power of others.

Individualism index (IDV)   the extent to which the individual is more important than the group. The USA scores very highly here.

Masculinity index (MAS)   the extent to which the roles of men and women are distinct with little or no overlap. Strictly traditional Islamic countries score highly here.

Uncertainty avoidance (UAI)   the extent to which people wish to reduce anxiety by reducing uncertainty. Such cultures like predictability, clear rules and stable structures. Japan scores highest in this dimension.

Long-term orientation (LTO)   the extent to which people attach importance to a long-term future rather than to tradition or the past or present. These cultures value thrift, perseverance and patience. For example, traditionally, parents in Northern European Protestant cultures impressed upon their children the importance of delayed gratification; chores had to be completed before play commenced.

Hofstede's system is extremely useful in looking at cultures on many levels, from the culture of an entire nation to that of a particular educational institution or class.

Hall's cultural dimensions

Although Hofstede's is the most famous theoretical construct designed to understand cultural dimensions, there are others. Edward T. Hall (1984) considered culture to be mainly subconscious unless challenged. He proposed an index consisting of two dimensions: high-context versus low-context, and monochronic versus polychronic (Hall 1959; 1969).

The high-context versus low-context dimension is concerned with the manner in which information is exchanged. It has two components:

- the context of the message (situation, history, people involved and so on);
- the content of the message (usually in the form of spoken or written words).

(Hall 1976)

High and low context

High-context cultures attach more importance to the transmitters and the surrounding context than to the message. For example, the fact that a message is delivered by someone in authority implies that it would be disrespectful to challenge it. Typical high-context cultures are Japan, China and Korea. Low-context cultures are more literal; information is mostly contained in the actual transmitted message with less attention paid to the transmitter or the context. North America, Scandinavia and Germany are examples.

Someone from a high-context culture such as China may feel that someone from a low-context culture such as the US is being rude and literal, whereas the person from the low-context culture may feel that the high-context person is being inscrutable.

Hall's ideas on high and low context cultures are useful to educators because they emphasize the subconscious communicative aspects of culture. Educators may not be aware of the way their cultural backgrounds influences the way they transmit information, nor of the way learners' cultures influences its reception.

M-time and P-time

Although not mutually exclusive, the monochronic (M-time) versus polychronic (P-time) dimension describes tendencies to view time differently. M-time cultures view time as linear, partitioned, scarce and not to be wasted. Timetables, schedules and deadlines are taken seriously. Germany is often seen as having an M-time culture. For P-time cultures, however, time is less tangible, more holistic, more flexible and defined by context rather than clock. Timetables are aspirational; people are more important. Stereotypically, tropical islanders are seen as 'laid back' and conforming to P-time cultures.

Conventionally, formal educational settings require an M-time approach with timetables, assessment dates and so on. This is balanced by the person-centred approach of P-time to allow for flexibility and compassion. Arguably, constructivist, child-centred education reflects a P-time approach and teacher-centred, whole-class methods reflect an M-time approach.

Habitus

Many manifestations of cultural diversity are seen in daily practices and behaviours that 'go without saying'. This is often referred to as 'habitus' and includes bodily habits, styles of moving, linguistic register and accent, tastes in food and clothing, and so on. In the 1970s, French sociologist Pierre Bourdieu argued that 'habitus' should also include personal constructs, belief systems and disposition. We are hardly conscious of our 'habitus' until we visit a foreign country or enter a different social milieu and are exposed to a habitus very different from our own (Bourdieu 1986).

Formal and informal education sometimes intentionally addresses aspects of the habitus – for example, children are taught 'good manners'. More often, however, habitus is acquired as a result of the general interactions during an educational career – for example, the importance that formal schooling places on punctuality prepares learners for the 'habitus' of the workplace.

Cultural reproduction and education

By passing on 'habitus', education reproduces culture, particularly those aspects of it that are seen 'above the waterline' in the iceberg (Figure 6.1). Education also has taken on the role of reproducing aspects of culture from below the waterline. Curricula include civics, citizenship and personal and health education; religious education and history also reproduce culture.

For example, in what has become known as the 'history wars', the Australian federal government from 1996 to 2007 consistently rejected history that presented white colonizers as invaders who destroyed indigenous culture. This thesis was decried as a 'black armband' view of history, and in 2007 a new, more 'neutral' and 'comprehensive' curriculum was mooted in the lead-up to a federal election (McIntyre and Clark 2004; Australian Government Department of Education, Science and Technology 2007). This example demonstrates that no subject is absolutely culture free. Even the decision to grant a topic the status of a subject worthy of study is itself a cultural statement.

Cultural capital

If education reproduces culture, it may also reproduce the cultural advantages enjoyed by privileged classes. To explain how this occurs, Bourdieu developed the idea of 'cultural capital' as part of his examination of differences in educational outcomes in France in the 1960s. He said that having certain cultural knowledge gives one an advantage. Just like financial capital, cultural capital is possessed more by some than by others, and with it comes status and power. Those who have cultural capital pass it on to their children and so the advantage is perpetuated. For example, a child who is surrounded by books and lives in a household in which both parents have benefited from higher education enjoys a certain cultural capital that is not available to those without these experiences.

According to Bourdieu (1986: 47), there are three types of cultural capital:

Embodied	This is personal. It includes accent, tone and the way an individual moves, as well as the traditions and beliefs passed on to that individual through socialization.
Objectified	This type consists of actual objects such as books and works of art. These need to be appreciated to be 'consumed'.
Institutionalized	This type consists of educational qualifications and academic credentials recognized officially by institutions. This cultural capital can be converted into financial capital by employment because higher paid jobs often require higher academic qualifications.

Bourdieu's notion of cultural capital that emphasizes access to literature, art, museums and galleries might seem outdated in the early twenty-first century, when the Internet makes books and art collections available online. However, not everyone has access to technology; students with broadband in their homes have a cultural and educational advantage.

Even more significant however, is the cultural capital that disposes people towards high culture and educational development which leads to success in education and employment. In addition, education can reproduce social and cultural inequalities insofar as teachers have been the successful recipients of cultural capital and, consciously or unconsciously, reproduce dominant values.

Educational implications of cultural learning theories

Educators responds to culture in two ways:	Theoretically in their cultural perspectives,
Educators may find the following theoretical constructs useful:	Practically in their culturally influenced pedagogical strategies.

- cultural awareness;
- enculturation;
- culture and knowledge, language and cognitive style;
- culture and motivation;
- cultural stereotyping;
- multicultural education.

Cultural awareness

Classrooms create their own cultures within which may be subcultures of social groups or other nationalities. From a constructivist perspective, teachers must be aware of their students' cultural backgrounds in order to understand how they construct knowledge and make sense of their worlds. This is important, regardless of whether teachers are working in their own culture, a foreign culture, or a mixed cultural context. Cultural dimension indices, such as those proposed by Hofstede, can help teachers reach greater understanding of the cultural diversity in their classrooms (see Table 6.1).

Table 6.1 Assessing classroom culture using Hofstede's indices

Hofstede's indicies	Related question for educator
Power distance	• How does the teacher distribute power in the classroom? • How do students respond to the distribution of power?
Individualism	• How far is the teaching directed at individuals or groups? • How cohesive is the class group?
Masculinity	• How does the teacher treat gender relations? • How much does gender influence learning?
Uncertainty avoidance	• How explicit are teachers about rules and procedures? • How do students perceive the value of rules and procedures?
Long-term orientation	• How do teachers explain aims and long-term goals? • How willing are students to persevere towards long-term goals?

Enculturation

According to Bruner (1996: 43), education is 'a complex pursuit of fitting a culture to the needs of its members and their ways of knowing to the needs of the culture'. In education systems, conscious attempts are made to pass on national and cultural history and tradition. This can be explicit in the case of schools run by religious denominations, or implicit in the content and delivery of the general curriculum. The curriculum includes everything that children experience at school – not just the subjects. Students are enculturated through interactions with teachers and peers – learning about social organization, power and status – and they also learn what is considered knowledge and what the culture considers worth learning. The culture may consider workplace skills more valuable than classical languages, for example, and reflect this in the curriculum.

Culture and knowledge

Meaning and knowledge are socially constructed and reflect the assumptions and worldview of the culture in which they have developed. What is seen as knowledge depends on cultural values. In a primitive society, knowledge of where to find food and water is far more important than knowledge of quantum theory or Greek philosophy. Subject choices made, and educational paths chosen, reflect the particular values of advanced societies.

The way that cultures create knowledge has implications for the distribution of power within those cultures. Foucault (1977) examined the cultural construction of mental illness, arguing that it was not until the nineteenth century that madness was seen as a medical condition. This new construction conferred power on psychiatry. Similarly, on the basis of their subject expertise and their institutional power, educators gain the power to diagnose educational failure or success, with long-term consequences for their students.

Culture and language

Language both reveals and transmits culture. Some cultural characteristics of language include the following:

Directness	For example, Americans avoid ambiguity and use precise language, whereas East Asian cultures use fewer words and are more vague.
Maintenance of relationships	Some cultures focus on objects and the relationships between them. Language is adapted to the status of the person addressed. For example, Japanese people use different grammatical structures for talking to men, women and people of lower and higher status.
Emotion	In the UK emotions are expressed obliquely and modifiers are used. In Korea there is more reserve and little demonstration of emotion.
Talk	African cultures make prolific use of proverbs, and the Greeks glorify rhetorical techniques.

(Samovar and Porter 2004: 146–52)

The way people think is influenced by the words and concepts they possess. A well-known example of this is the Sami natives of northern Sweden, who have 500 words to describe snow (Samovar and Porter 2004: 146). This enables them to make subtle distinctions about an important aspect of their experience. An educational example might be literature teachers or students, whose knowledge of technical terms such as irony, pathos and pathetic fallacy permit them to engage in deeper analysis, understanding and discussion. Hirst (1965) points out that the curriculum in fact consists of learning about ways of thinking in different disciplines.

Culture and cognitive style

Culture affects the way that we perceive and process the world. According to Samovar and Porter (2004: 242–3), the effects of culture can be identified in four cognitive styles:

- field independence versus field sensitivity;
- cooperation versus competition;
- trial and error versus 'watch then do';
- tolerance versus intolerance of ambiguity.

Field independence versus field sensitivity

Field-independent learners tend to ignore context and treat a subject directly. This is more typical of western cultures. *Field-sensitive learners* are more aware of broader contexts and of social dimensions. This may be a characteristic of Asian cultures, which emphasize relationships, respect and the preservation of 'face'.

Cooperation versus competition

The cognitive styles of some learner groups are cooperative, whereas others tend to be competitive. For example, Latino parents teach their children to work cooperatively in groups but North American parents teach their children to work on their own and to be competitive (Grossman 1984, quoted in Samovar and Porter 2004). The concept of individuality and competition runs through many North American discourses of education.

Trial and error versus 'watch then do'

Some people prefer to attempt something, fail and then try again until they get better at it. Others prefer to observe for a while before attempting a task. Cleary and Peacock (1998) argue that native American students prefer to watch activities until they feel competent enough to participate. In some Asian cultures, error is unacceptable and a cause of shame.

Tolerance versus intolerance of ambiguity

North American culture dislikes ambiguity and emphasizes clear aims and learning outcomes. At the same time, it allows for significant flexibility in teaching methods. East Asian cultures value ambiguity in knowledge, but their classrooms are highly structured and teaching methodologies are restricted.

Culture and motivation

Culture has a significant influence on what we value, and what we value in turn influences the factors that motivate us to learn. The sources of motivation are either extrinsic or intrinsic. Yao (1987) describes how Asian children are often motivated extrinsically – for example, they want to please parents and impress relatives. This may be less the case with students from western cultures that prize individual attainment and self-fulfilment. These students may be motivated intrinsically by their own desire to obtain good qualifications and jobs.

Similarly, cultural background may shape not only how students want to learn, but also what they want to learn (Samovar and Porter 2004: 247). For example, Japanese culture demands that children accurately memorize historical dates and mathematical formulae, and children are also expected to learn a musical instrument regardless of aptitude. Hispanic and native American students, on the other hand, 'prefer to learn information that is personally interesting to them' (Walker et al. 1989: 63).

Cultural stereotyping

Several of the theoretical constructs we have discussed above concern general differences among cultures, and we have drawn attention to them so that educators can be aware of the sources and types of cultural diversity in the classroom. At the same time, educators must be very careful not to make assumptions about learners, learning, and teaching practices from cultural backgrounds other than their own.

For example, on the basis of generally agreed western pedagogical principles, classrooms in Confucian-heritage cultures (CHCs) break all the rules. Classes are large – 40 or more students would not be unusual, teaching is often in the form of lectures, rote learning is highly valued, the teacher's authority is not challenged, the focus is on performance in highly competitive and stressful examinations, and educational financial resources and student support are minimal (Biggs 1996: 46–7). It would be culturally naïve for western teachers to ignore the subtleties of the relationships in CHC classrooms, to decry their methods or to dismiss their results. Students from such classrooms often outperform western students (including creatively) so it appears to be effective (Biggs 1996: 47).

Indeed, contemporary research (Biggs 1996; Tang 1996; Kember 2000; Watkins and Biggs 2001; Jarvis et al. 2003) debunks stereotypes about CHC learners, learning styles and teaching methods. For example:

- Skill in drawing can be developed by repeatedly copying a small number of examples very carefully. This skill can then be used creatively in original art work. This means that the western preconception that children should explore materials first and then develop skills can be reversed.
- CHC students are often said to be reluctant to engage with the teacher and other students in the western classroom. However, they are highly interactive outside the classroom. For example, the number of students who seek one-to-one interaction after class and interactions with other students is probably higher than among western students (Jarvis *et al.* 2003: 87).
- CHCs attribute success and failure more to effort than to ability. As a result, students spend more time studying outside of class and work harder than their western counterparts.
- Discussion is not common in CHC classroom settings (perhaps because it is viewed as a waste of valuable teacher time), but spontaneous student collaboration occurs when CHC students meet unfamiliar situations. Tang (1996) describes how 87 per cent of a student sample in Hong Kong University worked collaboratively without teacher instigation.

- Evidence does not support the idea that students from CHCs 'prefer passive learning and resist teaching innovation' (Kember 2000: 110). A study of 90 action learning projects in Hong Kong universities showed that when students are given the opportunity to adopt more active methods they do so, but teachers must prepare the ground carefully (Jarvis et al. 2003: 87).

Educators must remember that, although the brain and cognitive processes involved in learning may be similar for humans in general, pedagogy cannot be divorced from its cultural and social contexts.

Multicultural education

In the modern developed world, globalization and migration has meant that the multicultural classroom is becoming the norm, but there is debate about whether multicultural education is genuinely possible or desirable. Some call for the recognition of cultural diversity and emphasize the value of fostering it; others demand that the values, traditions and history of the dominant culture be given pre-eminence, as in the American custom of saluting the flag each morning before school starts. In some cases, the metaphor of the 'melting pot' – in which all cultures combine – has given way to the metaphor of the 'salad bowl', in which immigrant cultures and dominant cultures co-exist. The trouble arises when these cultures collide – for example, on religious issues such as the the wearing of the hijab at school (Lee 2003).

Even in monocultural classrooms, students bring to learning a range of backgrounds and learning styles. In the multicultural classroom with fewer shared cultural values, diversity may be more difficult to accommodate. In the next section, we suggest how a constructivist approach might be practically applied in these circumstances.

Practical advice to the teacher

A responsive pedagogy for cultural diversity can be implemented by means of procedural clarity, culturally sensitive meaning-making and culturally diverse teaching. It is also important to support the learning of all students.

Procedural clarity

Teachers should:

- be absolutely clear about norms and procedures;
- make sure that instructions are understood by obtaining feedback;
- guide students in class participation and discussion by making class rules explicit;

    ○   establishing clear rules for class discussion (taking turns, listening to everyone, contributing and not interrupting);

    ○   providing alternatives for those students who are less culturally inclined to participate in class discussion.

Culturally sensitive meaning-making

Constructivism tells us that teachers should make explicit efforts to help students engage in meaning-making. This needs to be sensitive and relevant to students' cultural values. To do this, teachers should:

- model respect by
    - ○ using inclusive language and inclusive examples;
    - ○ welcoming alternative viewpoints;
    - ○ asking students to produce projects describing particular cultural practices (for example, food);

- examine values by
    - ○ reflecting on the values implicit in the subject;
    - ○ reflecting on values that may be challenging to some cultures;
    - ○ respectfully exploring different value systems in relation to a topic;

- celebrate difference by
    - ○ asking students to provide examples of teaching topics relevant to their cultures;
    - ○ collecting culturally diverse materials for future use;
    - ○ eliciting information about preconceptions in the light of particular cultures.

Culturally diverse teaching

To make the most of their classrooms' cultural diversity, teachers should:

- learn as much as possible about students' cultural backgrounds by
    - ○ undertaking class surveys about cultural backgrounds;
    - ○ researching cultural backgrounds using the Internet;
    - ○ contacting and getting to know parents;

- teach tolerance by
    - ○ using icebreakers to introduce students to one another;
    - ○ celebrating and recognizing a range of religious festivals;
    - ○ using a range of culturally diverse sources.

Supporting student learning

Disadvantaged students will need additional or particular support. To avoid reproducing cultural and social disadvantage, teachers can:

- support students with language difficulties by
  - assessing language competence by means of early formative exercises;
  - teaching subject-specific vocabulary;
  - teaching the conventions of writing and speaking academic English;

- use assessment sensitively by
  - using a variety of assessment methods;
  - making clear the criteria for success;
  - using formative assessment and self-assessment in particular;
  - helping students to set personal goals.

Key ideas

- Human structures and meaning are culturally determined.
  - Culture is manifested in 'habitus' – the way things are done.
  - Culture determines the way we interpret the behaviour of others.
  - Cultures are diverse and contain many subcultures.
  - Language reveals and transmits culture.

- Culture determines what is considered worthy of study.
  - No subject is absolutely 'culture free'.
  - Learning involves learning about and within a culture.

- Formal education reproduces culture.
  - Educators' cultural perspectives influence how they view their role.
  - Educators' cultural perspectives influence their pedagogy.
  - The classroom itself has a culture.
  - Students' cultural perspectives influence how they construct knowledge.
  - Cultural background influences cognitive style and motivation.
  - Students are enculturated through interactions with teachers and peers.

Conclusions

This chapter explores cultural issues in education and raises the consciousness of educators to cultural diversity in education and how it is manifested in attitudes, behaviour, interpersonal relations and language. It contributes to a wider contemporary debate about differentiation in learning and how it can be achieved. It also offers some strategies for multicultural classrooms and alerts educators to their own culture and the way they may impose it.

However, while cultural diversity should be recognized and celebrated, the reality of multiple cultures in a classroom may mean that accommodating one culture may be disrespectful to another. There is also the opposite problem of cultural political correctness that attempts to avoid any cultural references in classrooms so that history and values are diminished. One of the functions of school is to transmit the culture of the surrounding society; yet, as many societies from Australia to Canada have found, there is an inevitable tension between the transmission of a culture and the accommodation of difference.

In one sense the world is becoming more homogenous culturally. Differentiation in education may provide a means of preserving and celebrating cultural identity, history and traditions.

References

Australian Government Department of Education, Science and Technology (2007) *Teaching Australian History*. http://www.dest.gov.au/sectors/school_education/policy _initiatives_reviews/key_issues/australian_history/default.htm (accessed 24 October 2007).

Biggs, J. (1996) Western misperceptions of the Confucian-heritage learning culture, in D. Watkins and J. Biggs (eds), *The Chinese Learner*. Hong Kong and Melbourne: University of Hong Kong Comparative Education Research Centre & Australian Council for Educational Research, 45–67.

Bourdieu, P. (1986) The forms of capital, in J. Richardson (ed.) *Handbook of Theory and Research for the Sociology of Education*. New York: Greenwood Press.

Bronfenbrenner, U. (1979) *The Ecology of Human Development*. Cambridge, MA: Harvard University Press.

Bruner, J.S. (1996) *The Culture of Education*. Cambridge, MA: Harvard University Press.

Cleary, L.M. and Peacock, T.D. (1998) *Collected Wisdom: American Indian Education*. Needham Heights, MA: Allyn and Bacon.

Foucault, M. (1977) *Discipline and Punish: The Birth of the Prison*. London: Penguin Books Ltd.

Hall, E.T. (1959) *The Silent Language*. New York: Doubleday.

Hall, E.T. (1969) *The Hidden Dimension: Man's Use of Space in Public and Private*. London: Bodley Head.

Hall, E.T. (1976) *Beyond Culture*. Garden City, New York: Anchor Press.

Hall, E.T. (1984) *The Dance of Life: The Other Dimension of Time*. Garden City, New York: Anchor Press/Doubleday.

Hirst, P. (1965) Liberal Education and the Nature of Knowledge, in R.D. Archambault (ed.) *Philosophical Analysis and Education*. London: Routledge.

Hofstede, G.H. (1991) *Cultures and Organizations: Software of the Mind*. New York: McGraw-Hill.

Hofstede, G.H. (2001) *Culture's Consequence: Comparing Values, Behaviors, Institutions, and Organizations Across Nations* (2nd edn). Thousand Oaks, CA: Sage.

Jarvis, P., Holford, J. and Griffin, C. (2003) *The Theory and Practice of Learning* (2nd edn). London: Kogan Page.

Kember, D. (2000) Misconceptions about the learning approaches, motivation and study practices of Asian students, *Higher Education*, 40(1): 99–121.

Lee, J.J. (2003) Expulsions over veil intensify French debate on secularity, *International Herald Tribune*, *19*, 21 October.

McIntyre, S. and Clark, A. (2004) *The History Wars* (2nd edn). Melbourne: Melbourne University Publishing.

Samovar, L.A. and Porter, R.E. (2004) *Communication Between Cultures* (5th edn). Belmont CA: Wadsworth.

Spencer-Oatey, H. (2000) *Culturally Speaking: Managing Rapport through Talk across Cultures*. London: Continuum.

Tang, C. (1996) Collaborative learning: the latent dimension in Chinese students' learning, in D. Watkins and J. Biggs (eds), *The Chinese Learner*. Hong Kong and Melbourne: University of Hong Kong Comparative Education Research Centre and Australian Council for Educational Research, 183–204.

Walker, B.J., Dodd, J. and Bigelow, R. (1989) Learning preferences of capable American Indians of two tribes, *Journal of American Indian Education*, [special issue]: 63–79.

Watkins, D. and Biggs, J. (2001) *Teaching the Chinese Learner: Psychological and Pedagogical Perspectives*. Hong Kong: University of Hong Kong Comparative Education Research Centre.

Yao, E.L. (1987) Asian-immigrant students: unique problems that hamper learning, *NASSP Bulletin*, 71(503): 82–8.

Chapter 7 Intelligence

Introduction

When you say to someone, 'That was not a very intelligent thing to do', what do you mean by 'intelligent'? If you open almost any psychology textbook and look up 'intelligence', you will encounter adjectives such as 'problematic', 'difficult', 'controversial' or 'disputed'. It may seem strange that a concept so apparently important to learning and education lacks a simple, clear and agreed definition.

History

In the nineteenth century, the German experimentalist Wilhelm Wundt investigated mental activities such as perception, discrimination and reflex action, making an association between these requirements for problem-solving and what we now call 'intelligence'. Another nineteenth-century experimentalist, Francis Galton, used measurement of abilities in pitch, colour and weight discrimination as indications of intelligence.

Whereas Galton looked at low-level cognitive functions, the French psychologist Alfred Binet, in the early twentieth century, preferred to look at higher-level functions (Binet and Simon 1916). He viewed intelligence as consisting of reasoning, comprehension and, in particular, judgement.

The idea of 'intelligence' began to surface in the early twentieth century, when psychology was establishing itself as a respectable branch of science. Intelligence was co-opted along with personality as one of the objects of a new interest in testing and psychometrics. Despite Binet's broadminded understanding of intelligence, the concept was conceived of quite narrowly in terms of reasoning and problem-solving. As the century went on, however, the definition broadened and returned to a position closer to Binet's as is seen in Table 7.1.

Table 7.1 Twentieth-century definitions of intelligence

Date	Theorist	Definition
1916	Binet; Terman	Intelligence is motivation and adaptation to the environment.
1927	Spearman	General intelligence, or 'g', underlies specific mental abilities.
1923	Boring	Intelligence is whatever an intelligence test measures.
1938	Thurstone	Intelligence consists of seven factors or primary mental abilities (spatial ability, numerical ability, verbal fluency, perceptual speed, inductive reasoning, verbal ability, meaning), which correlate with each other.
1958	Wechsler	Intelligence is the ability to act rationally and purposefully, and interact with the environment.
1963	Cattell	Intelligence includes the following factors: fluid intelligence – the ability to think logically and relate concepts through reasoning crystallized intelligence – the knowledge or skills acquired as a result of fluid intelligence.
1985	Sternberg	Intelligence is mental activity directed towards purposive adaptation to, and selection and shaping of, real-world environments relevant to one's life.
1986	Carroll	Intelligence can be thought of as a hierarchy: single general intelligence (like Spearman's 'g') group factors (for example, flexible thinking) specific abilities.
1993	Gardner	Intelligence is a collection of potentialities or abilities that allow us to solve problems or fashion products that are of consequence in a particular cultural setting or community.

Source: based on Davey (2004: 515).

This reveals several themes in contemporary understandings of intelligence:

- 'factor' theories (Spearman, Guildford, Cattell, Thurstone, Carroll, Gardner);
- cognitive processing (Binet and Terman, Wechsler, Cattell, Sternberg);
- adaptation to the environment (Binet, Wechsler, Sternberg, Gardner);
- relationship to culture (Binet, Sternberg, Gardner).

The sources of intelligence: nature or nurture?

The debate between nature and nurture with respect to intelligence is one of the most controversial in this field. To what extent are people 'born' intelligent? What is the relationship between intelligence and environment?

Nature

Twins offer a useful way of studying the issue.

Identical twins (monozygotic)

These come from a single fertilized egg that splits in two.

They have identical genetic makeup.

Fraternal twins (dizygotic)

These come from two eggs fertilized separately.

These twins are only as alike as any two siblings.

If inherited characteristics are important, monozygotic twins should be more similar in intelligence than dizygotic twins. The degree of similarity is measured statistically by a calculation called the correlation coefficient. Perfect correlation (twins with exactly the same IQ) would yield a correlation coefficient of +1.00. A review of 50 studies of the influence of genetics on intelligence by Erlenmeyer-Kimling and Jarvik (1963) revealed an average correlation of +0.87 for identical twins and +0.53 for fraternal twins. This indicates that twins are of similar intelligence but the degree of similarity is greatest with identical twins – a finding which has been explained by hereditary factors.

The IQs of identical twins have been shown to be very close, even when these twins are reared apart. Although some doubt has been thrown on some of the figures used, other studies still show a minimum correlation coefficient of 0.62 (Eysenck 1994: 15).

Fraternal twins show no greater closeness of IQ than brothers and sisters in the same family. The IQs of adopted children are closer to those of their natural than their adoptive parents. All of this seems to confirm the influence of genetics on intelligence.

Nurture

Despite the important of genetics, there is evidence that some key environmental factors have a significant influence on the development of intelligence.

Parenting

According to modern socio-cultural theory, thinking is formed as a consequence of social relationships (Vygotsky 2004). Parents are the primary socializers and so have a major role in the development of children's thinking skills.

Studies have shown that foster children generally have higher IQs than their biological parents, presumably because the environment provided by foster parents raises the children's intelligence (Eysenck 1994: 16). For example, Scarr and Weinberg (1976) found that the mean IQ of a group of 99 black children adopted by white, middle-class parents was 110. This is 25 points higher than the average IQ for black children in general (Eysenck 1994: 19).

Other elements of parenting important in the development of intelligence include parents' roles in the construction of identity through the modelling of behaviour and expectations they have of children. For example, parents might model curious and critical habits of mind, or interests in reading. They can also provide a consistent nurturing environment allowing for the development of routines and good habits associated with schoolwork and study.

Nutrition

Brains are physical organs, and it is not surprising that nutrition plays a vital role in their development and the related development of intelligence. The diet of premature babies made a significant difference to IQ eight years later (Davey 2004: 528). Giving vitamins and minerals to 6-year-olds made a difference to IQ (Benton and Cook (1991).

Schooling

In a classic study, Rosenthal and Jacobson told teachers that some of their pupils had high IQs and could be expected to bloom. In reality, the children had been selected randomly. Nevertheless these children went on to show an increase in IQ. The explanation for this was that the children received more attention from teachers because of the teachers' expectations (Rosenthal and Jacobson 1968).

Children who attend school regularly score higher on IQ tests than those who attend only intermittently. However, motivation has an influence on school attendance, and people with low IQs may not like to go to school; low IQ could be a cause rather than an effect of poor attendance.

Separating nature and nurture

As the discussion above suggests, it is difficult to untangle nature and nurture. Having the right biological parents is a good start, but the environment is critical in actualizing people's potential. The Canadian psychologist Donald Hebb claimed that 'asking whether intelligence is determined more by heredity or by environment is like asking whether the area of a field is determined more by its length or by its width: both are absolutely indispensable' (quoted in Eysenck 1994: 13).

Nevertheless, Hebb (1966) did make a distinction between two types of intelligence: type A, related to the genotype, and type B related to the phenotype.

Type A   *Genotype:*   the genetic makeup of an organism

Type B   *Phenotype:*   the observable, physical characteristics of the organism

Neither of these intelligence types is directly measurable, because type A is masked by experience, and only a tiny sample of the abilities associated with type B is measured by standard intelligence tests. Despite these difficulties, educators have a clear investment in understanding the extent to which the learning environment can enhance inherited intelligence: this will be discussed in more detail later in the chapter.

Intelligence testing

The Binet-Simon test

At the end of the nineteenth century in France, authorities noted that children from rural areas, although not mentally deficient, were doing poorly in school compared to their urban peers. In 1904, the French government asked *La Société Libre pour l'Etude Psychologique de l'Enfant* to appoint a commission to report and advise on the education of such children, as well as those with a genuine mental deficiency.

As members of the commission, Binet and his colleague Théodore Simon developed the Binet-Simon mental scale for identifying children requiring special education. The test was based on a range of tasks typical of children's abilities at various ages (see Table 7.2). This allowed children's mental abilities to be assessed relative to their peers so that an individual child's mental age could be established. From an educational point of view, this was seen as very useful because children could then be sorted into classes according to their mental ages.

Table 7.2 Sample tasks from Binet and Simon's tests

	Tasks
Age 4	Name objects (key, knife, penny).
	Repeat three figures.
	Compare the lengths of two lines.
Age 8	Compare two objects from memory.
	Count down from 20 to 0.
	Repeat five numbers.
Age 12	Produce more than 60 words in three minutes.
	Define three abstract words.
	Comprehend a jumbled-up sentence.

Source: Davey (2004: 516).

Binet was aware that the tests had a cultural dimension. For example, analogies such as 'hat is to head as shoe is to ...' require cultural knowledge. He recommended that the test should be given to children of similar backgrounds and he strove to remove cultural bias from it. But despite his nuanced understanding of its limitations, Binet's test was adapted in a less subtle way when it began to be used in America.

Intelligence quotient

Before the Binet-Simon scale was adopted in America, it was refined in 1912 by the German psychologist William Stern who first proposed the idea of the intelligence quotient (IQ). He suggested that the mental age of a child be divided by the child's chronological age and the result multiplied by 100 to give a measurement he called the IQ. If the two ages were the same, the IQ would be 100 and considered average. If a child had a mental age of 12 and a chronological age of 10, the IQ would be 12/10 x 100 = 120, and above average.

Comparison of chronological and mental age is not suitable beyond childhood, so IQ for adults is calculated by comparison with the average or the normal scores of a large number of people. This is called norm-referencing.

It is assumed that IQ scores are normally distributed in a population. This means that most scores are clustered near the mean or average, with fewer very high or very low scores. This produces the typical bell curve of what is known as the 'normal distribution' shown in Figure 7.1. The bell curve shows us that there are many people of average IQ but very few whose IQ is extremely high or extremely low.

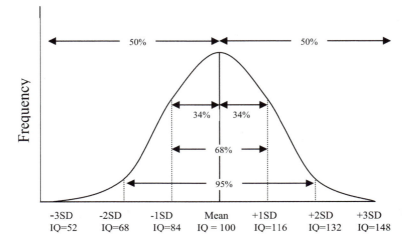

Figure 7.1 The bell curve of normal distribution.

The spread of IQ scores is measured by a statistic called the standard deviation (SD). In a normal distribution, 68 per cent of scores lie within one standard deviation (1SD) of the mean. Intelligence tests are designed to produce a mean of 100 and an SD of 16. So having an IQ of 116 (the mean plus 1SD) means that a person has a higher intelligence than 50 + 34 = 84 per cent of the population.

The Stanford-Binet test

Shortly after the publication of the Binet-Simon mental scale and its refinement by Stern, Louis Terman developed a version in English at Stanford University in the United States and standardized it with respect to a large American sample. Unlike Binet, Terman and his colleagues believed that intelligence was a fixed entity that could be accurately determined and could act as a basis for serious educational and vocational decisions. The Stanford-Binet test was guided not only by a benign desire like Binet's to help all children receive an education. The manual accompanying the test made the point that the test would result in 'curtailing reproduction of feeble-mindedness and in elimination of enormous amounts of crime, pauperism and industrial inefficiency' (Terman 1916: 26).

Contemporary tests

Stanford-Binet

The fourth edition of the Stanford-Binet test, published in 1986, made several advances over previous versions and allows the assessment of children as young as two years of age. It has 15 tests divided into four cognitive areas:

- verbal reasoning;
- abstract visual reasoning;
- quantitative reasoning; and
- short-term memory.

It has a high correlation with the Wechsler test (see below), with older versions of the Stanford-Binet test and with academic tests.

Wechsler

This is the most popular contemporary IQ test. It includes three tests for different age ranges, all in the same format: pre-school children aged 3 to 7, school children aged 6 to 16, and adults aged 16 to 74. The Wechsler Intelligence Scale for Children (WISC) consists of 13 subtests organized into six verbal tasks and seven performance tasks (see Table 7.3).

Table 7.3 WISC subtest

Verbal	Performance
1 *Knowledge*: things and events	1 *Picture completion*: identify missing part
2 *Similarities*: concept linkage	
3 *Arithmetic*: mental calculation	2 *Coding*: transcribe codes quickly
4 *Vocabulary*: word definition	3 *Picture arrangement*: sequence drawings
5 *Comprehension*: problem-solving	
6 *Digit-span*: digit-string recall	4 *Block design*: copy coloured mosaics
	5 *Object assembly*: complete jigsaw puzzles
	6 *Symbol search*: locate target shape
	7 *Maze*: find path in 2-D maze

Source: Based on Wood et al. (2006: 26).

Contemporary theories of intelligence

The statistician Charles Spearman (1927) noted that people who performed well on one of the Stanford-Binet tests of intellectual ability did well on other subtests. His statistical technique of factor analysis led him to attribute this correlation to an underlying general intelligence ('g'), manifested in the specific intelligences related to particular tasks. General intelligence is more important, because it can be directed towards the improvement of specialized intelligences. Because 'g' is the critical component, it represents a unitary intelligence.

Multi-factorial models

Table 7.4 shows a range of multi-factorial models of intelligence, in contrast to a unitary one.

Table 7.4 Factorial models of intelligence

Type	Theorist	Factors
General 'g'	Spearman (1927)	**Unitary:** one common factor
Dichotomous	Cattell (1963)	**Fluid:** speed of mental processing of new information **Crystallized:** use of previously acquired knowledge and skill
Triarchic	Sternberg (1985)	**Componential:** processing internal cognitive events **Contextual:** coping with the environment **Experiential:** bridging internal and external worlds
Hierarchical triad	Carroll (1986)	**Top:** general intelligence **Middle:** seven group factor abilities (crystallized, visual, auditory, speed, fluency, memory, fluid ability) **Bottom:** highly specific abilities (e.g. counting)
Multiple intelligences	Gardner (1993)	Several independent intelligences (linguistic, logical-mathematical, spatial, bodily kinaesthetic, musical, interpersonal, intrapersonal, naturalistic), which can be defined as collections of potentialities or abilities of value in a particular cultural setting

Source: based on Davey (2004: 519–20) and Eysenck (1994: 19–35).

The early theories stress cognitive processing as an isolated phenomenon, whereas later theories stress the importance of values, and the context in which people use their intelligence.

Multiple Intelligences (MI)

Gardner's multiple intelligences theory is the best-known of the multi-factorial theories and is the one of most relevance to classroom teachers as shown by his 'Project Zero' workshops run annually in the US (Harvard University 2007).

Gardner defines intelligence as a collection of potentialities or abilities that permits people to solve problems or make products which are of value in a particular cultural setting. For Gardner, the ability to act intelligently is driven by the goals, values and beliefs of that society (Gardner 1999). He argues that people do not have one intelligence, as measured by standard IQ testing, but several strengths or intelligences, resulting in a 'jagged intelligence profile'. Some of the evidence he offers for separate intelligences includes the way damage to parts of the brain affects specific abilities and the way savants with a low IQ may have an exceptional ability in one area.

The eight intelligences Gardner proposed are shown in Table 7.5.

Table 7.5 Gardner's multiple intelligences

Intelligence	Description	Exhibited by
Linguistic	The capacity to use language effectively	Poets, writers, politicians, teachers
Logical-mathematical	The ability to analyse and manipulate abstract relations	Scientists, mathematicians, accountants, programmers
Spatial	The ability to perceive visual and spatial patterns and represent visual and spatial images	Artists, architects, engineers, designers
Bodily-kinaesthetic	The ability to use the body expressively or skilfully	Athletes, surgeons, dancers, craftspeople
Musical	The ability to create, communicate and understand music	Composers, musicians, conductors, critics
Interpersonal	The ability to interpret moods, motivations and feelings of others, and to act accordingly	Parents, teachers, salespeople, counsellors
Intrapersonal	The ability to interpret personal feelings and build accurate self-representations	Meditators, actors, poets, reflective practitioners
Naturalistic	The ability to classify and use features of the environment	Farmers, botanists, geologists, explorers

Source: based on Gardner (1999).

There are other candidates for consideration as separate intelligences. For example, 'existential intelligence', which is an ability to consider questions of ultimate values and meaning (Gardner 1999). Goleman's popular theory of emotional intelligence has much in common with Gardner's intrapersonal and interpersonal intelligences (Goleman 1996).

There are some difficulties with MI theory. If all intelligences have equal ranking, the addition of more intelligences dilutes the significance of all. There is also the danger of labelling. MI theory may result in people being labelled not only according to traditional IQ measurements, but to eight other measurements as well.

Intelligence, gender and race

There are differences in scores and test results achieved by men and women and people from different racial backgrounds. Explanations for these differences are contested because of their political and social implications (Zuckerman 1990).

Gender

Women achieve higher scores on verbal reasoning tests, whereas men achieve higher scores on mathematical and spatial reasoning tests. Men's mathematical superiority is greater than women's verbal superiority (Benbow and Stanley 1983). Women's IQs tend to cluster around the mean whereas extremes of intelligence are more common in men as shown in Figure 7.2. Many controversies have arisen over the interpretations placed on these findings.

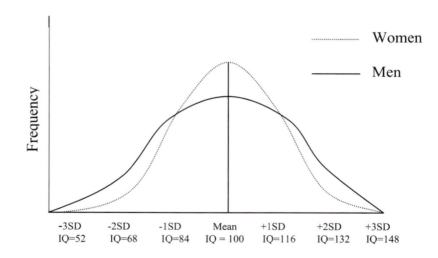

Figure 7.2 IQ variance of men and women.

Ethnicity

Ethnic differences in IQ have also been the subject of fierce debate. Scores have consistently shown that certain ethnic groups perform poorly on intelligence tests, and that such differences in intelligence have corresponding disadvantageous life outcomes (Herrnstein and Murray 1994). Such claims have been attacked on the grounds that it is too simplistic to treat intelligence as a single determining entity that predicts life chances and social outcomes.

Educational implications

The educational implications of ideas about intelligence can be categorized into those associated with theories and those associated with IQ testing.

Theories

If intelligence is completely determined by inheritance there would be little role for development. It is clear, however, that nature and nurture work together. Educators have always seen it as their role to provide an environment that stimulates intelligence and learning. That environment is structured by the curriculum.

Curriculum and classroom strategies

The components of intelligence identified by theory can helpfully guide curriculum planning and classroom strategy.

In the area of curriculum planning, the identification of fluid and crystallized intelligence can lead to a pedagogy that addresses both components. For example, in mathematics, the teaching of elementary mental arithmetic enhances speed of processing associated with fluid intelligence. The reinforcement of mathematical knowledge through regular homework and practice leads to the development of crystallized intelligence. Table 7.6 shows the curricular implications of a range of theories about intelligence, whereas Table 7.7 suggests how the theories might translate into various classroom strategies.

Table 7.6 Curricular implications of intelligence theories

Theory	Curricular implications
Unitary	• Standardized curriculum, diagnostic testing, scholastic attainment tests, IQ tests, large-scale national testing, norm-referenced testing
Fluid and crystallized	• Fluid: skills acquisition, task novelty, critical thinking, problem-based learning • Crystallized: spiral curriculum that embeds previous knowledge, task-based assessment, teaching for recall
Componential	• Emphasis on addressing cognitive skills, reasoning, planning, evaluating • Teaching and assessment of transferable skills

Theory	Curricular implications
Contextual	• Social constructivism, peer learning, situated knowledge, subject epistemology, values, communities of practice
Experiential	• Individualized curriculum, range of experience, practical curriculum, work-based and problem-based learning, reflective learning
Several independent intelligences	• Multi-faceted approaches, constructivism, teacher as learner/curriculum broker, variety of assessment methods

Table 7.7 Intelligence theories and classroom strategies

Theories	Classroom strategies
Unitary	• Subject-centred, whole-class teaching and testing • Compliance with national standardized methods and guidelines (for example, phonics as literacy method)
Fluid and crystallized	• Fluid: focus on student technique, explicit guidelines and modelling, variety of examples and tasks, development of expertise and speed • Crystallized: drawing on previous knowledge and experience, repetition and revision, link new knowledge to old
Componential	• Teaching critical thinking, reasoning strategies and meta-cognition • Use of learning style inventories, promotion of self-directed learning • Provision of tips, formulas and methods • Self-evaluation and formative assessment
Contextual	• Teaching for meaning • Teaching subject values in context • Subject relevance, field trips, integration with wider community, classroom visitors
Experiential	• Discovery learning, project-based teaching, practical and laboratory work • Reflective learning, learning journals and portfolios • Individualized learning plans
Several independent intelligences	• Student-centred teaching • Teaching for understanding • Teaching to the different intelligences and appealing to learners' strengths • Diagnostic self-testing, authentic assessment

IQ testing

Prediction

IQ testing has been used in the assessment of educational potential and for prediction of educational achievement. Although IQ tests cannot measure all types of intelligence, they have been shown to be reliable predictors of academic success; for example, Wechsler's verbal IQ score correlates well with achievement in elementary school (Jenson 1980).

Traditionally, the administrator of an IQ test offers no assistance to the test's subjects, and the measurement provides a snapshot of the learner's intelligence at that point in time. Newer tests provide a cognitive task to be performed by the learner. The novel aspect is that the tester offers assistance. 'The child's ability to profit from dynamic instruction is usually taken as the measure of the child's latent learning potential' (Sternberg 1986: 21).

One of the benefits of IQ testing is that it can provide a defensible basis for a teacher's expectations and may correct or confirm subjective perceptions. It can act as a diagnostic measure, signalling low or high IQ scores, which can be a useful guide in planning individual learning provided it does not act as a form of labelling, such as the English 11+ examination which determined children's educational opportunities.

Selection

Binet's original intention of testing as a means of identifying low-scoring learners in order to provide them with appropriate support is still evident in the diagnosis of learners of lower intelligence. This testing now falls to educational psychologists rather than teachers however. For reasons of equality, the use of IQ tests for selection has declined. They have been replaced by standard assessment tests (SATs), which measure linguistic and numerical achievement and are similar to standard IQ tests. Their purpose is for accountability and for maintenance of standards rather than selection.

Diagnosis

Intelligence tests are highly useful in the identification of students with special needs, indicating their likely difficulties and possibilities for progress. For example, the Wechsler test (WISC) assesses cognitive abilities overall and can reveal conditions such as dyslexia, which manifests itself in poor reading and writing skills on several of the WISC subtests, even when a child scores highly in other areas.

Remediation

Remediation generally involves interventions that aim to improve areas of weakness identified by intelligence subtests. For most conditions, early intervention is important. Research findings suggest that school-based interventions made as a result of intelligence tests need to be highly personalized, structured, intensive and consistent (Wood et al. 2006: 42).

Key ideas

There are several competing explanations of intelligence. For example, intelligence is:

- genetically determined by inheritance;
- develops through interaction with environment;
- a social and cultural construction.

Intelligence includes the following components, which may be in competition:

- fixed, innate potential;
- cognitive processing;
- quickness of mind;
- power of discernment;
- abilities related to practical survival (so it is learned and flexible).

Intelligence may be singular or multi-factorial. That is, it may consist of:

- a general underlying intelligence, known as 'g';
- a set of potentialities or strengths;
- a hierarchy of 'g', primary and specific factors.

Intelligence testing is characterized by a set of assumptions:

- Traditionally, intelligence is a fixed entity measurable by IQ tests;
- IQ scores are assumed to be normally distributed;
- Intelligence Quotient (IQ) compares an individual to the average;
- Modern intelligence tests assess a range of abilities.

Intelligence tests are used for:

- diagnosis and identification of learners with special needs;
- comparisons between social groups;
- academic and vocational selection.

Conclusions

The twentieth century saw a range of attempts to measure many individual characteristics such as personality, intelligence and creativity. Such attempts have met with many criticisms. For example, IQ testing has been criticized as being narrow on the basis of the range of attributes it tests, as being culturally biased, and as having potential for misuse in the service of political and social agendas.

Despite the different forms that IQ tests have taken in the twentieth century and beyond, there appears to be general agreement that key indicators of intelligence are speed and accuracy in cognitive processing and the importance of judgement and discernment. More latterly, IQ tests have also emphasized the importance of contextual factors and the idea of intelligence as a means of survival within an environment.

Some future directions of IQ testing are likely to include:

- greater alignment of testing and theoretical understanding;
- application of findings of cognitive science aided by brain-imaging;
- an emphasis on practical intelligence;
- an interest in qualities such as insight and wisdom;
- an interest in creativity.

Indeed, as cognitive science progresses, we can expect intelligence tests to have a shorter lifetime, to apply new knowledge and to use more dynamic forms of testing.

References

Benbow, P.C. and Stanley, J.C. (1983) Sex differences in mathematical reasoning ability: more facts, *Science*, 222: 1029–31.

Benton, D. and Cook, R. (1991) Vitamin and mineral supplements improve the intelligence scores and concentration of 6-year-old children, *Personality and Individual Differences*, 12(11): 1151–8.

Binet, A. and Simon, T. (1916/1973) *The Development of Intelligence in Children*. New York: Arno Press.

Boring, E.G. (1923) Intelligence as the tests test it, *New Republic*, 35: 35–7.

Carroll, J.B. (1986) Factor analytic investigations of cognitive abilities, in S.E. Newstead, S.H. Irvine and P.L. Dan (eds), *Human Assessment: Cognition and Motivation*. Dordrecht: Nyhoff.

Cattell, R.B. (1963) Theory of fluid and crystallized intelligence: a critical experiment, *Journal of Educational Psychology*, 54: 1–22.

Davey, G. (ed.) (2004) *Complete Psychology*. London: Hodder, Arnold.

Erlenmeyer-Kimling, L. and Jarvik, L.F. (1963) Genetics and intelligence: a review, *Science*, 142: 1477–79.

Eysenck, M.W. (1994) *Individual Differences: Normal and Abnormal*. Hove: Psychology Press.

Gardner, H. (1999) *Intelligence Reframed: Multiple Intelligences for the 21st Century*. New York: Basic Books.

Goleman, D. (1996) *Emotional Intelligence: Why it Can Matter More than IQ*. London: Bloomsbury Publishing.

Harvard University (2007) Project Zero. http://www.pz.harvard.edu (accessed December 2007).

Hebb, D.O. (1966) *A Textbook of Psychology* (2nd edn). Philadelphia: W.B. Saunders.

Herrnstein, R.J. and Murray, C. (1994) *The Bell Curve: Intelligence and Class Structure in American Life*. New York: The Free Press.

Jenson, A. (1980) *Bias in Mental Testing*. New York: Free Press.

McCall, R.B. (1979) The development of intellectual functioning in infancy and the prediction of later IQ, in J.D. Osofsky (ed.), *The Handbook of Infant Development*. New York: Wiley, 707–41.

Rieber, R. W. and Robinson, D. K. (eds) (2004) *The Essential Vygotsky*. New York: Kluwer Academic/Plenum Publishers.

Rosenthal, R. and Jacobson, L. (1968) *Pygmalion in the Classroom*. New York: Holt, Rinehart and Wiston.

Scarr, S. and Weinberg, R.A. (1976) IQ test performance of black children adopted by white families, *American Psychologist*, 31: 726–39.

Spearman, C. (1927) *The Abilities of Man*. New York: MacMillan.

Sternberg, R.J. (1985) *Beyond IQ: A Triarchic Theory of Human Intelligence*. Cambridge: Cambridge University Press.

Sternberg, R.J. (1986) The future of intelligence testing, *Educational Measurement: Issues and Practice*, 5(5): 19–22.

Terman, L.M. (1916) *The Measurement of Intelligence*. Boston: Houghton Mifflin.

Thurstone, L.L. (1938) *Primary Mental Abilities*. Chicago: University of Chicago Press.

Wechsler, D. (1958) *The Measurement and Appraisal of Adult Intelligence* (3rd edn). Baltimore, MD: Williams and Wilkins.

Wood, C., Sheehy, K. and Passenger, T. (2006) Understanding specific learning difficulties, in C. Wood, K. Littleton and K. Sheehy (eds), *Developmental Psychology in Action*. Oxford: Blackwell Press and Open University Press.

Zuckerman, M. (1990) Some dubious premises in research and theory on racial differences: scientific, social and ethical issues, *American Psychologist*, 45(12): 1297–303.

Chapter 8　Life course development

Introduction

Some older adults claim that they cannot learn as much or as well as they would like because their memory is not as good as it used to be. Is this claim valid? What are the implications of life course development for learning? This chapter addresses such questions.

By 'life course', we mean the sequence of events and experiences from birth to death, and their related physical and psychological states (Runyan 1978: 570). We begin with an overview of life course development, the models that have been used to describe it and the processes that are associated with various stages in the life course. We then examine a range of theories of life course development, contrasting holistic psychosocial and moral theories with the key cognitive, function-based theories most closely related to learning. The discussion highlights the learning processes and discusses the educational implications that flow from them.

Development

Development is not the same as change. Change is the difference between one state and another, whereas development is change that results from movement towards a goal. Various models – biological, cognitive and socio-cultural – have been proposed to describe development across the life course. It is worth noting that each model implies a different view of when and how learning takes place.

The most obvious kind of development we experience is biological: we are born, we get older and we die. Thus, a biological or maturational model of development suggests progression towards a plateau in adulthood, followed by decline, as shown in Figure 8.1. In this model, learning is usually associated with the earlier stages of life.

Other models extend the potential for development throughout the whole of the life course. Thus, a cognitive model focuses on changes in mental competence from infancy to old age. For example, research evidence highlights a decline in the ability to encode new information in working memory in older adults (Hedden and Gabrieli 2004). A socio-cultural model, on the other hand, looks at the roles and tasks that individuals assume from birth to death. These entail different learning motivations related to social identity at different stages.

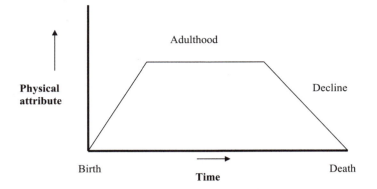

Figure 8.1 Biological/maturational model of development.
Source: Based on Sugarman (2001).

Processes of development

The changes associated with development may occur in an ordered sequence, concurrent with other changes, or dynamically in relation to the environment.

In the past, many psychologists applied an 'ordered change' framework to childhood and a 'stability framework' to adulthood. For example, Freud identifies the main stages of psychosexual development as occurring within the first six years of life and influencing all later experience. Piaget restricts his four stages of cognitive development to childhood, terminating at adolescence and the acquisition of formal reasoning. Such theories reinforce a sequential biological model.

On the other hand, development may occur on different fronts at the same time. For example, Piaget sees children's cognitive development as concurrent with the biological development of the nervous system. Adulthood may be characterized by stability in reasoning, which is paralleled by stability in socio-cultural roles typical of the middle stages of life. Old age is characterized by greater reflectivity, which occurs at the same time as the psychosocial integration of experience.

Another view suggests that individuals act on the environment, and the environment influences individuals dynamically through a variety of economic, geographic, historical, social and political factors. Bronfenbrenner's (1993) 'ecological' model is an example: it incorporates four enfolded systems, which impact on people's overall development (see Figure 8.2).

Each of these perspectives on developmental processes can be applied to the life course and related learning. For example, Piaget's ordered, sequential process for the acquisition of reasoning is useful in deciding on the appropriateness of learning experiences for children of different ages. The concurrent perspective reminds educators that learning must be linked to the demands of a particular life stage. For example, adults are most interested in learning material that is of relevance to them (Knowles 1984). The dynamic perspective indicates that there are many variables affecting people's learning – obvious ones such as parental and family background, and less obvious ones such as social and cultural influences.

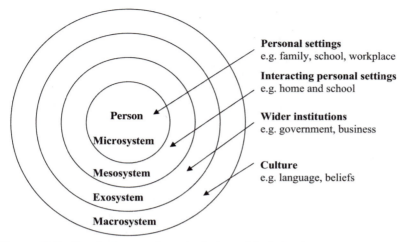

Figure 8.2 Bronfenbrenner's ecological model of development.
Source: Based on Bronfenbrenner and Morris (1998).

Age

The changes associated with development across the life course are to varying extents related to age, and it is important to note that developmental psychologists distinguish between different concepts of age.

Chronological age

This refers to the time since birth. This forms one criterion in all accounts of change. For example, people tend to reach puberty at a similar age. Changes in age-related characteristics such as height or body mass are most evident in childhood and in old age.

Biological age

This refers to the body's physical age, which is affected by chronological age, genetic factors and personal and environmental factors such as diet, exercise and health. In some deprived societies and social groups, people age very quickly; in others, there are patterns of longevity.

Social age

This includes a person's attitudes, behaviour and interests. For example, it is normal for children to go to school at a particular age. We talk about people 'acting their age', which assumes that there are ways of acting that are appropriate to different ages.

Psychological age

This refers to the way people cope with and adapt to life situations. The term is also used when talking about intelligence and problem-solving (Wood et al. 2002: 38). For example, Alfred Binet determined the cognitive abilities of 'normal' children at various ages and produced typical profiles for particular ages. Individual children were then evaluated to obtain their psychological or mental age (see Chapter 7, 'Intelligence').

Functional age

This is an integrated measure of performance on a range of scales that reflect the various chronological, biological, social and psychological aspects of age discussed above. It tries to define people in terms of their actual abilities rather than the length of time they have been alive (Wood et al. 2002: 38).

Categorization of people and processes according to age is useful for understanding aspects of daily life, but it is simplistic to see age as causing change or development. Age norms are averages, and most individuals deviate from them in some respect.

Theories of life course development

The most important theories relating to life course development can be categorized as psychosocial, moral and functional. Each theory presents a particular construction of development.

Psychosocial development

One of the most influential theories of psychosocial development was proposed by the German psychoanalyst Erik Erikson, who drew from the psychoanalytic tradition, which emphasizes the resolution of identity crises. Erikson's theory balances personal psychological development with the changing demands of society over the life course. In this theory, each stage of a person's life requires the achievement of a key psychosocial task, which itself involves the resolution of some crisis. For example, babies must form understandings of their world – is the world safe and dependable, or is it dangerous and inconsistent? Successful resolution of this 'crisis' develops hope and confidence for the future; failure leads to insecurity and avoidance.

Erikson identifies eight crises through the life course (see Table 8.1). To resolve these crises, people must locate themselves at some point between the positive and negative poles of a dimension. People acquire 'ego strength' when they resolve a particular crisis. This also involves personal learning, and people use the ego strengths they have acquired to tackle future crises. Failure to acquire ego strengths results in increasingly inadequate personal and social functioning.

Table 8.1 Erikson's eight stages of psychosocial development

Stage	Crisis	Learned strength
Infancy	Trust versus mistrust	Hope
Early childhood	Autonomy versus doubt	Will
Play age	Initiative versus guilt	Purpose
School age	Industry versus inferiority	Competence
Adolescence	Identity versus role confusion	Fidelity
Young adulthood	Intimacy versus isolation	Love
Middle adulthood	Generativity versus self-absorption	Care
Old age	Integrity versus despair	Wisdom

Source: Based on Sugarman (2001: 93).

Erikson's theory can be criticized on the grounds that too many of the stages or identity crises he posits deal with the early years in the life course, whereas old age, which might encompass 40 years or more, is allocated only one category. Therefore, American educationalist Robert Peck modified Erikson's stages by subdividing the last two stages and specifying more identity crises to be faced. He also sees old age as having more positive characteristics than Erikson did (see Tables 8.2 and 8.3).

Table 8.2 Peck's stages of middle age

Crisis	Learned strengths
Wisdom versus valuing physical powers	Coming to terms with loss of physical strength or attractiveness but gain of informed judgement
Socializing versus sexualizing	Seeing individuals in terms of their potential as friends rather than as sexual partners
Emotional flexibility versus emotional impoverishment	Ability to shift emotional attachments
Mental flexibility versus rigidity	Possibility of openness to new ideas

Source: Based on Peck (1968).

Table 8.3 Peck's stages of old age

Crisis	Learned strengths
Ego-differentiation versus work-role preoccupation	Redefinition of self
Body transcendence versus body preoccupation	Transcending physical decline
Ego transcendence versus ego preoccupation	Coming to terms with one's own death

Source: Based on Peck (1968).

Moral development

Moral development is an important construct in life development and its stages are parallel with the psychosocial ones. A concern with values and moral development is an integral part of the education process. Stages of moral development can explain how children respond to societal norms and behaviours. A key theorist is the US psychologist Lawrence Kohlberg, who sees morality as a developing process. The three stages in his theory of moral development shown in Table 8.4 are associated with childhood, adolescence and adulthood but Kohlberg suggests that most adults do not progress beyond the second stage (Colby and Kohlberg 1984).

Table 8.4 Kohlberg's theory of moral development

Stage	Characteristics
Pre-conventional	Punishment or reward consequences guide people's actions.
Conventional	People are motivated by obedience and respect for rules and authority.
Post-conventional	People assume personal responsibility and can generalize ethical principles.

Source: Based on Colby and Kohlberg (1984).

Functional theories

Functional theories specify what people are able to do or how they behave at particular stages. In this theoretical view, behaviour is seen as adaptive in evolutionary terms, serving physical, mental or social purposes. Here we consider the development of people's functionality at three distinct stages of the life course – childhood, adulthood and old age.

Childhood: Piaget

The best-known functional theory of children's cognitive development was proposed by Jean Piaget. Table 8.5 shows the stages in his theory of cognitive development.

Table 8.5 Piaget's theory of cognitive development

Stage	Characteristic
Sensori-motor 0–2 yrs	Infants: • experience the world through movement and senses • learn that objects continue to exist even when not in view • begin to represent behaviours through mental imagery or language.
Pre-operational 2–6 yrs	Children: • build a mental model of the world • are still egocentric, only seeing world from their own point of view • can perform mental operations such as addition only when objects are present.
Concrete operational 6–12 yrs	Children: • generate rules and principles based on their actions on the world • are able to understand only rules of which they have had direct experience • cannot yet use rules to generalize to situations not yet experienced • develop an ability to see other points of view.
Formal operational 12–	Young people: • are able to reason in a purely abstract and scientific way • are able to generate hypotheses about the world • are increasingly able to construct models that explain most experience.

Source: Based on Wood et al. (2002: 52–3).

For Piaget, these stages are predetermined, and closely linked to the maturation of children's nervous systems. Like the stages of biological growth, cognitive development and its processes cannot be directly accelerated.

Piaget considers that the development of internal models of reality involves the following internal processes:

- the development of schema – a mental representation of knowledge or action (for example, the child has a schema of a car with four wheels and a steering wheel);
- assimilation – the incorporation of new information into existing schema (for example, the child sees more types of cars that fit the schema);
- accommodation – the adaptation of an existing schema in the light of new information (for example, the child broadens the schema to include three-wheeled cars);

- equilibration – the balancing of the processes of assimilation and accommodation (for example, the child maintains a stable concept of a car despite variations);
- disequilibration – the inability to maintain the schema (for example, the child discards existing schema in the face of teleportation).

The power of Piaget's theory lies in his claim that children's intelligence develops towards increasing levels of abstraction, generality and stability in the transitions from the pre-operational to the formal operational stage. As part of this process, children also move from the personal to the social, taking on other perspectives and developing the ability to appreciate other points of view.

On the other hand, Piaget has been criticized for his limited view of intelligence, which fails to take account of cultural values or kinds of reasoning other than the formal scientific type: 'We are not simply victims of genetically determined cognitive predispositions' (Kincheloe and Steinberg 1993: 300). Another criticism is that Piaget assumes that formal reasoning is reached in adolescence and fails to develop further. Many researchers now recognize that adult thinking continues to develop and become more dialectical and tolerant of ambiguity (Sugarman 2001: 109–34).

Childhood: Vygotsky

The Russian psychologist Lev Vygotsky agreed with Piaget that there are stages of development but felt that they are less biologically determined. Vygotsky, whose ideas are discussed in Chapter 4, believed that parents, teachers, peers and wider culture develop children's functional abilities, including inner talk, thought and intelligence. Some of the ideas of Vygotsky and Piaget are compared in Table 8.6.

Table 8.6 Piaget's and Vygotsky's theories of development: a comparison

Piaget	Vygotsky
Children's intellectual potential develops through interaction with the world.	Social interaction is necessary for intellectual development.
Children move from the personal to the social.	Children move from the social to the personal.
Stages of intellectual development are predetermined like physical development.	Stages of intellectual development may be accelerated by social interaction and support.
Social development is a consequence of intellectual development.	Intellectual development is a consequence of social development.

Adulthood

In the past, adulthood was considered largely within biological frameworks and was seen as the peak of development. Cognitive development did not receive much attention beyond childhood. More recently, theorists and researchers have come to see adulthood as a period that has its own sub-stages, although research has focused more on adult roles and responsibilities rather than on cognition.

Some of the most important work in this area has been done by the US educationalist Marcia Baxter Magolda (1992), who outlines a view of epistemological development derived from research with cohorts of university students. She claims that there are four discrete and sequential stages in the adult acquisition of knowledge, each characterized by a particular view of knowledge.

1. *Absolute stage* Knowledge exists, is certain and needs to be acquired.
2. *Transitional stage* Knowledge exists but is not so certain and needs to be discovered.
3. *Independent knowing* Knowledge is relative, personal, contested and needs to be defended.
4. *Contextual knowing* Knowledge is socially constructed and needs to be evaluated on the basis of acceptable evidence.

Baxter Magolda points out that students rarely achieve the final stage while at college, and it may be that greater experience of the world is necessary (Baxter Magolda 1992).

The epistemological characteristics of Baxter Magolda's final stage are consistent with the claim that adult reasoning is often contradictory and embedded in context. According to other research (Riegel 1973; Kramer 1989), mature adult thinking requires an ability to live with complexity and ambiguity; and reasoning needs to be flexible and open. It is characterized by:

- an awareness that knowledge is affected by values and cannot be neutral;
- a tolerance of contradiction and ambiguity;
- an acceptance of different perceptions;
- an ability to integrate contradictions into a dialectical whole;
- an intuitive understanding based on experience.

Old age

Old age is associated with cognitive changes, some of which may be seen as development rather than decline (see Table 8.7). Although it is common to assume that people's cognitive functionality declines with age, it is important to make a distinction between fluid intelligence, which is associated with the speed of cognitive processing, and crystallized intelligence, which relates to increased knowledge. Thus, older people generally think more slowly, but this is balanced by an increase in what they know (Wood et al. 2002: 44).

Table 8.7 Biological and cognitive aspects of ageing

Change	Effect
Bodily appearance	Gain in weight. Decrease in physical attractiveness.
Psychomotor performance	Declining speed in large movements and reduced fine control in small movements. Longer decision times. More conscious monitoring of performance.
Vision and hearing	Diminishing ability to discriminate components of visual display. Slower adaptation to light change. Loss in hearing.
Learning and memory	Impaired retrieval from short-term memory. Decreasing ability to sustain attention.

Source: Based on Sugarman (1986: 53–63).

Fluid intelligence

David Wechsler (1972), who devised the Wechsler Adult Intelligence Scale (WAIS), proposed that 'fluid intelligence', as measured by IQ tests, declines with age as does physical ability.

The greatest decline in cognitive performance occurs in attention and memory function, particularly in 'information retrieval'. Indeed, brain imaging shows a decline of activity in the hippocampuses and frontal lobes of older people, areas implicated in memory and in planning. Thus, older people remember past events better than recent ones. This is known as Ribot's Law. Older people are also less likely to organize new material in ways that facilitate effective learning. Such decline can be diminished if memory is exercised and relied on for everyday activities such as shopping; an example of 'situated', contextual learning. Health, social and environmental conditions also play a part in halting the decline of fluid intelligence. For example, performance on cognitive measures can be improved if an individual regularly engages in aerobic activities such as walking. Other strategies such as heightening emotional states can help offset memory decline too. For example, older people who were taught to learn scripts by enacting the emotional states of the characters showed a higher recall and recognition than those who simply learned the script (Wood et al. 2002: 43–5).

Crystallized intelligence

Older people do better than younger ones on tasks requiring experience, practical knowledge and vocabulary. The judgements of older people are also often more sophisticated than those of younger adults. Collectively, these characteristics are known as 'crystallized intelligence'. Greater crystallized intelligence means that older people excel at the types of social and cultural learning that are carefully avoided by standard IQ tests, although Sternberg's (1985: 45) definition of intelligence (see Chapter 7, 'Intelligence') does recognize the importance of purposive understanding in real-world environments.

When considering the life course developments associated with older age, we also need to take into account the wisdom of older people and their ability to reflect on, and come to terms with, experience and mortality in ways that are difficult at more active stages of life. For many older people, life experiences lead to an integrated philosophy of life that make older age satisfying and meaningful and that may be passed on to others by:

- maintaining social and cultural values;
- acting as mentors to pass on what has been learnt;
- improving society through social activism;
- emphasizing some existential dimensions of life undervalued in contemporary society.

(Jarvis 2001: 108–9)

Educational implications of life course development theories

Diverse educational implications arise from life course theories. Taking a chronological approach, we will deal with implications for the education of:

- people throughout the life course;
- children;
- younger adults;
- adults;
- older adults.

Throughout the life course

A review of formal education throughout the world shows that it is directed at the young, with chronological age as a key marker of intellectual level. This is consistent with the framing of education in relation to biological models of development, which see human development as reaching its peak in adulthood and then declining. On the other hand, socio-cultural and cognitive models of development suggest that development continues throughout the life course, leading directly to the view that people learn throughout their lives, and may therefore require and seek educational opportunities and provision. Theories of lifelong learning discussed in Chapter 9, 'Adult learning', build on this idea.

Learning throughout the life course:

- Programmes should be devised to cater for all stages of the life course.
- The potential inclusion of people at different stages of the life course should be considered in the design of educational programmes.
- Informal and formal educational opportunities should be available throughout the life course.

- Groups should be supported in devising their own learning opportunities.
- Research should to be carried out into the learning styles and requirements of different age groups.
- Implicit assumptions about age-related ability should be examined and challenged.
- Access policies should be accommodating to all groups.
- Learning outcomes should reflect the expectations and needs of students at different stages in the life course.
- Teachers' roles should vary according to the age and nature of students.
- Teaching methodologies should address the different learning styles of adults and children.
- Assessment practices should be negotiated in the light of learning outcomes and learner needs.

Children

The implications of Piaget's and Vygotsky's theories for classroom practice are discussed in Chapter 4.

Younger adults

The four stages in Baxter Magolda's theory of epistemological development discussed above have corresponding implications for learning and teaching practice, as shown in Table 8.8.

Table 8.8 Educational implications of Baxter Magolda's theory

Knowledge	Teacher role	Student role	Assessment test
Absolute	Impart knowledge	Absorb knowledge	Recall of knowledge
Transitional	Facilitate understanding	Understand and apply	Comprehension and application
Independent knowing	Support individual views	Defend individual view	Presentation of argument
Contextual knowing	Collaborator	Constructor of situated knowledge	Evaluation of knowledge claims

Adults

Learning opportunities for adults, even in the most advanced societies, are still poor in comparison with the opportunities provided by compulsory childhood education. The nature of adult learning and its associated pedagogy is discussed in Chapter 9, 'Adult learning'. Here it is important to note how the educational implications of the way adults think and reason can be applied in practice (See Table 8.9).

Table 8.9 Educational implications of adult thinking

Adult thinking characteristics	Educational implications
Knowledge is value-laden.	Make values explicit in curriculum and in teaching.
Adults can tolerate contradiction and ambiguity.	Model reflective practice and reflexivity.
Adults can accept different perceptions.	Provide opportunities for airing opposing views
Adults can integrate contradictions into a dialectical whole.	Encourage discussion, debate and critical thinking.
Adults have intuitive understanding based on experience.	Draw on learners' personal experience and life histories.

Older adults

Learning itself reduces cognitive decay. In the US, a longitudinal study was conducted for many years with a contemplative order of nuns. It found that elderly nuns who exercised their minds through reading, doing crosswords puzzles and maintaining a positive attitude lived longer and resisted age-related cognitive decline (Snowdon 2001).

There are economic and social benefits in providing formal and informal educational opportunities for older people. Doing so might reduce the burden of care associated with diseases such as dementia. Studies in Canada, the US and the UK show that educational programmes for older adults increase optimism, mental flexibility and confidence. This may act as a form of empowerment, with older people in care settings taking more responsibility for their lives. For example, a research study conducted in a nursing home in the US divided residents into two groups. One group was given responsibility for everyday decisions; the others were passive recipients. Within a short time, the empowered group enjoyed higher levels of mental alertness and the death rate dropped by 10 per cent (Jarvis 2001: 122–5).

Various educational opportunities for older people have emerged since the 1960s. For example, in the US, the Institute for Learning in Retirement was founded in the early 1960s. It subsequently became the Elderhostel Institute Network, which still provides summer school and university education opportunities for older people. Similarly, the University of the Third Age (U3A) emerged in France in the 1970s to provide an informal liberal education for older people. It has spread to other countries and taken different forms. In the French model, the local university takes responsibility for the U3A. In the UK model, the U3A are voluntary self-initiated groups with interchangeable teacher and learner roles (Jarvis 2001: 2).

Educational self-help movements for older people have spread to other countries with the support of governments. The next wave of demand for access to further and higher education may come not from ethnic groups or the economically disadvantaged, but from older learners.

Key ideas

- The life course has distinct stages.
- Learning changes with life stages.
- Biological development theories suggest a peak in adulthood, followed by decline.
- Socio-cultural models explore difference in roles and tasks rather than decline.
- Biological models suggest sequenced change.
- Sociocognitive and cultural models suggest contingent, concurrent development.
- An ecological model suggests a collection of interacting systems, which a person inhabits at particular life stages.
- Concepts of age include the chronological, biological, social, psychological and functional.
- Psychosocial theories involve the resolution of key conflicts particular to each stage.
- Stage developmental theories concentrate on childhood.
- Stages of moral development parallel those of cognitive development.
- Ageing involves biological and cognitive change that affects learning.
- Fluid intelligence (speed in cognitive processing) declines with age.
- Crystallized intelligence (knowledge and wisdom) does not decline.

Conclusions

This chapter shows how theories and models of life course development move away from a narrow biological focus to an interest in socio-cultural experience and cognitive functioning. It focuses the attention of educators on the different stages and demands of the life course and suggests some pedagogical strategies to respond to them, emphasizing a holistic, constructivist approach that sees meaningful learning continuing long after childhood.

However, the many positive ideas discussed are not necessarily matched by funding support. From a theoretical perspective, the wide diversity of approaches in life course development may threaten the field's coherence in making its case. More research is needed, as childhood studies dominate the theory's evidence base.

Nevertheless, the theories do offer the educator some counter arguments to prejudice and ageism and suggest some case to be made for the allocation of more resources to adult learning. Some of the issues and understandings in relation to adult learning are further explored in the next chapter.

References

Baxter Magolda, M. (1992) Students' epistemologies and academic experiences: implications for pedagogy, *Review of Higher Education*, 15(3): 265–87.

Bronfenbrenner, U. (1993) Ecological systems theory, in R. Wozniak and K. Fisher (eds) *Specific Environments: Thinking in Context*. Hillsdale, NJ: Erlbaum, 3–44.

Bronfenbrenner, U. and Morris, P.A. (1998) The ecology of the developmental process, in R. Learner (ed). *Handbook of Child Psychology, Vol 1: Theoretical Models of Human Development*. (5th edn). New York: Wiley, 993–1028.

Colby, A. and Kohlberg, L. (1984) Invariance sequences and internal consistency in moral judgement stages, in W.M. Kertines and J.L. Gewirtz (eds) *Morality, Moral Behaviour and Moral Development*. New York: John Wiley.

Hedden, T. and Gabrieli, J.D.E. (2004) Insights into the ageing mind: a view from cognitive neuroscience, *Nature Reviews Neuroscience*, 5: 87–97.

Jarvis, P. (2001) *Learning in Later Life: An Introduction for Educators and Carers*. London: Kogan Page.

Kincheloe, J.L. and Steinberg, S.R. (1993) A tentative description of post-formal thinking: the critical confrontation with cognitive theory, *Harvard Educational Review*, 63(3): 296–320.

Knowles, M. (1984) *Andragogy in Action*. San Francisco, CA: Jossey-Bass.

Kramer, D.A. (1989) Development of an awareness of contradiction across the life span and the question of post formal operations, in M.L. Commons, J.D. Sinnott, F.A. Richards and C. Armon (eds) *Adult Development: Comparisons and Applications of Development Models*. New York: Praeger.

Peck, R. (1968) Psychological developments in the second half of life, in B. Neugarten (ed.) *Middle Age and Ageing*. Chicago: University of Chicago Press.

Riegel, K.F. (1973) Dialectical operations: the final period of cognitive development, *Human Development*, 16: 346–70.

Runyan, W.M. (1978) The life course as a theoretical orientation: sequences of person-situation interaction, *Journal of Personality*, 46(4): 569–93.

Snowdon, D. (2001) *Aging With Grace: What the Nun Study Teaches us about Leading Longer, Healthier and More Meaningful Lives*. New York: Bantam Books.

Sternberg, R.J. (1985) *Beyond IQ: A Triarchic Theory of Human Intelligence*. Cambridge: Cambridge University Press.

Sugarman, L. (1986) *Life-Span Development: Concepts, Theories and Interventions*. London: Methuen and Co.

Sugarman, L. (2001) *Life-Span Development: Frameworks, Accounts and Strategies* (2nd edn). Hove: Psychology Press.

Wechsler, D. (1972) 'Hold' and 'don't hold' tests, in S.N. Chown (ed.) *Human Aging*. New York: Penguin.

Wood, C., Littleton, K. and Oates, J. (2002) Lifespan development, in T. Cooper and I. Roth (eds) *Challenging Psychological Issues*. Milton Keynes: Open University Press.

Chapter 9   Adult learning

Introduction

When we think of education, we think of children being instructed by adults. Durkheim defined education as 'the influence exercised by adult generations on those who are not yet ready for social life' (1956: 71).

The chapter questions this position. It begins by considering some key definitions in adult education, and goes on to outline its extensive and venerable history. Although adult education is a relatively new phenomenon, its antecedents are in early vocational education, working peoples' institutes and community action movements. We describe and evaluate more recent developments, including the emergence of andragogy and transformative thinking. The chapter also provides an overview of important areas of concern in contemporary adult learning theory and practice. Areas selected for discussion include those concerning adults' access to education, power relationships, and the rise of instrumentalism in education. Finally, we outline the practical implications of adult learning theory for learning and teaching practices.

Definitions

Changes over time in the terminology of adult education indicate shifts in the perspectives of educationalists and policy makers. The terminology evolved from 'adult education', which indicated the separate provision of informal education to adults, to 'recurrent education', which implied an extension of school education. 'Recurrent education' was replaced by 'continuing education', which pointed to a broadening of provision, covering both informal, non-accredited learning and accredited educational provision. This term gradually subsumed the more traditional 'adult education' (Tight 2002 : 39–43).

A major change in emphasis, from 'education' to 'learning' is signalled by the emergence of the term 'lifespan learning', coined in the 1960s by the American adult educationalist Cyril Houle, as a result of his research into adults' self-directed learning (Houle 1964). The currently accepted terminology, endorsed by the Organization for Economic and Cultural Development (OECD) is 'lifelong learning' (Tight 2002: 39). As John Field points out, 'lifelong learning' incorporates learning from every aspect of our lives – social relationships, environment, society and culture. For Field, 'we cannot stop ourselves from being lifelong learners' (2000: vii–viii). Figure 9.1 outlines the evolution of this terminology.

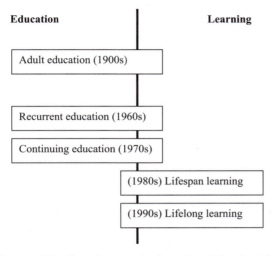

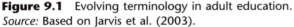

Figure 9.1 Evolving terminology in adult education.
Source: Based on Jarvis et al. (2003).

Origins of adult education

Adult education originated in historical initiatives and movements in Britain, Scandinavia and North America. These initiatives often emphasized the use of experience and group collaboration, key learning principles which survive to this day.

Working-class education

Technical institutes were the forerunners of contemporary adult education. They developed in the mid-nineteenth century in industrialized countries and centres, teaching technological subjects and crafts to factory workers and apprentices, and subjects such as book-keeping to clerical workers. Sometimes the workers themselves set up institutes. Towards the end of the nineteenth century in England, many of these technical institutes established themselves as a 'new niche' in the formal educational sector, becoming technical colleges and later polytechnics (Merricks 2001: 4).

Another significant development in England was the founding of the Workers' Educational Association (WEA) in 1898 by Albert Mansbridge. The WEA often attracted eminent academics to heavily industrialized towns in order to deliver lectures on politics or economics to mass working-class audiences. This had the aim of encouraging workers' participation in liberal education for its own sake, rather than to rise above their existing class and employment (Merricks 2001: 4).

We see the emergence of a discourse of adult education in the 1920s through the work of Basil Yeaxlee. He believed that adults have a right to continuing education, not simply to compensate for the failures of formal schooling, but as a legitimate pursuit. He advanced a student-centred approach to learning, claiming that adults form a heterogeneous learning group whose needs cannot be met by formal classroom teaching methods. Yeaxlee also argued that adult education should be grounded in practical and community initiatives, and that these settings provide the authentic conditions for learning (Yeaxlee 1929).

Scandinavian rural adult education

Study circles and folk high schools developed in the nineteenth century, were the beginnings of self-organized adult education in Scandinavia. Study circles originated in rural settings, as adults met to develop practical skills in woodwork, farming, fishing and accounting. In this way the participants directed and fulfilled their own learning needs. These study circles still survive in Sweden today, although depleted by the disintegration of rural communities and the influence of mass communications. Folk high schools built on the idea of study circles. They concentrated on the further development of skills and practical knowledge and there was no formal assessment. Folk high schools made no social distinctions and provided education without any charge many, years before the introduction of free education in countries such as Britain (Bjerkaker 2004: 220–5).

North American democratic and community education

The philosopher and educationalist John Dewey was writing early in the twentieth century, at a time of huge immigration into the US. This shaped his belief that education enabled individuals from diverse ethnic backgrounds to participate fully in civic life and decision-making. Education therefore ensured the stability of democratic society. Dewey also maintained that education should not stop with the end of formal schooling; adults have important learning experiences throughout their lives that contribute to their intellectual growth (Dewey 1902; 1966).

The American educationalist Edward Lindeman, working in the 1920s, viewed adult education as a means of personal development. His work focused on reforming existing educational structures, including the tradition of the adult educational curriculum to elevate subjects over learners. For Lindeman, experience was 'the adult learner's living text book' (Lindeman, 1989: 7). He believed that adult learners have a repertoire of practical knowledge, skills and experiential resources on which to draw. He thought small-group discussion essential to the adult learning process because it allows experiences to be shared, interpreted and placed in meaningful contexts.

Moses Coady is associated with a more radical branch of adult education. This priest, educator and socialist was a leader of the Eastern Canadian Antigonish movement, which originated in the 1920s as a means of empowering impoverished rural workers. This movement encouraged people to share their common experiences and knowledge on topics related to their working lives. In time, courses were offered on a range of subjects of interest to the community (Coady 1939). This was an early form of community development, underpinned by the belief that the goal of education is to initiate social reform through the raising of consciousness and political action.

A final figure in this overview is Cyril Houle, who claimed that all individuals, irrespective of age or social status, have a propensity towards learning. People have different motivations for learning, causing them to engage in independent study projects. Houle shifted the focus in adult education towards people's own reasons for engagement in learning, signalled by his term 'lifeplan learning' (Houle 1961: 15–16).

Recent developments in adult learning

Since the 1970s, investigations have concentrated on the differences between children's and adults' learning. This has led to an interest in the potential of adult education to facilitate personal development and critical reflection on the social and political conditions of people's lives. The theories that underpin these developments are those of andragogy, transformative learning and critical thinking.

Andragogy

The work of the US educationalist Malcolm Knowles in the 1970s and 1980s has had a pervasive influence on adult education. He is best known for developing the theory of 'andragogy' – 'the art and science of teaching adults' – as opposed to that of 'pedagogy' – 'the art and science of teaching children' (Knowles 1980: 43). He identified four ways in which adult learners are different from child learners: 'self-concept', 'experience', 'readiness to learn' and 'orientation to learning'.

Self-concept Adult learners are self-directing, independent and responsible for their own learning needs. They undertake study programmes because they want to learn what is meaningful, and relevant to their lives. Adults need to match subject matter to their own learning goals.

Experience Adults have a reservoir of practical examples, skills and knowledge that can be used and reused in new learning situations. Knowles argued that experience must be central to the adult learning process in order for learning to be meaningful.

A readiness to learn Adults are internally motivated to seek out new learning methods and knowledge. They participate actively in learning processes for personal reasons.

An orientation to learning Adults are problem rather than content-oriented. They work best in environments where they can apply reasoning abilities, and where they can draw on their self-concept, experience and readiness to learn.

Andragogy is learner-centred and constructivist in nature because it assumes that the defining feature of adult education is the meaning that individuals attach to their learning. The theory has been important in developing a methodology of adult teaching and learning. However, it can be criticized on two grounds. First, it is debateable whether all adults are as self-directed as Knowles's North American cultural assumptions would suggest. Learners in eastern parts of the world respect authority and expect to follow the lead of the teacher (Jarvis et al. 2003: 87). Second, the clear division Knowles proposes between adult and child learners may be exaggerated. Learner-centred education, in which children are encouraged to take control of their own learning, and teachers to develop learner autonomy, is a key tenet of all constructivist practice.

Transformative learning

The American educationalist Jack Mezirow developed the theory of 'transformative learning' in the 1970s. It claims that when individuals engage in critical reflection they reach a deeper understanding of their personal experiences, assumptions, or of political and social structures. When adults question their existing frames of reference they discover new perspectives, which may result in a reframing or a transformation of meaning. He thought that such perspective transformations could also be used by communities of adult learners where it could act as the basis for collective social action, through a challenge to imposed and distorting meaning perspectives (Mezirow 1991). The theory has been influential for its combining of personal and social goals but can be criticized for the view that people can transform their lives through rationality, discounting emotional, subconscious or cultural influences.

Critical thinking

Other theories of critical thinking have been developed. For the US educationalist Stephen Brookfield, critical thinking does not mean opposing, but interrogating an existing situation or piece of information. It involves thinking about one's own thinking and taking a deep approach to learning. He suggests four components of critical thinking:

- recognizing and challenging assumptions;
- identifying the context in which assumptions are made;
- being willing to explore alternative perspectives;
- engaging in thoughtful scepticism.

(Brookfield 1987: 7–9)

Brookfield (1995) also proposes ways in which teachers of college and adult students may use critical reflection for professional and self-development. He sees teaching as a political process, with teachers needing to examine and challenge their own and other hegemonic assumptions about the nature of teaching. Hegemonic assumptions are promoted by powerful interests to protect the status quo, and are internalized by teachers. They include the assumptions that:

- teaching is a vocation, which often leads to teacher 'burn-out';

- teachers need to be rated as 'excellent' in student evaluations (very much a North American concern);
- good teachers will be able to meet all of their students' needs all of the time.

When teachers engage in critical reflection on such assumptions, it can:

- increase their ability to take 'informed action';
- develop a rationale for their classroom practices;
- reduce a tendency to blame themselves for aspects of student learning outside their control;
- increase student trust by modelling thoughtful and responsible behaviour.

(Brookfield 1995)

Contemporary concerns in adult learning theory and practice

Theorizing about adult learning gives rise to discussions about its capacity to help people analyse and challenge social and political norms. Some of the most important areas of concern in contemporary adult learning theory and practice relate to understanding and dismantling the barriers that prevent adults from taking full advantage of learning opportunities. These may be summarized as concerns about:

- access and equity;
- power structures in adult education;
- instrumentalism in education.

Access and participation

Since the 1960s, equity and equality in accessing lifelong learning opportunities has emerged as a major issue (Tight 2002: 142–6). Even in the most advanced countries, some people do not or cannot participate in education, putting themselves and their families at risk of social and economic exclusion. This has consequences for broader society with certain groups alienated or disengaged from society. Barriers to participation vary – in some societies, cultural norms exclude women or certain ethnic or religious groups from education. In others, the main barriers are psychological and social, with some disadvantaged groups seeing education as 'not for the likes of us'.

The inclusion and rights of all citizens to access basic, further or higher education is now set as a policy target by governments in most advanced countries. Three major objectives have been identified internationally in relation to educational equity:

- ensuring the right of all citizens to participate in education;
- developing the concept of the learning society;

- ensuring that justifications, principles and measures taken by policy-makers and institutions are adequate to promote lifelong learning.

(Cooper 2001: 2)

The US moral philosopher John Rawls provides a compelling justification for the fair distribution of educational opportunities. He argues that education is an absolute good which, if all citizens are to attain, requires not equal but equitable – that is, fair – opportunity and access (Rawls 1999). It is not enough to give everybody the same access to educational opportunities; some groups may require more opportunities and support. For example, early 'access initiatives' to encourage students from disadvantaged backgrounds into higher education were not very successful because they concentrated simply on entry for such students, but failed to support them adequately when they were enrolled. Positive discrimination and ongoing support for some disadvantaged groups might be necessary to ensure a 'just' distribution.

Access initiatives in different countries have prioritized different groups. In Britain, for example, one 'equity' group is unemployed men who traditionally exclude themselves from education and training. Research has identified factors such as mistrust in formal education or poor school experiences as contributory factors (McGivney 1998). Australian research on equity groups shows that the nature of disadvantage is complex and dynamic, requiring initiatives at local, institutional and national levels (Ferrier and Heagney 2001: 83).

Power structures in adult education

Radical adult education thinkers such as Freire and Habermas are dealt with in the constructivism chapter. We deal here with radical perspectives from women's viewpoints and community education which are not covered elsewhere in this book.

Community and women's education

Concerns about ways in which power structures in adult education reproduce those of broader society are articulated by the community and women's education movements. These movements have tended to take a more social and structural approach to learning than advocated by theorists coming from individualistic North American traditions. The feminist writer Nell Keddie argues that adult education must move beyond individualism, which, she claims, encourages competitiveness, endorses middle-class values and uniformity. She asserts that adult education has largely failed to 'identify or identify with the needs of those who reject the premises on which individualism is based' (Keddie 1980: 64).

Jane Thompson, the radical feminist adult educator sees a link between knowledge and the status quo, claiming that sexism and self-interest now permeate adult education, which has abandoned its earlier concern with social change (Thompson 1983). For example, adult education in many countries is managed by men, although women form the majority of adult education students. Similarly, community-led initiatives in education have often been appropriated by powerful educational bodies, displacing the community group whose interests are the primary ones.

Thompson argues the role of women's education is to raise political awareness so that the contributions women make to 'really useful knowledge' can lead to more direct roles in decision-making (Thompson 2007: 35).

Thompson claims that much educational discourse is framed within a deficit model of learning in which experts know what learners require. Feminist and community theorists raise issues such as the extent to which the key stakeholders in learning can get their voices heard and the ownership of their learning acknowledged.

The main disadvantage of these discourses is their tendency to remain situated at a local level. Advocates are unable to get their voices heard at the level of democratic decision-making.

Instrumental education

Governments often justify funding for adult education on instrumental grounds, such as the needs of the knowledge economy. On this view, a highly educated workforce is an economic resource that gives the nation a competitive advantage. Lifelong learning can mean lifelong employability and an ongoing capacity to contribute to this resource. International and national bodies have issued policy statements on 'lifelong learning', which has become part of an accepted discourse on the purpose of education. For example, 'learning for life' was adopted as a worldwide priority by UNESCO in the 1990s, with an emphasis on 'lifelong retraining' (Tight 2002: 39). According to Field, 'lifelong learning' has become a convenient label for modernizing educational and vocational systems for purposes of economic competitiveness (Field 2001: 11).

The benefit to learners and educational providers in such a focused view of education lies in the economic support provided by governmental and international agencies to adults undertaking vocational training or retraining. Aligning with government rhetoric also provides increased resources to educational institutions. The disadvantage in such a narrow view is that it ignores the learning needs of those outside the labour market, and leads to the downplaying of liberal and non-vocational education. There is an increasing concern about this direction as it affects curriculum planning, provision and the outcomes of education.

A more benignly instrumental justification for adult education appears in the growing importance attached to continuing professional development (CPD). CPD is based on the claim that members of professions need to continue to learn throughout their working lives if they are to maintain personal and professional competence. This goes beyond knowledge of professional practice; it involves a commitment to holistic personal development along with the updating of skills. Continuing professional development is encouraged and supported by professional associations and institutes because it is seen as meeting the needs of the profession. For the individual, CPD maximizes potential and provides opportunities for demonstrating continuing competence (Nicholls 2001: 23–5).

These instrumental approaches to adult and lifelong learning can be criticized on the grounds that they treat people as economic units and neglect the whole person and their culture. As Gelpi points out, a more appropriate role for lifelong learning theory and practice is to express and implement values of democracy, equity and fairness (Gelpi 1980).

Educational implications of adult learning theory

Practical learning and teaching strategies associated with some of the ideas above are presented here.

Origins of adult education

The history of adult education indicates four recurrent emphases:

- education as a practical preparation for career and working life;
- education as a humanistic, life-enhancing activity;
- education as a form of democratic activity;
- education as a form of social action.

To help learners prepare for careers in trade and technical areas, teachers should:

- draw on the learners' prior experiences, knowledge and skills;
- model the skills or behaviour to be learned;
- diagnose learners' present knowledge and skills;
- give many opportunities for practice;
- utilize problem-based learning scenarios;
- provide relevant and authentic learning experiences;
- use project work and case studies;
- test mastery of skills and knowledge through their practice.

To promote humanistic education, teachers should:

- acknowledge and attempt to address the social, behavioural, emotional, moral and spiritual aspects of learning;
- acknowledge that learning can be informal;
- promote self-directed learning;
- be student rather than subject-centred;
- recognize moral, aesthetic and social values;
- make connections between different subjects;
- give learners freedom to pursue individual interests;
- encourage sharing, collaboration, discussion and debate;

- respect adults' experience and cultures.

To promote education as a form of democratic activity, teachers should:

- model tolerance and openness to difference;
- encourage debate and respectful listening;
- encourage adult learners to share and voice their thoughts and feelings;
- encourage learners to question their own and others' assumptions;
- use case studies and problem-solving methods to elucidate issues;
- promote social values and citizenship;
- provide reasoning and linguistic tools to examine argument;
- look for opportunities to promote social and civic values.

If learners are to participate in education as a form of social action, teachers should:

- show that knowledge is value-laden;
- identify the ownership of knowledge;
- be explicit about their own values;
- work with learners to identify the learners' social and political circumstances;
- help learners to discover oppressive social structures affecting their lives;
- diminish the power distance between themselves and their students;
- establish a reciprocal relationship with learners, sharing teaching and learning;
- implement a curriculum that raises consciousness of social issues;
- engage in joint social and political action to tackle injustice.

Andragogy

The theory of andragogy claims that adults learn in a different way to children and will use different learning techniques that require different teaching strategies. When teaching adults, teachers should:

- create a climate of cooperation;
- help learners to identify their needs and set goals;
- justify the relevance of what is taught;
- present learning as tasks to be undertaken or problems to be solved;
- take account of learners' backgrounds and experience;
- provide opportunities for self-directed learning;
- encourage learners to plan the curriculum and evaluate their own learning;
- use the experience of learners as a teaching resource;
- facilitate students in identifying their learning styles and strengths;
- show how the learning can be of immediate relevance;
- use collaborative group discussion, case studies, project work and study groups.

Transformative learning

Since transformative learning results from an interrogation of personal experience, teachers should:

- encourage reflective dialogue with peers to examine assumptions;
- focus on learner experiences;
- recognize initial and ongoing learner needs;
- promote analysis of learners' motivation;
- engage learners in examining and resetting goals;
- teach principles of reflective practice;
- encourage learners to explore and discuss the meanings they attach to experience;
- use tools such as learning logs and journals to record experience and reflection;
- encourage the self-regulation of learning.

Critical thinking

Brookfield (1995) claims that to engage in genuinely critical thinking and reflection, learners and teachers need to get outside their own perspectives and experiences, which can be difficult. He suggests that teachers view their practice through the following four 'lenses', which can reveal new ways of seeing and understanding themselves:

- their personal histories as learners and teachers – for example, using learning journals or reflective portfolios;
- their students' perspectives – for example, using student feedback from critical incident questionnaires (see Brookfield 1995: 115–17), student performance, informal feedback and formal evaluations;
- their peers' perspectives – for example, using peer observation and review;
- theoretical frameworks from the literature.

The benefits of critical reflection include:

- a deepened understanding of the ideological foundations of the curriculum;
- protection from burnout for teachers;
- an appreciation of professional development;
- the ability to integrate connections between processes and learners' experiences;
- the discovery of an authentic voice.

Power structures in adult education

Theories of radical education suggest that the uncovering of power structures, and enabling these to be critiqued is the first stage of positive action to combat oppression. Feminist and community educators should:

- state their personal positions on gender and power issues;
- uncover the forces that contribute to the oppression of individuals and communities;
- analyse the ways in which power is manifested in the 'hidden curriculum';
- unite with others to combat injustice and oppression;
- take coordinated action for self-determination;
- challenge or subvert oppressive systemic structures;
- find ways of promoting their own agendas;
- claim control of their domain;
- identify community shared values and experience.

Instrumental approaches to adult education

We have already stated some criticisms of an instrumentalist view of adult education. However, we are not unrealistic, and realize that adult educators and teachers work in a climate where the demands of the knowledge economy dictate the educational agenda. In order to promote a lifelong learning agenda, teachers should:

- keep up to date on vocational and economic trends;
- identify and teach key transferable skills;
- forge links between business and educational sectors;
- design courses targeted to the needs of the economy;
- devise ways of accrediting the prior experiences of learners;
- promote formal and informal work-based learning;
- facilitate ongoing CPD with part-time and flexible programmes;
- encourage course evaluation by external stakeholders.

Key ideas

- Learning needs to be relevant and consistent with learners' educational goals.
- Learners are self-directing in nature and can assume responsibility for their own learning.
- Learners have a huge reservoir of experience to draw from and therefore learn best when new information is grounded in real and practical examples.
- Critical reflection is a key feature of adult learning, allowing learners to assess implications of decision-making and sense-making processes.
- Contextualizing new subject matter promotes meaning-making processes.
- Learners are autonomous and self-regulating, which implies that they both direct and diagnose their own learning needs.
- Learning is optimized and enhanced through social, collaborative and discursive practices. Thus strategies such as group discussion, project work, case studies, problem-solving scenarios and situated learning experiences all promote adult learning.

Conclusions

A survey of the development of adult education shows a movement from the 'heroic age' of adult education in the early twentieth century, when the education of adults and communities was pursued with an almost missionary zeal, to a more recent concern for fulfilling the training requirements of the economy and industry.

Lifelong learning creates the discourse of a 'learning society', in which the majority of 'citizens have become permanently learning subjects', whose 'performance as adult learners is at least in part responsible for determining their life chances' (Field 2000: 38). Although it is presented as having a range of social outcomes, lifelong learning actually represents a turn away from the socialist focus of early adult education to a new focus on the individual.

These two perspectives highlight a fundamental dichotomy in adult education between emancipation and socialization. Can, and should, the aim of adult education be to help people free themselves from those conditions that limit their thinking and acting? Or should it prepare them to accept and conform to their eventual roles as workers and consumers in a capitalist society? When assessing the various strands of adult learning theory and practice, it is helpful for teachers to bear these questions in mind.

References

Bjerkaker, S. (2004) The study circle for learning and democracy, K. Brosnan, M. Walker et al. in D. Saunders (eds) *Learning Transformations: Changing Learners, Organisations and Communities*. London: Forum for the Advancement of Continuing Education, 220–5.

Brookfield, S. (1987) *Developing Critical Thinkers: Challenging Adults to Explore Alternative Ways of Thinking and Acting*. San Francisco, CA: Jossey-Bass.

Brookfield, S. (1995) *Becoming a Critically Reflective Teacher*. San Francisco, CA: Jossey-Bass.

Coady, M.A. (1939) *Masters of their own Destiny: the Story of the Antigonish Movement of Adult Education through Economic Cooperation*. New York: Harper.

Cooper, M. (2001) Introduction, in L. Thomas, M. Cooper and J. Quinn (eds) *Access to Higher Education: The Unfinished Business*. Staffordshire: Institute for Access Studies, Staffordshire University and the European Access Network.

Dewey, J. (1902) *The Child and the Curriculum*. Chicago University of Chicago Press.

Dewey, J. (1966) The Dewey school, in F.W. Garforth (ed.) *Dewey's Educational Writings*. London: Heinemann.

Durkheim, É. (1956) *Education and Sociology*. New York: The Free Press.

Ferrier, F. and Heagney, M. (2001) Disadvantage is complex: targeting special groups is not enough!, in L. Thomas, M. Cooper and J. Quinn (eds) *Access to Higher Education:*

The Unfinished Business. Staffordshire: Institute for Access Studies, Staffordshire University and the European Access Network, 83–96.

Field, J. (2000) *Lifelong Learning and the New Educational Order*. Stoke-on-Trent: Trentham Books.

Field, J. (2001) Lifelong education, *International Journal of Lifelong Education,* 20 1–2: 3–15.

Gelpi, E. (1980) Politics and lifelong education policies and practice, in A.J. Cropley (ed.) *Towards a System of Lifelong Education*. Oxford: Pergamon.

Houle, C.O. (1961) *The Inquiring Mind*. Madison, WI: University of Wisconsin Press.

Houle, C.O. (1964) *Continuing Your Education*. New York: McGraw-Hill.

Jarvis, P., Holford, J. and Griffin, C. (2003) *The Theory and Practice of Learning* (2nd edn). London: Kogan Page.

Keddie, N. (1980) Adult education: an ideology of individualism, in J.L. Thompson (ed.) *Adult Education for a Change*. London: Hutchinson.

Knowles, M. (1980) *The Modern Practice of Adult Education* (revised edn). Englewood Cliffs, CA: Prentice Hall Regents.

Lindeman, E. (1989) *The Meaning of Adult Education*. Oklahoma: Oklahoma Research Centre for Continuing, Professional and Higher Education.

McGivney, V. (1998) *Excluded Men*. Leicester: NIACE.

Merricks, L. (2001) The emerging idea, in P. Jarvis (edn). *The Age of Learning: Education and the Knowledge Society*. London: Kogan Page.

Mezirow, J. (1991) *Transformative Dimensions of Adult Learning*. San Francisco, CA: Jossey-Bass.

Nicholls, G. (2001) *Professional Development in Higher Education: New Dimensions and Directions*. London: Kogan Page.

Rawls, J. (1999) *A Theory of Justice,* Cambridge, MA: Harvard University Press.

Thompson, J.L. (2007) 'Really Useful Knowledge': linking theory and practice, in B. Connelly, T. Fleming, D. McCormack and A. Ryan (eds) *Radical Learning for Liberation 2*. Maynooth: MACE.

Thompson, J.L. (1983) Women and adult education in M. Tight (ed.) *Educational Opportunities for Adults,* London: Croomhelm and the Open University.

Tight, M. (2002) *Key Concepts in Adult Education and Training* (2nd edn). Abingdon: Routledge.

Yeaxlee, B.A. (1929) *Lifelong Education: A Sketch of the Range and Significance of the Adult Education Movement*. London: Cassells.

Chapter 10   Values

Introduction

Values are hard to define. Most synonyms of the term relate to purposes, goals, priorities, ethics and 'the good'. But the term can also include people's desires and needs – what they consider to be most important in their lives. Values can be normative too, setting out what people or society should do or aspire to doing. Thus the meaning of 'values' varies with context.

In the educational context, 'value' or 'values' can refer to the important – even invaluable – role that education has in achieving fundamental moral, social or individual goals. It can also refer to the specific values held by educators, such as commitments to 'education as a right', pluralism or 'equality of opportunity'.

It is important for teachers and scholars to consider the value of education because of the unthinking importance we attach to it. This is reflected in the fact that education has become one of the largest items of government spending in many advanced countries. In Britain, for example, spending on education outstrips spending on defence (Holford and Nicholls 2001: 145). Many countries are now increasing the percentage of GDP that they devote to education (Budge et al. 2002: 97). Also worthy of examination are the cultural and individual values that determine the policies to which teachers are subject and the practices that they use everyday. It is necessary for teachers to uncover their values so that they can evaluate and improve their practice.

In this chapter, we consider the value of education from moral, religious, political and social, economic and individual perspectives. We move on to the values held by teachers, particularly those that relate to educational policies and practices. Towards the end of the chapter, there is an overview of the implications of values in education, with special attention to the influence of social values and also to the relationship between values and the curriculum.

The value of education

Some people look to the past for the meaning and purposes – the value – of education, promoting, for example, its moral or religious value. Others claim it has an indispensable social and political value and remains an important collective social activity. Emerging discourses position education as an enabler of national and global economies, and also as fulfilling individual ambitions and enhancing individualistic lifestyles. Where do these values of education come from?

Moral value

One of the oldest and most venerable traditions of thought sees education and knowledge as forms of virtue. The Greek philosophers, Plato and Aristotle, along with later medieval thinkers, related education to the acquisition of virtue and the 'summum bonum' – the good life. The good life is defined not as a life of pleasure, but a life given over to a striving for higher ideals, truth and knowledge – a life of denial and self-sacrifice, of self-awareness and reflection. Socrates' famous aphorism that 'the unexamined life is not worth living' (Plato, Apology 38a) makes a clear link between knowledge and value, and also suggests that the most important thing that people can do is evaluate what they consider to be valuable.

Increasingly, moral development has come to be seen as the province of the educational system. In the past, and in many societies, moral values were seen as the responsibility of the family and of religion. With the decline of both institutions, however, there is a growing social awareness that, in many cases, the only opportunities that people have to develop their moral thinking is through formal education. Classes in citizenship or values are attempts to provide what is now seen as an important perspective on life. The view that education is basically a moral training in how to live well or rightly is the basis for many of the claims discussed below.

Religious value

The view that education inculcates eternal truths is the religious version of the philosophical claim above. Within this view, the value of education can be measured by the extent to which it prepares individuals and society for lives lived in accordance with universal laws of existence, God's laws or specific religious edicts. For traditions such as the Confucian, Hebraic, Islamic and Christian, education becomes a prerequisite or prelude to a spiritual life, both here and hereafter. The British philosopher R.M. Hare remarks:

> For myself, I have found it impossible to discuss education without bringing in religion. One's attitude to religion will impinge powerfully on one's approach to education. ... the irrational side of our nature, from which none of us can escape, needs to be educated and religion, interpreted broadly to include humanistic beliefs, is the only way of doing this.

(quoted in Cairns 2001: 57)

In the past, monastic educational systems often took on this spiritual or religious responsibility, particularly in homogenous societies such as found in Christian Europe. The influence of this tradition can still be seen in the mandatory inclusion of religious education in the primary and secondary school curricula of many countries. But as societies have become more globalized and culturally diverse, this specific educative role has been increasingly assigned to the family or faith group. This has led to the phenomenon of 'faith schools' in the UK and sectarian colleges or universities, especially in the US, where there is a proliferation of privately funded universities. The promotion of 'intelligent design' theories and attacks on evolution in faith-based schools and colleges in the US and UK illustrates the problems that may arise when one set of basic values conflicts with another. A related problem arises when religious values are at odds with secular educational values, as seen in France in 2003, after two Muslim sisters were expelled from their school for refusing to take off their veils (Lee 2003).

Political and social value

The idea of education as a tool for promoting political, social and cultural values is as long-standing as the traditions of moral and religious education. For example, this view of education underpinned Plato's vision of the ideal society in *The Republic*. Since the Enlightenment, education has taken on the role of 'creating and recreating the social order' (Skilbeck 1989: 20), as we see in the seventeenth-century English philosopher Thomas Hobbes' argument that education teaches people obedience to the 'sovereign authority' of the state: 'Public Ministers have the authority to teach or to enable others to teach the people their duty to the Sovereign Power, and instruct them in the knowledge of what is right and wrong' (Hobbes 1651/1991: 167). Durkheim and other nineteenth-century sociologists maintained the view that this was education's main value and function. For Marx, however, the value of education lay in empowering people to make class-based challenges to dominant ideologies as part of their struggle against oppression.

Since the nineteenth century, education has increasingly been seen as a bureaucratic arm of the state as well as an economic force. The growth of the modern state led to an interest in the education of state functionaries, which led in turn to the establishment of the modern university as well as technical institutes such as the University of Berlin founded in 1809. This Prussian model, developed by the nineteenth-century diplomat Wilhelm von Humboldt, emphasized practical and applied skills – in science and technology, modern languages and business – and developed newer types of awards such as the PhD.

In the early twentieth century, John Dewey saw education as an integral element of the democratic process. He proposed that an educated population is able to exercise critical social and personal judgement, which promotes democratic values that are best suited to large and culturally diverse societies. But it is important to note, as Pierre Bourdieu does, that education can be a source of oppression, insofar as access to educational opportunities represents a form of 'social capital' (see Chapter 5, 'Social learning'), which dominant groups in society can use and invest to reproduce and maintain social inequalities and privileges. Jürgen Habermas nevertheless argues that the value of education may lie in the insight it gives people into their oppressed states, as well as the language for communicating and combining with others (Habermas 1992). Indeed, a great deal of critical thinking in the twentieth century, including Marxism, feminism and post-structuralism, has maintained that the chief value of education lies in the potential it gives people to recognize and challenge dominant economic and social power.

Economic value

In the 1960s, the western discourse of education spoke of child-centredness, progressive pedagogies and mixed ability teaching. By the 1980s, this discourse had shifted such that its chief vocabulary is now economic: it refers to students as 'consumers', and requires of education and educational institutions virtues such as efficiency, effectiveness and accountability (Carr and Hartnett 1996).

Education has become part of the 'knowledge economy', and is now regarded as a marketable product under the World Trade Agreement. Private educational institutions are behaving like corporations, competing for customers, marketing their products and emphasizing accountability to shareholders (Jarvis and Preece 2001: 220–2). And just as some educational institutions are behaving like corporations, many corporations are behaving like universities. In 1995, there were over 1000 corporate universities in the US (Jarvis and Tosey 2001). 'From socio-cultural enclaves … one of whose main functions has been the construction of … citizens with cultivated minds and souls [universities] are being metamorphosed into sites for the production of instrumental knowledge and the acquisition of marketable skills' (Kazamias 2001: 2).

Schools are also behaving like businesses in competing for student customers, but evidence from Australia, New Zealand and the UK shows that market models applied to school education reinforce inequities and inequalities in education (Ball 1993: 14). Unfortunately, in a competitive environment, there will be both winners and losers. In the business world, the weakest perish. In contrast, in education it is precisely the weakest – for example, those who cannot afford the privileges of a private school education – who need to be protected. We should remember, however, that despite the encroachments of these inequitable values, a pure market in education may be unrealizable: in most countries, the state still controls the supply of and demand for education (Mace 2001: 75).

We should also remember that every discourse produces a counter-discourse. There is now a growing resistance to narrow economic and vocational views of education, in favour of a more holistic approach and a concern for the individual. For example, the UK Dearing Report published in the UK in 1997 argues that education is 'founded on respect for the rights of the individual and the responsibilities of the individual to society as a whole' (quoted in Merricks 2001: 12).

Individual value

The view that the value of education lies in the ability it gives people to fulfil themselves is characteristic of western cultures. The acquisition of knowledge is part of what makes us human, as is the pursuit of individual well-being and happiness. This way of thinking about education can be seen in the hedonistic utilitarian argument that the purpose of life is to maximize pleasure and happiness and to avoid pain, both for the individual and for society as a whole. Although these arguments may appear to give too much priority to pleasure, the idea of education as a means of self-fulfilment is also associated with some very respectable thinkers. For example,

Cardinal Newman in the nineteenth century argued that universities should offer a liberal education because of the importance of fully developing the whole person.

There are links here with some of the most influential developmental theories of the twentieth century, including Maslow's hierarchy of needs (see Chapter 11, 'Motivation'). Kohlberg's hierarchy of moral development and Baxter Magolda's typology of epistemological development (for more on Kohlberg and Baxter Magolda, see Chapter 8, 'Life course development'). In these theories, formal and informal learning has a role to play in the emergence of maturity, which is characterized by self-empowerment and an ability to locate personal values within the context of specific knowledge.

The extent to which education fulfils the purposes discussed above has been much debated. Education is an 'essentially contested concept', the purpose of which is continually redefined and challenged in the light of political and social priorities (Carr and Hartnett 1996: 19).

The values of teachers

It is important to consider not only the value of education, but also the values espoused, either consciously or unconsciously by teachers, and by the systems within which they work. These values are perhaps most evident in educational policies and practices.

Policies and values

The late twentieth-century massification of education in advanced societies, which has seen many more young people go on to some form of higher education, suggests a re-orientation from the meritocratic and elite values – to which education subscribed in the past – to democratic ones. This shift has been fostered by government policies that delay the age at which young people enter the labour market, as well as a higher demand for qualifications, which often correlate with high earning power and prestige. The most important implication of these changes is that greater participation in education is linked to social inclusion, and non-participation to social exclusion. From this arises an important question: how do we ensure educational participation and social inclusion?

Policies that promote access to education for socially excluded groups have been developed in many countries since the 1960s. They have their origins in the US civil rights campaigns and rely on the assumption that education is a fundamental right to which all are entitled. This is the thinking developed by the American moral philosopher John Rawls, who claims that education, together with health and minimum standards of living, are 'absolute goods' for all citizens. Educational provision and resources should not be allocated on the basis of their return to the society or state, but on their value in enriching the lives of citizens who have an entitlement to them as a matter of equity (Rawls 1999).

At first glance, this seems uncontroversial. But many commentators on discourses of social inclusion point out the confusion that arises between the terms 'equity' and 'equality'. According to Rawls, equity implies a fair distribution of resources. Equality, on the other hand, implies an equal distribution of resources. Consider, for example, learners from socially excluded backgrounds attempting to access higher education. The institution may demonstrate a commitment to equality of opportunity in that members of such backgrounds may receive assistance with fees or enrol through special selection and entrance procedures. This may still fall short of equity, however, because other students will already possess greater socio-cultural advantages – for example, they might be more familiar with education and qualifications through parental role models, ways of speaking and academic know-how. Therefore, it might be more equitable to make extra allowances for disadvantaged groups by providing additional academic or social support in order to achieve not simply 'equality of access' but 'equality of outcome' (Rawls 1999: 391).

Practices and values

Teachers' values shape the way teachers view themselves and the way they view their students, and one influences the other. This has implications for how teachers approach their everyday practice.

Although teachers can include a wide variety of people – including parents – here we refer to those who are paid professionals with professional values. The values or paradigms of teachers generally fall into one of two categories:

- teaching as an art, consisting of human, ethical and value-laden activity;
- teaching as a craft, consisting of a set of skills, which entail few values.

(Squires 1999)

The values associated with teaching as an art are personal and intuitive, characterized by qualities such as affection for both subjects and students (Squires 1999). Where teachers value teaching as an art, they may:

- be more learner-centred in their classroom teaching, showing an 'unconditional positive regard for learners' (Rogers 1959). According to Rogers, 'teachers facilitate the learning of students; you cannot teach a person directly' (Rogers 1951);
- adopt a traditional liberal-humanist view of the curriculum as a set of valued high-status subjects, each of which represents a 'unique way of experiencing and understanding the world' (Golby 1989: 35). The teacher's role is to initiate students into the 'mysteries' of a knowledge-based curriculum.

The values and personalities of such teachers may be more important than their training. For example, research in Ireland indicates that teaching incompetence is founded on personal rather than technical failure, and cannot therefore be remedied by skills training. The issues for administrators may be that of entry to the profession rather than that of skills-based remediation (Carlile 2000).

On the other hand, the values associated with the perception of teaching as a craft or applied science elevate straightforward, empirically verifiable principles and objectives that can be defined, demonstrated and mastered. Training can provide the knowledge and skills necessary to acquire these skills.

Most effective teachers recognize that they need to incorporate both Paradigms into their practice. The processes of classroom interaction need to be respectful and person-centred, while not losing sight of effective technical methods of achieving teaching objectives and facilitating learners in achieving learning outcomes.

Policy, practice and values: a case study

Marquand (quoted in Lawton and Cowen 2001: 22–4) gives an example of the way that the values of late twentieth-century England have influenced educational policy and practice. He argues that these values fall into two categories, which can be expressed as binaries:

- individualism and free choice in education versus collectivism and social engineering;
- self-fulfilment versus responsibility and obligations to society.

Marquand provides a chronological account of conflicts and confluences between the two categories over the twentieth century, showing the way that different decades have veered between collectivist and individualist principles, as shown in Table 10.1. Notice that collectivism and individualism recur in active and passive forms.

Table 10.1 Educational values and implications in twentieth-century England

Stage	Values	Educational implications
1: 1940s–1950s	Active collectivism	Optimism and implementation of secondary education for all
2: 1950s–1970s	Active collectivism	Selection seen as socially divisive Value of equal opportunity and pluralism
	Passive individualism	Importance of play in school Child-centred curricula
3: 1970s–1980s	Active individualism	Consumerism Parental choice
	Passive collectivism	Concern about educational standards
4: mid-1980s–1990	Active individualism	Vocationalism in education Benchmarks and educational efficiency

Source: Based on Marquand (1996: 21–4).

Educational implications of values

One of the most obvious arenas in which the practical implications of educational and teachers' values are felt is the curriculum. In this section, we discuss the growing role of the curriculum in transmitting various values. This has come about partly because the decline of religion as a major moral influence on people's lives has demanded other means by which values – social responsibility, obedience to the law, respect for others – can be instilled. Therefore, a recent trend in values education is towards explicit instruction in subjects that inculcate values. The shaping role of values is seen not only in what is taught in the curriculum, but in other curricular practices, such as planning, assessment and administration.

Citizenship education

The teaching of citizenship is a response to multicultural societies that can no longer guarantee shared values and allegiance to the state. The 1998 Crick Report (Advisory Group for Citizenship and the Teaching of Democracy in Schools) in the UK had as its primary aim the promotion of citizenship. As a result, curriculum planners in Britain are now required to show how citizenship and values can be incorporated into every disciplinary area (Holford and Nicholls 2001: 144).

Community education

The rise of values education can also be seen as a reaction to the decline in community participation in modern urban societies. This decline has had serious consequences – for example, David Putnam (2000) concludes that a lack of community involvement is a key factor in rising teenage violence and crime, exemplified in the Columbine High School shootings in the US in 1999. Therefore, educational initiatives that encourage service to the community are being developed. One such strategy is to award academic credits to students for service undertaken in the community, just as students can gain academic credits for work-based learning.

Curriculum planning

Curriculum planning is another area where explicit values are becoming prominent. This was not always the case: in the mid-twentieth century, for example, value-free education was seen as a positive thing. This position was associated to some extent with the behaviourist tradition, from which developed a technical-rational approach to curriculum planning (Tyler 1949). The behaviourists had little interest in the overall aims or purposes of education, and were more concerned with verified procedures and strategies of learning and instruction to achieve measurable learner outcomes. This is why they emphasized the science and technology of instruction, which is still favoured by instructional design (ISD) models of education. On the other hand, constructivist models of learning claim that individuals construct knowledge and meaning by synthesizing new information with prior constructs, which of course include values.

A more recent model is a social interactivist one, which is based on the idea that the aims and content of the curriculum should be determined by key stakeholders, who ensure that the curriculum represents their particular values (Golby 1989). For example, industry, as a key stakeholder, promotes the inclusion of core transferable skills to meet its needs.

Curriculum assessment

What values are reflected in decisions about assessment? Who is valued in the assessment process? Traditional norm-based assessment compares candidates with respect to the average performance of the group. Since this form of assessment allows students to be compared and ranked, it reflects the values of top performers and of the selectors who wish to identify them by a simple mechanism.

Recent assessment strategies have rejected norm-referencing in favour of criterion-referencing, which means that people's performance is measured in relation to stated criteria. For example, to pass a driving test, people must demonstrate that they can do a three-point turn, reverse park, obey traffic signals and so on. Criterion-referenced assessment places a value on personal achievement rather than on utilitarian competitive ranking.

Curriculum administration

In relation to the administration of the curriculum, two main issues arise – ownership and transparency.

Who owns the curriculum? That is, whose values are most important in determining the form and content of the curriculum? Learner-centred values would suggest that the learner should decide what is to be learned and how. For example, community groups often come up with innovative curricular ideas and may even receive funding for these. But their initiatives must be channelled through formal educational providers that force conformity to formal, institutional and bureaucratic procedures. This leads to the disempowerment of a major stakeholder and an imposition of the values of the institution. For example, in community education there is the view that no one should fail and that formal assessment is unnecessary. For the institution however, measurement and accreditation of learning is a priority. There is likely to be a clash of values between the institution's desire for efficiency in delivering qualifications and the community's desire to meet urgent social needs.

The curriculum consists not only of the subjects learners study, but of all the experiences learners have in educational settings. The values that shape these experiences are not necessarily transparent, however. The concept of the 'hidden curriculum' refers to values that are not articulated but may still guide the way the curriculum is experienced. For example, the popularity of closed-book examinations as opposed to more authentic forms of assessment may result from a hidden curriculum that values bureaucratic convenience over pedagogical validity. Unfortunately, the victims of the hidden curriculum tend to be learners, whose learning experience is compromised.

Key ideas

- 'Values' can refer to the role that education plays in achieving human goals.
- 'Values' can refer to the specific values held by teachers.
- Education is closely associated with the moral, religious, social, political, economic and individual values of particular times and societies.
- Teaching may be viewed as a value-laden art.
- Alternatively, teaching may be viewed as a value-free set of technical skills.
- Values are expressed at many levels from government policy to classroom practice in directing what is considered worthy of being taught and to whom.
- The curriculum is a major tool in the transmission of values.
- The curriculum can be seen to represent the values of certain stakeholders.
- Curriculum values need to be articulated, so that they may be challenged, agreed or confirmed.

Conclusions

You may not agree with the values that currently shape policy and practice in your educational context, but it is worth remembering, as this chapter has shown, that education is never value-free. Even the apparently value-neutral educational ideologies espoused in the mid-twentieth century are invested with particular ideas and commitments.

Values-driven education has important benefits. It can encourage the development of socially responsible attitudes and behaviours, and fill the gap left by the decline of social institutions such as the church and the family. It empowers people to challenge the ideologies that underpin any oppression or inequality they experience and can provide exemplars of values in action.

On the other hand, the values in and of education can entrench rather than counteract social privilege and the moral and political values of certain social and political classes. It can strengthen the hold of certain discourses, such as the 'knowledge economy' and contribute to the social exclusion of those who do not share its values.

For these reasons, it is critical that teachers, students of education, and educational bureaucrats examine and reflect on the values that guide their everyday work. Values need to be made explicit in order that they may be affirmed, challenged or rejected, allowing teachers to act in good faith for the ultimate benefit of their students.

References

Ball, S. (1993) Market forces in education, *Educational Review*, 7(1): 8–11.

Budge, I., Hofferbert, R., Keman, H., McDonald, M. and Pennings, P. (2002) Comparative government and democracy: modelling party democracy across 16 countries, in H. Keman (ed.) *Comparative Democratic Politics: A Guide to Contemporary Theory and Research*. London: Sage.

Cairns, J. (2001) Religious perspectives, in J. Cairns, D. Lawton and R. Gardner (eds) *World Yearbook of Education: Values, Culture and Education*. London: Kogan Page.

Carlile, O. (2000) *Incompetent Teachers in Irish Voluntary Secondary Schools: Principals' Perceptions, Attitudes and Reactions*, unpublished Doctoral Thesis, University of Hull.

Carr, W. and Hartnett, A. (1996) *Education and the Struggle for Democracy: The Politics of Educational Ideas*. Buckingham: Open University Press.

Golby, M. (1989) Curriculum traditions, in B. Moon, P. Murphy and J. Raynor (eds) *Policies for the Curriculum*. London: Hodder and Stoughton.

Habermas, J. (1992) Further reflections on the public sphere, in C. Calhoun (ed.) *Habermas and the Public Sphere*. Cambridge, MA: MIT, 421–61.

Hobbes, T. (1651/1991) *Leviathan*, R. Tuck (ed.) New York: Cambridge University Press.

Holford, J. and Nicholls, G. (2001) The school in the age of learning, in P. Jarvis (ed.) *The Age of Learning: Education and the Knowledge Society*. London: Kogan Page.

Jarvis, P. and Preece, J. (2001) Future directions for the learning society, in P. Jarvis (ed.) *The Age of Learning: Education and the Knowledge Society*. London: Kogan Page.

Jarvis, P. and Tosey, P. (2001) Corporations and professions, in P. Jarvis (ed.) *The Age of Learning: Education and the Knowledge Society*. London: Kogan Page.

Kazamias, N. (2001) General introduction: globalization and educational cultures in later modernity: the Agamemnon syndrome, in J. Cairns, D. Lawton and R. Gardner (eds) *World Yearbook of Education: Values, Culture and Education*. London: Kogan Page.

Lawton, D. and Cowen, D. (2001) Values, culture and education: an overview, in J. Cairns, D. Lawton and R. Gardner (eds) *World Yearbook of Education: Values, Culture and Education*. London: Kogan Page.

Lee, J.J. (2003) Expulsions over veil intensify French debate on secularity, *International Herald Tribune*, 19, 21 October.

Mace, J. (2001) Economic perspectives on values, culture and education: markets in education – a cautionary note, in J. Cairns, D. Lawton and R. Gardner (eds) *World Yearbook of Education: Values, Culture and Education*. London: Kogan Page.

Marquand, D. (1996) Moralists and Hedonists, in D. Marquand and A. Sheldon (eds) *The Ideas that Shaped Post-war Britain*. London: Fontana.

Merricks, L. (2001) The emerging idea, in P. Jarvis (ed.) *The Age of Learning: Education and the Knowledge Society*. London: Kogan Page.

Putnam, D. (2000) *Bowling Alone: The Collapse and Revival of American Community*. New York: Simon and Schuster.

Rawls, J. (1999) *A Theory of Justice* (revised edn). Cambridge, MA: Belknap Press of Harvard University Press.

Rogers, C. (1951) *Client-Centered Therapy: Its Current Practice, Implications, and Theory*, Boston, MA: Houghton Mifflin.

Rogers, C. (1959) Significant learning in therapy and in education, *Educational Leadership* (Alexandria, VA), 16: 232–42.

Skilbeck, M. (1989) A changing social and educational context, in B. Moon, P. Murphy and J. Raynor (eds) *Policies for the Curriculum*. London: Hodder and Stoughton in association with the Open University.

Squires, G. (1999) *Teaching as a Professional Discipline*. London: Falmer Press.

Tyler, R.W. (1949) *Basic Principles of Curriculum and Instruction*. Chicago: The University of Chicago Press.

Chapter 11   Motivation

Introduction

Why is it that some individuals engage in tasks that consume large amounts of their free time and effort? What drives athletes, musicians and artists? Why do people persevere in difficult tasks rather than simply giving up? The answer is that they are motivated. The word 'motivation' comes from the Latin *movere* – 'to move'. It refers to the set of factors that 'move' people so that they respond.

Motivation is an important factor in academic success. When students are motivated to learn, academic achievement is significantly increased. A motivation towards learning can stem from numerous sources – for example, from external sources such as assessment requirements or the expectations of parents or teachers.

Motivation for learning can also be internal such as the enjoyment of learning and problem-solving in a particular subject area. Another internal motivator is the desire for academic recognition and status.

This chapter attempts to clarify the nature of motivation and outlines the role of motivation theory in learning. It explores the ways motivation is related to academic success. The chapter begins with a brief account of the evolution of motivation theory.

It then looks at motivation in terms of content and process theories. Content theories concentrate on the extrinsic and intrinsic needs, factors and orientations that motivate individuals. Process theories concentrate on the cognitive states experienced and strategies used in satisfying needs and achieving goals.

Finally, the chapter explores some educational strategies suggested by motivation theory.

Development

The evolution of motivation theory can be traced through the development of other major theories of human behaviour and learning, including Cartesian dualism, Darwinism, Freud's drive theory and theories of needs including Maslow's hierarchy. More recent theories include humanistic and person-centred approaches.

Inspiration

Primitive societies believed that people were driven by the gods or their internal manifestations in the form of the daemon – a supernatural force which possessed and impelled them to action without their consent.

Dualism

The Greek philosophers believed that humans were made up of two parts – a lower part concerned with the body and its appetites, and a higher part associated with a rational pursuit of ultimate well-being and happiness. This pursuit involved the identification of aims and the means to achieve them.

The seventeenth-century French philosopher René Descartes proposed a fundamental duality of mind and body. According to the Cartesian view, motivation is an act that begins in the mind and goes on to influence the mechanistic body which is completely separate.

Biology

The nineteenth-century British naturalist Charles Darwin viewed animal motivation and behaviour as largely instinctive, acting as a mechanism to meet survival needs. The Austrian psychiatrist Sigmund Freud proposed that there are subconscious psychic and emotional needs which impel behaviour.

Early twentieth-century 'drive' theories, associated with behaviourist theories of stimulus and response relationships, also emphasize the role of motivation in satisfying physiological needs in order to maintain bodily homeostasis or equilibrium.

Cognition

Drive theory does not take account of the fact that people's behaviour may not always be a reaction in order to reduce drives. 'We eat when we are not hungry and seek shelter when we are not cold and, although we clearly like to be in a state of equilibrium, whether physically, emotionally or cognitively, there is more to human motivation than the reactive behaviours that achieve balance' (Brown et al. 1998: 60). Cognitive elements also play a part. People have expectancies, ambitions and goals which motivate them to realize their futures proactively.

Modern theories of motivation display an awareness of a combination of behaviourist reaction to stimuli and cognitive processes in which people seek to determine and control their environments.

Motivational theories have developed from a perception of uncontrolled and uncontrollable external forces to a nuanced understanding of personal agency in response to a multitude of factors.

Content theories of motivation

Content theories focus on the factors that motivate people. These factors can be physiological, social or psychological (Reeve 2005: 103). The best-known theory, and the most influential in showing the relationship between different types of needs, is that of the American psychologist Abraham Maslow.

Hierarchy of needs

In Maslow's hierarchy (see Figure 11.1, lower needs are associated with drives which must be satisfied or reduced in order to move on to the next level, although some needs could be satisfied simultaneously. For example, ownership of a home might simultaneously meet physiological, safety and self-esteem needs.

Although lower level needs are seen as drives which respond to deficiencies, higher level needs are more like aspirational goals which may not be fully achieved.

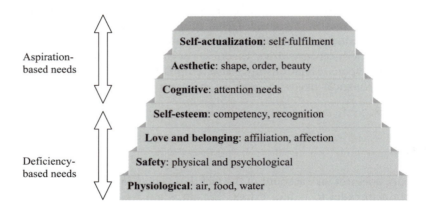

Figure 11.1 Maslow's hierarchy of needs.
Source: Based on Child (1997: 55).

The value of Maslow's theory to teachers is its appeal to common sense, its incorporation of a number of motivation factors within one model and its recognition that higher level motivational factors may depend on lower. For example, school initiatives related to healthy eating may improve mental concentration and so promote learning (Woteki and Filer 1995).

In spite of its usefulness to educators, Maslow's theory may be criticized on a number of counts. Complicated constructs like 'self-actualization' are hard to define and measure. It also raises the question whether the height of human achievement is to be found in self rather than in altruism, in community and in dedication to a higher cause.

There are other theories from the same period as Maslow that recognize a qualitative difference between deficiency needs and aspirational needs. These follow.

Hygiene factors and motivators

The Polish-American scholar Frederic Herzberg and his colleagues held a two-factor theory of motivation (Herzberg et al 1959). Corresponding to Maslow's deficiency needs, they refer to 'hygiene factors', or maintenance needs which do not stimulate motivation but prevent dissatisfaction. Their work-related research identified hygiene factors such as pay and working conditions. Recent commentators on education have pointed out that classroom hygiene factors such as heating, lighting and seating can have a little-recognized but adverse effect on student learning (Bleakley 1998: 170–1).

Once hygiene factors have been satisfied, Herzberg's theory refers to 'motivators' such as achievement, recognition, responsibility and promotion. Similarly, in a learning context, students are motivated by the subject being studied, the achievement of learning objectives, the recognition of that achievement, and by the sense of personal autonomy in learning.

Extrinsic and intrinsic factors

An analysis of Maslow's theory shows a division into extrinsic and intrinsic motivators:

Extrinsic motivators: factors external to the individuals that motivate them to respond, e.g. high grades, praise or money;

Intrinsic motivators: factors internal to the individuals that are rewarding in themselves without the need for incentives, e.g. self-esteem.

Typical extrinsic motivators in education include punishments such as reproof, low grades or rejection, and rewards such as high grades, acceptance and praise. An experiment from the 1920s quoted by Child (1997) investigated the effect of praise and reproof on 10-year-olds undertaking work in mathematics. They were divided into four groups:

A praised group: consistently praised regardless of performance;

A reproof group: consistently criticized regardless of performance;

An ignored group: in the same room but neither criticized nor praised;

A control group: undertaking the same tasks in a different room.

The results showed that the 'praised' group did significantly better than all the other groups. The poorest performing group was the control group which received no feedback from teachers or others (Child 1997: 59–60).

Generally, intrinsic motivation is more effective and lasting than extrinsic motivation (Gagné and Medsker 1996: 169). Intrinsic motivation is much more likely to help learners to:

- engage in tasks and pursuits on their own initiative, resulting in self-directed and self-regulated learning strategies over long periods of time;
- involve themselves in deep rather than surface learning;
- experience increased levels of self-satisfaction, self-efficacy and competency.

McGregor's X and Y theory

The attitudes displayed in teacher praise and reproof described above is reflected in two contrasting, stereotypical management styles, described by the American social psychologist Douglas McGregor (1960). X-type managers exercise tight control, assuming that workers require extrinsic motivation in order to act. By contrast, Y-type managers are more trusting in their view that workers are intrinsically motivated and should be given opportunities and responsibilities (see Table 11.1).

Table 11.1 McGregor's X and Y theory

X-type managers think subordinates	Y-type managers think subordinates
are lazy and work-shy	find work natural and empowering
must be coerced and controlled	are self-directed and committed
avoid responsibility	want to accept responsibility

Source: Based on McGregor (1960).

In the field of education, X-type teachers will tightly manage all aspects of the learning experience, using traditional whole-class teaching methods with extensive monitoring of performance. Punishments and rewards will be used to drive student behaviour. While this may be successful in the short term, it is difficult for the teacher to maintain, and only works while the control is strictly monitored.

Y-type teachers encourage students to engage with the tasks independently and believe that learner motivation is greatly increased when students set their own learning goals. This in turns promotes learner responsibility and autonomy. This assumes that students have the maturity to think for themselves. It may not suit all cultural types and it may not ensure that teaching objectives are achieved.

Deci and Ryan (1987) have produced a more sophisticated model which identifies extrinsic and intrinsic factors as the ends of a continuum. Learners are motivated by factors which can be partly extrinsic and partly intrinsic. They propose two intermediate points, 'identified' and 'introjected' which combine these factors in varying amounts (see Table 11.2). Deadlines are mostly extrinsic but may be internalized. Personal delight in solving a problem is mostly intrinsic. Choice of subject however, is determined partly by an intrinsic liking for the subject and partly by extrinsic course requirements. They also have a category called amotivation which describes a state of motivational indifference (Deci and Ryan 1985).

Table 11.2 Examples of motivational orientations

IM	ID	IJ	EM
Intrinsic	**Identified**	**Introjected**	**External**
Student studies a subject for stimulation	Student enjoys the subject but it is also a course requirement	Although not liking the subject the student has to do it as a course requirement	Student has no interest in higher education but goes to college because of parental pressure

Brown et al. (1998: 66–7) reports a research study of Welsh undergraduates which describes how these motivational orientations vary over the course of an undergraduate programme. Although the students were consistently motivated over time, the type of motivation varied depending on whether they were young or mature students and on the stage of the course and assessment schedules, with extrinsic motivation higher at the end of the first year, presumably due to assessment. Mature students scored consistently higher on internal motivation.

Social or person-centred needs

Maslow places social needs between the satisfaction of external drives and the attainment of internal goals. These social needs relate to people's desire for attention, recognition and acceptance.

The American sociologist Elton Mayo (1933) is best known for the Hawthorne studies which found that a group of factory workers increased their output when they were observed. They worked harder, not because of a concern to maintain output but because they thrived under the attention given to them.

A study carried out in the Sunderland Business School in the UK showed that a lack of individual attention to students resulted in their demotivation (Thompson 1998: 130–1). Teachers need to be conscious of student perception and the importance of being attentive to students, though this advice may be unrealistic in an educational climate of large numbers and increasing teacher workloads.

The American psychologist Carl Rogers points out to teachers the importance of recognition and acceptance of students. In order to motivate learners teachers should:

- empathize with learners and offer 'unconditional positive regard';
- facilitate rather than dictate the learning experience;
- be authentic and honest in their interactions with learners;
- help students identify and clarify their own experiences and values.

(Feinberg and Feinberg 2001)

Rogers' approach is suited to the exposing and sharing of learners' values but teachers also need to examine, explore and evaluate them. His individualistic stance is not always suitable for educational enterprises which stress the importance of learning communities and peer interactions.

The theories discussed above have identified specific extrinsic and intrinsic motivating factors. The next set of theories relates to the cognitive processes involved in the creation of intrinsic goals, the recognition of external forces and the consequent behavioural decisions.

Process theories of motivation

Although there is considerable overlap with content theory, process theories focus on the cognitive, dynamic and social processes that develop, encourage and sustain motivation in individuals.

Expectancy theory

This suggests three cognitive factors in relation to motivation.

Anticipation: of the gain or reward

Expectation: of achieving this

Importance: of success to the learner.

(Cohen et al. 2004: 178)

Expectancy refers to people's perceptions of, and judgements about their own abilities. High expectancies based on previous success increase students' chances of accomplishing learning goals. Learners with high expectations are more likely to persist and commit themselves to achieving desired results. A study by Sears (1940), reported by Child, divided a group of children aged 10 to 12 into three groups:

a)   those who had been successful,
b)   those who had been unsuccessful, and
c)   those who had been differentially successful (successful in some subjects but not in others).

The children were presented with tasks and asked to estimate how long it would take to complete them. Their estimates were compared with the time actually taken. The children with a background in success were realistic in their estimations; those with a background of failure under or over-estimated the time and the differential group was realistic in the subject in which they had a background of success (Child 1997: 67). Learners who had been successful in the past were able to estimate accurately the prospects of future success. Learners who had previously been unsuccessful, however, did not have the knowledge background on which to base accurate predictions; they did not know what they did not know.

It is important to note that expectancy hinges firmly on people's self-esteem and self-efficacy.

Self-esteem   refers to people's perceptions and evaluations of their own *worth* – for example, very shy people may feel they have nothing of value or worth to give to a decision-making process.

Self-efficacy   refers to people's perception and evaluation of their own *ability* within specific areas – for example, learners with high levels of self-efficacy in mathematics are more likely to enjoy challenging mathematical situations and problem-solving.

According to Bandura (1977), a learner's self-efficacy is affected by:

- past performances;
- vicarious experiences (seeing a role model able to do it);
- persuasion by teachers or peers;
- physiological and emotional cues.

Self-esteem and self-efficacy underpin expectancy insofar as people who believe they can accomplish difficult tasks persist for longer and work harder to achieve desired outcomes (Bandura 1982).

Learned helplessness

'Learned helplessness is the psychological state that results when an individual expects that life's outcomes are uncontrollable' (Reeve 2005: 238). When people doubt their own ability, they shun activities and their feelings of self-doubt became more entrenched. Certain over-prescriptive teaching methods, where the teacher determines all aspects of the learning experience, may contribute to student passivity and learned helplessness. Instead, teachers should facilitate students' active learning by setting achievable goals and by employing strategies such as scaffolding, coaching and modelling. Teachers should empower learners by offering choices. The increased autonomy results in increased motivation and a decrease in helplessness.

Attribution theory

This theory explains how people account for their successes or failures. People generally attribute their successes to their own abilities and their failures to uncontrollable causes such as external circumstances (Weiner 1986). This may be an evolutionary strategy in that people need to feel that their own actions can bring about changes in the world. The concept of control is implicit in attribution theory. 'Locus of control' refers to people's beliefs about the extent to which they have control over their own situations or destinies. Learners with a strong internal locus of control are self-determining, usually expecting they have the power to change events and circumstances in their lives. They are more likely to be proactive in their learning. Since they have an internal locus of control, they take more pride in their success and feel greater shame in failure.

People with an external locus of control can avoid ultimate responsibility. Learners, for example, may attribute their failure to external circumstances or bad luck rather than to their own lack of effort. Teachers may challenge this belief by setting attainable goals and supporting learners in the achievement, gradually withdrawing support as confidence is gained.

The ARCS model of motivation was developed in order to integrate motivational strategies into training programmes.

A Attention
R Relevance
C Confidence
S Satisfaction

In order to be motivated, the learner needs to attend to the material, see its relevance, be confident that they can learn it and achieve satisfaction from the learning (Keller and Kopp 1987).

Goal setting

Goal setting is the process of defining what needs to be achieved and then specifying objectives that will aid and facilitate achievement. But the goals people set are affected by their goal orientation. Goal orientation refers to the types of achievements to which individuals are attracted. Dweck (1986) distinguishes between performance goals and learning goals.

Performance goals

These focus directly upon end results – for example, to pass an examination in multimedia studies. This may be perceived by the learner as a measurement of innate, unchangeable capability. Research shows that learners with high self-confidence sustain their efforts to achieve performance goals but those with low self-confidence tend to give up.

Learning goals

These are concerned with learning – for example, to be able to incorporate video sequences into multimedia presentations. This may be perceived by the learner as a skill that can be acquired and improved upon. Research shows that learners of both high and low self-confidence sustain their efforts (Dweck 1986).

Educational implications of motivation theory

Some educational implications of the theories discussed have already been demonstrated. Maslows' hierarchy of needs can be categorized into three types:

- physiological needs;
- social needs;
- cognitive and existential needs.

We now offer some practical strategies under these three headings.

Meeting physiological needs

- Make sure the room is adequately ventilated.
- Make sure the room temperature is appropriate for learning.
- Ensure that students have access to a water fountain or drinkable water.
- Encourage healthy eating and physical exercise.
- Establish regular learning routines.
- Provide learners with rest periods and short breaks between classes.
- Ensure that learners take regular breaks and receive fresh air.
- Avoid lengthy periods of passive listening.
- Provide a range of physical and mental activities.
- Schedule difficult cognitive activities when energies are highest.
- Arrange the seating to suit the teaching methodologies used.
- Accommodate students with eyesight or hearing problems.
- Create a safe classroom or laboratory environment.
- Provide extrinsic rewards such as prizes or privileges in the early stages of learning.
- Use mixed teaching methods and multimedia to stimulate and maintain learner interest.
- Be consistent and aware of the amount and type of feedback produced.

Meeting social needs

- Use *small group* formations for project work and learning activities.
  - Allocate specific roles to individuals working in groups.
  - Train groups in the development and analysis of group processes.
  - Promote affiliation and loyalty to the group.
  - Use role-play to teach difficult interpersonal skills like conflict resolution.
  - Promote peer learning through 'friendship' and randomly allocated groups.

- Use *large group* formations to provide socialization opportunities.
  - ○ Promote a culture of openness and respect where bullying is unacceptable.
  - ○ Respect different viewpoints while allowing them to be challenged.
  - ○ Teach social, communication and collaborative skills.
  - ○ Promote a sense of classroom community (e.g. use 'we' in teacher talk).
  - ○ Allow 'friendship' groups for academic support but vary their composition.
  - ○ Create a sense of identity (school houses, or academic departments).
  - ○ Use inter-group competition and cooperation.
  - ○ Encourage clubs and societies.
  - ○ Encourage study groups and homework clubs.
  - ○ Engage in whole class extra-curricular activities.
  - ○ Have whole school events in which all can participate.

Meeting individual needs

- Know and use the names of learners.
- Listen, acknowledge and value all learner contributions – even when incorrect.
- Do not make comparisons between learners; do not put people down.
- Use humour positively – not at the students' expense.
- Teach assertiveness techniques.
- Arrange for learners to have a degree of autonomy, control and responsibility.
- Plan for attainable goals and learning outcomes.
- Provide additional help or remediation where necessary.
- Build success into activities.
- Provide encouraging, constructive and positive feedback.

Meeting cognitive needs

Keller's ARCS motivational model will be used as an organizing principle in the following suggestions for the teacher:

Attention

- Arouse the interest or curiosity by presenting challenging or intriguing material.
- Present materials in more than one form to appeal to the different styles of learners.
- Vary activities and stimuli to maintain interest.

Relevance

- Relate new material to previous learning and show how it can be used.
- Link teaching to the achievement of external long-term goals such as gaining employment.
- Identify and cater for learners' personal needs such as affiliation or self-esteem.

Confidence

- Create clear achievable goals and criteria for success.
- Challenge the learners with tasks that are neither too difficult nor too easy and offer support until they achieve mastery.
- Provide constructive and timely feedback interpreting difficulty or failure as a need to change learning strategy rather than an indication of ability.

Satisfaction

- Arrange opportunities to try out learning and experience success or failure.
- Give students the opportunity to enjoy the satisfaction of applying their learning in an immediate and authentic way.
- Make assessment fair and transparent so that learners perceive it as equitable.

(Gagné and Medsker 1996: 174–9)

Meeting existential needs

Self-actualization is an autonomous stage of learning in which the learners take control of their own learning goals, choice of methods and evaluation. Self-actualized learners are likely to be mature learners who will have developed autonomy and high expectations and so will not need motivational encouragement from the teacher.

Learners themselves will decide if assessment is appropriate or necessary and, if so, whether they intend to submit to it. They may also have acquired a complete mastery of a subject area. Schön pointed out that a possible strategy is to ask such learners to reflect on their mastery so that their tacit internalized knowledge and intrinsic motivations are made explicit so that they can be shared with other learners (Schön 1987).

Praise, punishments and sanctions as motivators

Punishment was used in the past as a method of discipline in education. However, modern theories show that punishment is not as effective a motivator as praise. Punishment indicates only the misdemeanour – not the desired behaviour. It is less predictable in its effects. For instance some pupils may enjoy the attention. They may see it as an arbitrary imposition by the teacher and it may support their feelings of learned helplessness.

Although not as effective as praise, sanctions are superior to punishment. Sanctions are consequences of behaviour agreed by both teacher and student so there is shared responsibility. The student therefore has some control and some incentive to change.

Behaviour modification programmes to change disruptive and anti-social behaviour in school children make use of reward and sanction, based on behaviourist principles.

Praise is the most natural and frequently used motivational method by teachers. Praise should:

- be simple, direct and unambiguous and expressed naturally;
- specify the behaviour being praised;
- be given for effort, care and persistence;
- include verbal and non-verbal responses;
- be offered appropriately so that learners are not isolated;
- be for learning rather than compliance;
- not be overdone so as to suggest a lowering of standards.

(Brophy 1981: 5–32)

Key ideas

- Motivation is concerned with the identification of needs, the establishment of goals, and the determination of action.
- Motivation theory developed from philosophical, biological and psychological roots.
- Extrinsic and intrinsic needs can be ranged hierarchically.
- Learners may be motivated by varying amounts of extrinsic and intrinsic motivational factors as well as by social influences.
- Motivation is affected by cognitive states such as self-esteem, self-efficacy, expectancies and their attributions of the cause of success and failure.
- Motivation is affected by the nature of the goal pursued.
- Teachers may hold stereotypical attitudes about the motivation of their students.

Conclusions

It could be argued that most motivational theory emanates from a western male, white, middle-class, individualistic perspective and may need to be broadened or mediated to take account of gender, social class and non-western cultural factors.

Self-actualization may not be the pinnacle of human achievement. Members of non-western cultures may believe that conformity to the norms of religion, society or family take precedence.

Motivation theory shows that there are some variables about which the teacher can do very little. Expectations of success or failure in learning are formed by the child's home and cultural background and teachers may be unable to motivate an adolescent boy whose peer group is antagonistic and alienated from learning.

However, motivation theory gives teachers an appreciation of the multiplicity of factors affecting student motivation and learning and offers a range of models to understand it and some strategies that may be used to increase motivation. Classroom activities have an impact on learners' self-esteem and identity over and above the instruction received and knowledge acquired.

Motivation theories emphasize the importance of learners as people with feelings and identities that teachers need to respect.

References

Bandura, A. (1977) Self-efficacy: towards a unifying theory of behavioral change, *Psychological Review*, 84: 191–215.

Bandura, A. (1982) The self and mechanisms of agency, in J. Suls (ed.) *Psychological Perspectives on the Self*. New Jersey: Lawrence Erlbaum Associates.

Bleakley, L. (1998) Learning as an aesthetic practice: motivation through beauty in higher education, in S. Brown, S. Armstrong and G. Thompson (eds) *Motivating Students*. London: Kogan Page in association with the Staff and Educational Development Association (SEDA), 165–172.

Brophy, J. (1981) Teacher praise: a functional analysis, *Review of Educational Research*, 51: 5–32.

Brown, S., Armstrong, S. and Thompson, G. (eds) (1998) *Motivating Students*. London: Kogan Page in association with the Staff and Educational Development Association (SEDA).

Child, D. (1997) *Psychology and the Teacher* (6th edn). London: Cassell.

Cohen, L., Manion, L. and Morrison, K. (2004) *A Guide to Teaching Practice* (5th edn). London: Routledge Falmer.

Deci, E. and Ryan, R. (1985) *Intrinsic Motivation and Self-determination in Human Behavior*. New York: Plenum.

Deci, E. and Ryan, R. (1987) The support of autonomy and the control of behavior, *Journal of Personality and Social Psychology*, 53(6): 1024–37.

Dweck, C.S. (1986) Motivational processes affecting learning, *American Psychologist*, 41: 1040–8.

Feinberg E. and Feinberg, W. (2001) Carl Rogers, 1902–87, in J.A. Palmer (ed.) *Fifty Modern Thinkers on Education: From Piaget to the Present*. Abingdon: Routledge, 49–53.

Gagné, R.M. and Medsker, K.L. (1996) *The Conditions of Learning: Training Applications*. Fort Worth: Harcourt Brace College Publishers.

Herzberg, F., Mausner, B. and Snyderman, B.B. (1959) *The Motivation to Work* (2nd edn). New Jersey: John Wiley.

Keller, J.M. and Kopp, T.W. (1987) An application of the ARCS model of motivational design, in C.M. Reigeluth (ed.) *Instructional Theories in Action*. New Jersey: Erlbaum.

McGregor, D. (1960) *The Human Side of Enterprise* (25th Anniversary Printing). London: McGraw-Hill.

Mayo, E. (1933) *The Human Problems of an Industrial Civilisation*. New York: MacMillan.

Reeve, J. (2005) *Understanding Motivation and Emotion*, (4th edn). New Jersey: John Wiley.

Schön, D. (1987) *Educating the Reflective Practitioner: Toward a New Design for Teaching and Learning in the Profession*. San Francisco, CA: Jossey-Bass.

Thompson, G. (1998) The effect of stressors on student motivation: a report of work in progress at Sunderland Business School, in S. Brown, S. Armstrong and G. Thompson (eds) *Motivating Students*. London: Kogan Page in association with the Staff and Educational Development Association (SEDA), 123–32.

Weiner, B. (1986) *An Attributional Theory of Motivation and Emotion*. New York: Springer-Verlag.

Woteki, C.E. and Filer, L.J. (1995) Child health, nutrition and physical activity, in *Dietary Issues and the Nutritional Status of American Children*. Illinois: The Human Kinetics Publishing Company.

Chapter 12   The learning body

Introduction

Many primary schools now timetable short periods of physical exercise before pupils attend mathematics classes. Provided it is not so strenuous as to lead to exhaustion, such exercise has been found to promote alertness. But how does the physical experience of being 'wide awake' contribute to the mental activity of learning to do fractions?

One answer is that exercise increases blood flow and oxygen to specific areas of the cerebral cortex, which encourages neuronal activity and in turn facilitates the fast processing of information. To put it more simply, physical activity stimulates the brain. This shows that the body has a part to play in cognition and learning, once considered purely mind-based activities. This chapter will explore the role of the body in learning by examining relevant theories arising from neuroscience, cognitive and social psychology and philosophy. These theories have a range of educational implications, which we will outline towards the end of the chapter.

The body in educational traditions

The ancient Greeks considered that the body and its development were important. The emphasis on bodily prowess was shown through major public events like the Olympic Games. We inherit the word 'gymnasium', which is both a place of exercise and a place of learning, from the Greek 'gumnasion' where youths exercised naked. Powerfully influenced by Cartesian dualism, traditions of formal education over the last three hundred years, especially in Western Europe, have laid more emphasis on the intellect than on the body.

However Rousseau, in his famous text *Émile* published in 1762, recommends the inclusion of physical exercises in the education of children.

> To learn to think we must therefore exercise our limbs, our senses, and our bodily organs, which are the tools of the intellect; and to get the best use out of these tools, the body which supplies us with them must be strong and healthy. Not only is it quite a mistake that true reason is developed apart from the body, but it is a good bodily constitution which makes the workings of the mind easy and correct.

> (Rousseau 1762/2007: 99)

In nineteenth-century England, education for the upper classes began to emphasize the importance of physical activity for boys, making explicit connections between education, physical prowess and England's place in the world – as shown in the famous quotation attributed to Wellington that 'The battle of Waterloo was won on the playing fields of Eton' (Chambers 1997).

In this period, the 'Muscular Christianity' movement in English public schools reverted to Greek ideals of physical perfection, with the belief that team sports build character and leadership qualities. A parallel movement, the Young Men's Christian Association (YMCA) was founded in the 1840s in London to serve the mind, spirit and bodies of young working men. It soon spread to the United States where members commissioned buildings with gymnasia and swimming pools and set up exercise drills (YMCA 2007).

Germany and the Scandinavian countries have long recognized the importance of physical exercise and exposure to fresh air as part of a healthy lifestyle. Physical education programmes, including some for girls, were developed in the 1840s by Adolf Spiess, the founder of school gymnastics in Prussian schools (Eichberg 1986: 99).

In spite of these developments, physical education has not been seen as a priority in mainstream western education. However, a recent health concern about sedentary lifestyles and poor diets has created a renewed interest in the physical education curriculum and the development of the body as well as the mind.

Definitions of the body

The body is more than a physiological object. It is involved in every aspect of our lives – in our thinking and feeling, our identity, our self-awareness and self-understanding. It is the medium through which we experience and interpret the world. Shilling (1993) argues that the body is an unfinished biological and social project and the more we know about our bodies, the more we are able to control, intervene and alter them. The body therefore needs to be defined in biological, psychological, sociological and philosophical terms.

Biological constructs

The body is a set of physiological systems – respiratory, digestive, nervous, reproductive, lymphatic and endocrine – working together to achieve homeostasis and equilibrium without much conscious control or monitoring. But, if teachers limit their understanding of learning to a reductionist set of biological responses, it will result in a mechanistic behaviourist approach where all learners are expected to respond in the same way to a given set of stimuli.

Personal constructs

The attitudes and beliefs we hold about our bodies are reflected in images we construct of ourselves – in how we present ourselves. The body is a means of self-representation; according to the British sociologist Anthony Giddens, the body is central to the formation of personal identity and the pursuit of lifestyles (Giddens 1991). A feature of modernity is the undertaking of ongoing 'body projects' through the use of personal trainers, dietary and exercise regimes and cosmetic surgery. In educational settings students may represent themselves and construct their identities through bodily projects like drama, dance, gymnastics and sport – as in the case of adolescent rugby players who take food supplements to increase in size and weight.

Sociological constructs

The body is also the means by which we relate to others. Bourdieu argues that our gestures, our use of space and the physical distance we keep from other people are also physical and form our 'habitus', a concept discussed in Chapter 6, 'Cultural learning' Dieting, hairstyle, body-building, body-piercing and tattooing can be seen as social practices that establish group identity. School authorities often try to establish a cohesive group identity through the regulation of bodily appearance by means of dress codes and prohibitions on excessive bodily decoration.

Power constructs

The body is also an object upon which power is exerted. The French philosopher Michel Foucault claims that power involves the regulation and control of the human body. In *Discipline and Punish* (1977) he traces the genealogy of punishment for deviancy as an evolution from public, gruesome torture and execution to private, physical confinement in jail, internalized, personal self-regulation. There has been a parallel evolution in the 'technology' of punishment from instruments of torture and execution to prisons, health farms and expensive drug rehabilitation centres. The history of school discipline shows a similar genealogy, moving from externally imposed physical punishment, to confinement and detention, to the internal regulation of homework and self-study.

Phenomenological constructs

A phenomenological view of the body provides rich 'insider' accounts of what experience 'feels' like. The body is not only an object – it is subjectively experienced. The body is not 'just some body, some particular physiological entity, but my (or your) body as I (or you) experience it' (Merleau-Ponty 1964: 166). Our bodiliness may extend beyond the limits of our body – for example, towards something at which we are pointing. Constructivist views of learning also see the learner as engaged in a process of meaning-making which must include the meaning of the body.

Metaphorical constructs

Many of the metaphors we use to describe our mental states or our experiences of being in the world are sensory: 'my blood froze'; 'my heart leaped'; 'the hair stood on the back of my head'. According to George Lakoff (1993), metaphors show that cognition has its roots in bodily experience. 'The mind is inherently embodied' (Lakoff and Johnson 2000: 1). The American evolutionary psychologist Steven Pinker disagrees in part, arguing that metaphors are not sufficient in themselves to permit thinking; there are underlying rules of thought that allow them to be used (Pinker 2007: 259). Educators too have their bodily metaphors: courses are 'run', arguments are 'weighed' and students 'struggle' with ideas until they 'grasp' them. The word 'remembering' itself contains an echo of physical members and calls to mind a child counting the fingers of one hand.

Impedimentary constructs

There is a long tradition of the body as an impediment, holding back mental activity. Many philosophical and religious traditions stress the renunciation of the body. The body is represented as a tiresome bundle of demands which must be satisfied in order that the real business of thinking and learning can proceed. School breaks and holidays involve a temporary discontinuity when the real business of education is interrupted by the needs of the body.

Mind–body relationships

The constructs above show that although the body is a centre of physiological activity, it is much more than this. Similarly, the mind is much more than a centre of psychological activity. The relationship between brain and mind is hugely complex and the subject of fierce debate. Some would completely dismiss 'mind' as an irrelevant concept, seeing consciousness as an accidental by-product of intense neuronal activity. Evolutionary psychologists however, hold that consciousness, like language, is an adaptive advantage, developed through processes of Darwinian selection (Rose 2005: 138–9).

When we talk of 'mind' we refer to the human mental states of self-awareness, intentionality, agency and empathy that do not at first glance appear to have anything to do with the body. On the other hand, it is obvious that the brain, a physical organ, is involved in all mental activity – as the American Nobel prize-winner in physiology Eric Kandel, claims, 'Of course, the mind is a product of the brain' (Dobbs 2007: 34). We subscribe to the view of the mind and brain, not as separate entities, but as different constructions of the same set of events. Educators can view reading as a deliberate conscious cognitive activity as well as a response to neurons firing in the visual cortex. Problems with reading such as dyslexia can be interpreted either as a result of poor reading strategies or as a consequence of neural disorganization in the left hemisphere of the cortex – an area responsible for language function (Rosenzweig et al. 2005: 594).

The brain architecture

The adult human brain is a greyish-pink gelatinous mass weighing about 1.4 kg or 3 lb. It contains about 100 billion brain cells or neurons with one million billion connections between them, all bathed in cerebro-spinal fluid which acts as a shock absorber and carries nutrients and other chemicals (Blakemore and Frith 2005: 11).

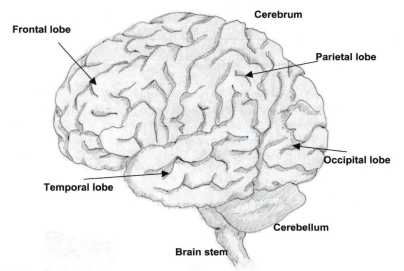

Figure 12.1 The brain.

Viewed externally the brain has three parts: the cerebrum, the cerebellum and the brain stem (see Figure 12.1).

The cerebrum is the largest part of the brain accounting for 85 per cent of its weight and consisting of two large hemispheres with a highly folded exterior called the cerebral cortex. The left and right hemispheres of the cerebrum are separated by a deep longitudinal fissure. They are connected by bundles of nerve fibres – the largest of which is called the corpus callosum. There are five lobes of the cerebrum detailed in Table 12.1.

Brain function

It has been claimed that the brain operates as a series of modules performing different cognitive functions such as face recognition, speech, or emotion regulation (Rose 2005: 101). Brain abnormalities offer evidence for discrete modules in the brain

(Rosenzweig et al. 2005: 603). For instance, people born with Williams Syndrome are proficient in language and social interaction but IQ tests show them to be mentally deficient. Certain areas have been shown to have a major responsibility for specific cognitive functions as shown in Table 12.1.

Table 12.1 Brain lobes and related responsibilities

Lobe	Some related responsibilities
Frontal	Planning, selecting and inhibiting responses, decision-making
Parietal	Arithmetical calculations, knowing where things are spatially
Temporal	Language processing
Occipital	Visual recognition
Insula	Regulation of emotional reactions and cravings

Left-hemisphere and right-hemisphere specialization

There have been some cases where drastic treatment for epilepsy involving the cutting of the corpus callosum, produced a 'split brain' with little interaction between left and right hemispheres. This reveals a specialization of function in each hemisphere that is masked by interconnection and integration in normal brains (Rozenzweig, et al. 2005: 597). The cognitive modes in which each hemisphere specializes is shown in Table 12.2.

Table 12.2 Left and right hemisphere cognitive mode specialization

Left hemisphere	Right hemisphere
Phonetic	Non-linguistic
Sequential	Holistic
Analytical	Synthetic
Propositional	Gestalt
Discrete temporal analysis	Form perception
Language	Spatial

Source: Rosenzweig et al. (2005: 603).

In the past, researchers assumed that the left hemisphere was usually dominant but modern research has moved away from this notion to suggest co-functioning, with specialization of function (Rosenzweig et al. 2005: 597). These ideas have implications for educational practice which will be explored in the latter part of the chapter.

Brain plasticity

Despite the specialization described above, research shows a certain amount of brain plasticity where brain regions can vary their usual function. This can happen in two ways – by compensation or by development. Damage to certain brain areas or deprivation of sensation can lead to neurons adapting to a new role to compensate. For example, when researchers blindfolded sighted adults continuously, after only five days the visual cortex, deprived of visual stimulation, took over some of functions of hearing and feeling. The visual cortex was activated when they felt Braille dots. 'The seeing brain was now hearing and feeling' (Begley 2007: 114–15).

Brain plasticity is also evident in the development of the child and adolescent. The infant brain has multiple neural connections between many parts of the brain with the potential to take on many different functions. For example, if life-threatening conditions require a toddler to lose the left hemisphere which controls language, the functions of learning to talk, read and write can all be taken over by the right hemisphere (Begley 2007: 76).

Teenage brains also continue to develop new neurons, especially in the frontal lobes which control high-level functions of planning, judgement and emotional regulation. Neurological pruning also takes place at this time so that unused neural pathways die out to improve efficiency. It is only at the age of about 25 that this growing and pruning diminishes and the brain looks adult (Begley 2007: 113). If a subject studied in primary school is not continued, then it will be lost. Teachers have always known the importance of revision and continuous use. 'Use it or lose it' is a well-worn cliché.

Even when adults learn – acquiring new knowledge or mastering a new skill – the brain changes in a physical way. Neuroscientists have found that skilled performers have more than an average number of neural connections between the areas of the brain relating to that skill. 'Cells that fire together, wire together' (Robertson 1999: 49). For example, regular piano practice results in an expansion of the basal ganglia, cerebellum and the motor cortex related to finger movement. Apparently, for a skilled pianist, just thinking about playing the piano leads to measurable changes in the motor cortex (Begley 2007: 151). London taxi drivers develop an enlarged area of the hippocampus responsible for spatial memory as a result of needing and using a detailed knowledge of the city (Rosenzweig et al. 2005: 548).

Physical development

The development of the brain is integrated with development of the rest of the body over the life course and each stage has implications for learning.

- *Pre-birth* The development of cognition requires a particular set of environmental conditions. Proper development requires adequate maternal nutrition and lifestyle. Nutritional deprivation in the womb leads to impaired growth, intelligence and responses to learning after birth.
- *Infancy and childhood* Body image is formed from the reactions of parents and teachers and perceived physical comparisons to others. Children learn as a result of their physical actions on materials in the world, and the process of making sense of these.

- *Teenage years* Body image is very important, for example in terms of attractiveness to the opposite sex. Adolescents also extend their categorization of themselves and others to include personality traits. Intellectual and emotional learning is intense with social learning often taking priority.
- *Adulthood* With maturity, identity is grounded more on roles and responsibilities than on body image. The frontal lobe area of the brain matures leading to more control and less impulsivity and risk-taking. Learning is related to social roles.
- *Old age* Body image is not so important. The body slows up, and the brain also slows up with a decline in fluid intelligence as shown in Chapter 8 (p. 122). The importance of reflection on life events suggests that learning has become more integrated, hence the attribution of wisdom to older people.

Learning physical skills

Much of what we learn is physical. For example, we learn to walk, dance, drive, hold a pencil, write and speak. All these require the body and muscles to learn certain routines. People gradually learn to perform well-rehearsed physical actions automatically. Thinking about such automatic skills may even interfere with their performance. However, teaching a skill and passing on a skill may require conscious awareness and an explicit statement of how the skill is carried out for the purposes of sharing (Schön 1987: 24–5).

People usually acquire a physical skill in stages. Benjamin Bloom, whose cognitive taxonomy was discussed in Chapter 2, also identified the stages of skills acquisition which he termed 'psychomotor'. These stages range from knowing the sequence of physical operations to internalized performance as shown in Table 12.3.

Table 12.3 Stages of psychomotor development

Stage of development	Starting a stationary car
Unconscious mastery	Able to start car without thinking about it
Conscious control	Able to perform complete sequence of action while thinking about it
Coordinated performance	Able to use clutch and gear stick-shift together
Partial performance	Able to depress the clutch
Procedural task knowledge	Knowing how to start a car

Source: Based on Bloom and Krathwohl (1956).

The first stage of Bloom's psychomotor taxonomy can be learned by observing and enacting the expert behaviour of others. This is known as modelling, and requires physical enactment. Bandura, whose work is reviewed in Chapter 4, describes how we observe and model the behaviour of more expert performers, thus trying out new skills (Bruning et al. 2004).

Chemical balance in the body and hormonal systems also influence learning. These are too complex to be discussed here. However, teachers need to be aware of the importance of such systems and the need to maintain appropriate hydration and blood sugar levels. The issue of nutrition and chemical enhancement of learning is discussed later in the chapter.

Educational implications of the learning body

As we have seen, the body is central to the individual and social experiences of everyone and this must be taken into account in formal education. Educationalists need to take a holistic view of education, incorporating all elements of personhood, recognizing the importance of physical expression and promoting social interaction. Everything we learn – knowledge, practical skills or cultural values – has a physical dimension, of which teachers should be aware. Learning is most effective when the learning activity:

- is connected directly to physical experience, and
- includes the physical presence of others.

Connecting to physical experience

Teachers should:

- provide spaces for individual and group learning: break-out spaces, alcoves, tables to facilitate social learning;
- provide educational settings that take account of the needs of the body: drinking fountains, toilets, ventilation, ergonomic furniture;
- create rich stimulating sensory environments for learners: water, plants, animals, musical instruments;
- start sessions with younger learners with some form of physical exercise to increase the blood supply to the brain: stretching, yawning, action songs, action games;
- include physical education as an important subject at all levels: use gymnastics, sporting activities, games; value physical education in assessment and accreditation;
- encourage frequent changes of the environment to stimulate different aspects of brain or physical development:
  - o have frequent breaks between sessions of teacher talk;
  - o encourage movement between classrooms;
  - o arrange field trips, use laboratory work;
- encourage movement between learning sessions and classes: have a variety of learning locations; where possible, let rooms be bases for teachers so that students move;

- consider physical and real-world activities appropriate to subject and learner: environmental surveys (e.g. soil sampling, traffic surveys), school trips;
- include physical activities as part of assessment strategies: use authentic assessment of psychomotor skills; e.g. life-saving and First Aid examinations, practical laboratory work.

Physical presence of others

Other people are important in learning, both as physical presences and as observable proof that desired or desirable goals can be achieved. Teachers are more than mere transmitters of knowledge. They are, as Bruner says, 'human events, who create a social world which connects to the social world of the learner' (Bruner 1986: 126).

Teachers should:

- build relationships between themselves, their students, and the subject matter:
  - use student names and relate to them as individuals;
  - keep in touch with students informally in corridors and playgrounds;
  - share personal feelings about their subjects;

- be aware of body language;
  - consider furniture placement and teacher location;
  - take account of the body language communication of learners;

- be aware that, as teachers, they embody the values of their subject and profession:
  - maintain an appropriate physical and psychological distance;
  - consider the importance of personal appearance, grooming and dress;
  - be aware of the propensity of personal mannerisms to annoy;

- allow learners appropriate personal space: take account of gender and cultural differences;
- move around the classroom, except when giving instructions;
- be aware of learning as a social activity:
  - be sensitive to possible social isolation or bullying;
  - encourage group work and problem-based learning;
  - set up school hobby clubs and societies;
  - encourage peer collaboration and challenge;
  - stage school plays and encourage group music-making.

Embodied and distance education

Embodiment can sometimes be an impediment to learning. The necessity to be together in the same place at the same time, can be a serious barrier to learners, especially adults with many commitments. Online learning allows the possibility of transcending space and time limitations, and permits vicarious experience and the efficient, enhanced transfer of information.

However, the lack of physical presence leads to other problems. In order to take account of the physical aspect of learning at a distance teachers should:

- incorporate some form of physicality into their programmes:
    - use photographs and biographical details of the instructional designers and authors;
    - make use of web-cam and audio linking, video-conferencing and other communicative technologies;
    - use the social networking capabilities of the web to create learning communities;

- consider the multi-sensorial capabilities of technology:
    - use sound, vision, touch, animations, interactivity;
    - expand physical capability in exploring virtual environments;

- facilitate rapid communication and feedback:
    - set up online tutorials using web-cam and Voice Over Internet Protocol (VOIP);
    - use web-conferencing;
    - make use of a range of input devices to capture many aspects of embodiment.

Although new technologies have gone some way towards reproducing physical presence in a virtual environment, there remains much physical learning which requires the practice of physical skills in a real environment.

The importance of practice

Recent educational research and practice has focused on the conditions necessary for skilled performance or mastery of a subject area.

To facilitate skilled psychomotor performance, teachers should:

- break a skill down into smaller units or sub-tasks;
- be explicit about the sequence of actions required;
- model correct performance;
- allow learners to learn by trial and error;
- gradually combine sub-skills to integrate sequences;
- insist on constant practice so that neural pathways are established;

- link learning to physical places and routines.

Learning enhancement

Since learning is a physical activity, it can be enhanced by physical means. Diet, exercise and artificial supplements can enhance learning. Water, exercise and a diet high in Omega 3 and 6 fish oils have been identified as promoting more effective mental activity and the development of neural pathways (Kiefer 2007: 58–63). Drugs such as Ritalin are now widely used by psychologists to control attention deficit hyperactive disorder (ADHD) in children. The World Health Organization (WHO) claims that Ritalin is now being widely used as a learning enhancer by normal students (Rose 2005: 260).

Popular psychology has interpreted the concept of left-brain right-brain specialization to imply that one side of the brain may be dominant over the other, for example, that left-brain logical thinking is dominant over the right-brain creative or emotional thinking. Inventories of left-brain right-brain attributes such as that shown in Table 12.4 are sometimes used in education in association with learning style inventories.

Table 12.4 Left and right brain thinking

Left brain thinking	Right brain thinking
Logic	Intuition
Calculation	Creativity
Recognition	Spatial awareness
Detail and patterning	Holistic overview
Caution	Risk-taking
Detachment	Emotion

Although it may have some use as a metaphor, research does not support such a simple dichotomy – for example, language in left-handed people is housed in both hemispheres. According to the neuroscientist Sarah Blakemore, it is questionable whether left- and right-brain categorization should be applied in education, and it may even act as a barrier to learning (Blakemore and Frith 2005: 60).

Key ideas

- Formal western education has laid more emphasis on intellect than body.
- There has been some interest in physical education historically.
- The body is more than a physiological object.
- The body is a set of physiological systems.
- The body is a set of personal constructs used to formulate identity.
- The body is the means by which we relate to others.

- The body is an object upon which power is exerted.
- The body is subjectively experienced.
- Embodiment is common in metaphor.
- The body has been seen as an impediment holding back mental activity.
- The mind and brain are different constructions of mental events.
- Different brain parts have major responsibilities for different functions.
- The brain operates as a series of functional modules.
- The left and right hemispheres work together but specialize in different cognitive modes.
- Brain regions can vary their usual function through development or to compensate for damage.
- In learning, the brain changes in a physical way.
- Brain performance can be enhanced naturally and artificially.
- Brain development is integrated with the development of the rest of the body over the life course.
- Much learning involves the acquisition of physical skills.
- Skills develop by increasing the integration of sub-tasks until they become automatic through practice.
- Observing experts modelling performance gives learners an overview of a skill to be acquired.

Conclusions

This chapter emphasizes the importance of the body and embodiment and seeks to redress the traditional view of education as a purely mental activity. The chapter draws attention to aspects of learning such as the physical environment and to the physiological needs of learners.

Knowledge of neural processes has been found to be important in understanding and tackling learning disorders such as dyslexia and ADHD. A knowledge of neural processes could be useful in the future to enhance the learning of the general population.

Many learning disabilities are spectrum disorders ranging from mild to severe, so an exploration of the neurological substrates of such disorders and remedial strategies may help a variety of learners.

Likewise, chemical and nutritional enhancement of learning need not be confined to remediation. Just as the medical use of drugs enhances and prolongs physical life, so their educational use may enhance and prolong intellectual life.

However, this chapter does not simply concentrate on the brain and the body as biological entities. There is a danger in presenting a reductive view of learning based on observable neuronal phenomena, ignoring the personal, social, subjective and metaphorical constructs of embodiment and their influence on learning.

Learning combines mind and body. It is a holistic experience, seeking as the Latin motto proclaims, 'Mens sana in corpora sana' – a healthy mind in a healthy body.

References

Begley, S. (2007) *Train Your Mind, Change Your Brain: How a New Science Reveals Our Extraordinary Potential To Transform Ourselves.* New York: Ballantine Books.

Blakemore, S. and Frith, U. (2005) *The Learning Brain: Lessons for Education.* Oxford: Blackwell Publishing.

Bloom, B. and Krathwohl, D. (1956) *Taxonomy of Educational Objectives: Handbooks 1 to 3: The Cognitive, Affective and Psychomotor Domain.* London: Longmans Green.

Bruner, J.S. (1986) *Actual Minds: Possible Worlds.* Cambridge, MA: Harvard University Press.

Bruning, R.H., Schraw, G.J., Norby, M. and Ronning, R.R. (2004) *Cognitive Psychology and Instruction* (4th edn). New Jersey: Pearson, Merrill Prentice Hall.

Chambers (1997) *Chambers Biographical Dictionary* (ed M.Perry). London: Chambers.

Dobbs, D. (2007) Eric Kandel: from mind to brain and back again, in *Scientific American Mind,* Oct/Nov.

Eichberg, H. (1986) The enclosure of the body – on the historical relativity of 'health', 'nature', and the environment of sport, *The Journal of Contemporary History,* 21(1): 99–121.

Foucault, M. (1977) *Discipline and Punish: The Birth of the Prison.* London: Penguin.

Giddens, A. (1991) *Modernity and Self-identity: Self and Society in the Late Modern Age.* Cambridge: Polity Press.

Kiefer, I. (2007) Brain Food, *Scientific American Mind,* 18(5): Oct/Nov.

Lakoff, G. (1993) The contemporary theory of metaphor, in A. Ortony (ed.) *Metaphor and Thought,* (2nd edn). New York: Cambridge University Press.

Lakoff, G. and Johnson, M. (2000) *Philosophy in the Flesh.* Cambridge, MA. MIT Press.

Merleau-Ponty, M. (1964) *Signs* (trans. Richard C. McCleary). Evanston, IL: Northwestern University Press.

Pinker, S. (2007) *The Stuff of Thought.* New York: Viking Penguin.

Robertson, I. (1999) *Mind Sculpture: Unleashing your Brain's Potential.* London: Bantam Press.

Rose, S. (2005) *The 21st Century Brain: Explaining, Mending and Manipulating the Mind.* London: Jonathan Cape.

Rosenzweig, M.R., Breedlove, S.M. and Watson, N.V. (2005) *Biological Psychology: An Introduction to Behavioral and Cognitive Neuroscience* (4th edn). Sunderland, MA: Sinauer Associates, Inc.

Rousseau, J.J. (1762/2007) *Émile, or On Education.* Sioux Falls: NuVision Publications.

Schön, D.A. (1987) *Educating the Reflective Practitioner: Towards a New Design for Teaching and Learning in the Profession.* San Francisco, CA: Jossey-Bass.

Shilling, C. (1993) *The Body and Social Theory.* London: Sage Publications.

YMCA (2007) History of the YMCA. http://www.ymca.net/ (accessed Nov. 2007).

Chapter 13   Language and learning

Introduction

As you pass a classroom or lecture theatre you are likely to hear people talking: teachers imparting information or asking questions, and learners responding and asking their own questions. In most educational settings language is the medium of learning and teaching. This chapter explores language and its relationship to learning. It does not address the scientific elements of philology and language usage, but concentrates on topics of practical use to the teacher.

The importance of language

By language we mean the socially shared conventions that govern communication using words, symbols or gestures. Because communication and language are central to all forms and levels of education, they deserve special consideration in a book on educational theory. Learning a language is the main intellectual exercise undertaken by a young child. Language is a prerequisite for engaging in formal education and has both a social and cognitive role. Tables 13.1 and 13.2 illustrate some of the socio-cultural and cognitive roles of language in relation to curriculum and classroom activities.

Table 13.1   Socio-cultural roles of language in relation to the curriculum

Communication Teacher and students	Transaction Teacher and students	Enaction Teacher
Articulating and sharing curricular values	Agreeing curricular values	Adapting, mediating and clarifying values
Communicating and sharing curricular objectives	Negotiating group learning contracts	Inducting students
Transmitting and receiving curricular content	Negotiating content and processes of learning	Laying down procedures and ground rules
Giving and receiving feedback	Negotiating success criteria	Delivering written or spoken judgements

Table 13.2 Cognitive roles of language in relation to classroom activities

Teaching	Learning	Thinking
Calling for attention	Listening	Focusing attention
Stating aims and learning outcomes	Developing expectations	Guiding perception
Reminding learners about previous classroom activities	Responding to questions	Drawing on memory
Suggesting learning methodology and activities	Planning of learning process	Guiding perception and meta-cognition
Presenting material in verbal or written form	Listening, reading, writing, psychomotor skills	Using memory for encoding and recall of information, promoting thinking
Initiating and provoking class discussion	Talking, debating, challenging, confirming	Reinforcing or reconfiguring mental constructs
Offering encouragement or challenge	Accepting, justifying, excusing, querying	Supporting or changing mental constructs
Testing, using written or verbal forms	Answering in verbal or written forms	Recalling from memory and re-enforcing existing knowledge

Socio-cultural functions of language

Language as a social activity

Etienne Wenger argues that learning is inherently a social activity as learners participate in communities of practice, in which novices are inducted into specific ways of thinking and talking about the world (Lave and Wenger 1991). Such communities offer their own 'discourses' or forms of language usage so that members can share common interests, identify each other, and distinguish their community from others.

A family is the most immediate learning community encountered by the child, and within which it learns language along with social roles and codes of behaviour. Next is the school where concept formation and symbolic representation form a shared linguistic process, situated in a learning community where teachers and children jointly construct meaning.

Language facilitates the construction of personal meaning and social identity. Individuals develop a sense of self and explore their identities by what they say to themselves, and by what others say to them. Individuals and groups tell stories about themselves, which encapsulate their histories, values and ambitions. Language does not reflect reality, it constructs it.

Language as a sociocognitive activity

The Russian constructivist psychologist Vygotsky claimed that thinking develops and meaning is constructed through language – a cultural tool developed over centuries. One reason that language is such an effective tool is that it does not have to be reinvented by every speaker, but can be appropriated immediately (Leont'ev 1981). An individual's ideas are shared with others through language and this joint participation in language becomes internalized as individual thought. Social communication therefore develops into internalized thinking (Vygotsky 1962).

As the child acquires subject knowledge, language for thinking is simultaneously 'appropriated'. A child's experience is mediated firstly through social interaction and language as the child learns to talk and make complete sentences. This social speech is then used to guide and direct action as the child engages in 'private speech' with themselves. This 'private speech' often consists of abbreviated sentences or phrases spoken aloud as the child engages in a difficult task. This is the beginning of 'verbal thought' and with it, the development of the self-regulation of thinking (Bodrova and Leong 2003: 161).

Learners come to an educational setting with a certain amount of cognitive ability and knowledge; the teacher brings a more sophisticated cognitive ability and a greater level of knowledge. Through the medium of language, teacher and learner interact. The teacher encourages, gives examples, supports and affirms ideas, offers analogies and metaphors and challenges existing ideas in order to assist thinking in a process termed 'scaffolding' (Wood et al. 1976: 89–90). This interaction becomes internalized as cognitive change in the learner. Vygotsky called the intellectual space in which these interactions occur the 'zone of Proximal Development' (ZPD). Through the processes of social interaction, the learner can learn more than they could achieve alone (Vygotsky 1962).

For Vygotsky, schooling develops formal thinking skills and theoretical knowledge. For example, learning to read leads to far-reaching changes in the nature of children's knowledge and use of language, which leads in turn to more analytical ways of thinking. Children acquire self-regulation through language, learning to take on different perspectives and feedback. However, language usage itself may be different for different groups, as shown by research on cultural language codes.

Cultural language codes

Writing in the 1970s, the English sociologist Basil Bernstein attributed children's variable educational performance to the forms of language used by the different social classes. He singled out middle-class and working-class language registers (Bernstein, 1977). Compare these exchanges between a parent and child:

Middle-class parent: Would you mind moving those books off the chair so that I can sit down?

Working-class parent: Get those off there.

The middle-class parent uses an elaborated code of language where all the communication is contained within the statement. This offers the possibility of abstraction and complexity. The elaborated language code confers an advantage in the formal educational setting where language mastery is so important. The restricted language code used by the working-class parent requires physical presence and gestures to convey meaning. There is little abstraction. It limits language to the present time and present place. This restricted language code is an impediment to educational and vocational progress. For Bernstein language codes are part of a vicious circle reinforcing economic and social divisions in society. They lead to divergent aspirations for children from different social classes, and to different teacher and learner expectations of school performance.

The US Headstart Project of the 1960s aimed to enhance the linguistic abilities of young African-American children on the assumption that it would lead to improved educational and vocational opportunities. President Johnson claimed that 'children who have never spoken, learned to talk' (Wood 1988: 90). Empirical studies of the time showed that such children often used a single word for a sentence, for example, 'hebigdaw' for 'He's a big dog' (Wood 1988: 91). This expression is now not regarded as evidence of linguistic deprivation but as an example of a distinctive imaginative language known as Ebonic or African-American speech. This simplifies consonants ('daw' for 'dog') and uses the verb 'to be' to indicate continuous action ('he be gone' for 'he is frequently gone'); (Samovar and Porter 2004: 154–5).

Bernstein's work failed to take into account the complexities of different cultural and social linguistic forms. The idea that language and social class are clearly correlated has revived however, with concepts of cultural and social capital and the 'reproduction' and 'transmission' of dominant social class values in education (Bourdieu 1977). Teachers may have higher expectations of children with whom they share a common language, making communication easier than with other children (Wood 1988: 113).

Socio-political uses of language

Different fields of knowledge have an associated language that determines what is perceived, valued and legitimized. The French sociologist Foucault claims that knowledge is embedded in 'discourses' – all the language and practices associated with a field of knowledge. Those who control the discourse, control access to the knowledge, its meaning and its language (Peters 2001: 170–4). The discourse of education reveals that the legitimacy of the knowledge possessed by teachers lends legitimacy to the power that they wield. For example, many educational terms have undertones of power, as well as their surface meaning. Teachers are 'authorities' – they *have* authority in their classrooms and they *are* authorities in their subject area. Similarly 'discipline' refers both to the subject being studied and the control that the teacher exercises over classroom events (Hoskin 1990: 30). The discourse of assessment in education – its use of 'grades' and 'passing' or 'failing' has been shown to be threatening to the self-identity and self-esteem of adult learners (Murphy and Fleming 2000).

Paulo Freire, the South American educationalist, worked with peasants and landless workers on literacy projects. He saw literacy acquisition as highly political, involving a critical scrutiny and assimilation of the words which are culturally and politically relevant to an oppressed group. Through reading, these peasants can learn how the dominant discourse contributes to their oppression – 'reading the word' became 'reading the world'. Language can therefore act as a source of empowerment, enabling oppressed people to develop counter-discourses that challenge current political realities (Freire 1982).

This idea is developed by Jürgen Habermas, the German philosopher, in his theory of 'communicative rationality' (Morrison 2001: 215–23). By this he claims that liberation from misleading social or bureaucratic forces can flow from a group's commitment to:

- a shared construction of reason;
- the principles of mutual understanding;
- a critical evaluation of the claims put forward in argument.

Although the concept of 'communicative rationality' appears quite abstract, it is used as the basis for a number of innovative educational programmes in peer-talking in English schools discussed in the later part of this chapter.

Political correctness in language

It is no longer acceptable to describe learners as 'mentally deficient', or to use 'he' to refer to people in general. Feminists claim that sexist language reinforces sexist thinking. Teachers now encourage inclusive language that avoids the labelling of people and challenges prejudice and stereotypical thinking. Concepts of political correctness are based on the Sapir-Wharf hypothesis (SWH) that language does not simply reproduce, but influences the thoughts and categorizations that speakers make (Whorf 1956).

Cognitive functions of language

There is sound empirical evidence for a link between language and thinking. For example, the vocabulary spurt in children before their second birthday coincides with an increased ability to categorize, though it is difficult to say whether the words or the concepts come first (Quinn and Oates 2004: 54–6). A range of hypotheses have been proposed to explain the relationship between language and thought as Table 13.3 shows.

Table 13.3 Relationship between language and thinking

Hypotheses	Theorist
Language is thinking.	Watson: 1920s
Language affects the way people think.	Whorf: 1956
Thinking develops from acting on the world but talk with others facilitates this process.	Piaget: 1967
Thought and language have different roots but gradually integrate.	Vygotsky: 1962
There is a movement from action to visualization to symbolic representation as language.	Bruner: 1964

Source: Based on Child (1997: 224).

Stages of children's linguistic development

Piaget is the major theorist on the cognitive development of children but, unlike Vygotsky, he does not accord language a high place. For Piaget, children construct knowledge by developing increasingly sophisticated hypotheses drawn from their actions on the world (Piaget and Inhelder 1969). This cognitive development leads to language development, as illustrated in Table 13.4.

Table 13.4 Piaget's developmental stages: cognitive and linguistic development

Stage	Action on the world	Cognitive development	Language development
Sensory-motor Age 0–2	Children interact with objects in front of them	Early categorization and comprehension	Babbling, single-word speech
Pre-operational Age 2–6	Children play with and act on objects They engage in imaginative play	Increase in categorization Elementary logical thinking (e.g. faulty theories of conservation of liquids) Egocentricity	Vocabulary spurt Use of 'this' and 'that' as referents Facility to acquire a second or third language without accent
Concrete operational Age 6–12	Children experiment with materials and form hypotheses about the observable world	Appreciate multiple perspectives Engage in correct logical reasoning about observed objects	When not understood, children re-formulate and clarify their language May acquire a second or third language without accent

(contd)

Stage	Action on the world	Cognitive development	Language development
Formal operations Age 12	Individuals discover rules and principles socially and intellectually Formal education fosters language and thinking	Develop independent thinking Reason with abstract, hypothetical, and contrary-to-fact information	Further development of abstraction in language More difficulty in acquiring other languages without accent

For Piaget, intellectual development is a predetermined developmental process which cannot be accelerated, so teaching is relatively unimportant. Instruction could impose the teacher's language or solutions on children without their having gone through the necessary processes of understanding. However, there is a role for language. It can be used to ask questions that unsettle children's current thinking so that they consider new hypotheses. For example, if children think feathers fall more slowly than stones, the teacher could ask what would happen if the feather and stone were dropped on the moon where there is no air. Peers are more effective than teachers in provoking such cognitive dissonance since they have less power than teachers to impose meaning or 'correct' solutions (Wood et al. 2006: 205).

Language acquisition

Imitation

A common-sense view of language acquisition is that a child learns language from hearing it spoken (Skinner 1957). Young children learn grammar by repeating what they hear and then generalizing the rules – for example, adding 's' to plurals and 'ed' to past tenses. However, children's facility in generating sentences they have never heard before cannot simply be explained by imitation.

Innate language

The structural linguist Noam Chomsky claims that language learning cannot be reduced to responses to stimuli. For Chomsky, language involves the knowledge of a set of innate or inherent language rules that enable a speaker to say something never spoken before, and a listener to hear and understand it. Children are born knowing the deep structure of language, for example the difference between verbs and nouns. According to Chomsky, this capacity for language reflects the uniqueness of the human mind, differentiating humans as a species from others (Chomsky 1972).

Language and evolution

The American evolutionary psychologist Stephen Pinker claims that language was a key factor in human evolution, caused by a significant mutation in the vocal tract, which led to the production of an expressive variety of sounds, and ultimately to speech (Pinker 1994). Language has probably existed for over a million years and every one of more than 5000 human cultures has developed language (Bruning et al. 2004: 244). Language and the brain may have co-evolved, with language evolving to match brain processes that categorize the world in different ways. This in turn shaped the structure of the brain to fit language's increasing demands on it (Rose 2005: 133).

The innate potential of young children for language learning allied to their brain plasticity and developmental stage may account for their facility in language learning and may have something to contribute to decisions about foreign language teaching in primary and secondary school.

The chapter has shown that language has socio-cultural and cognitive dimensions. Since these are the central concerns of teachers, the next section draws out some of the educational implications.

Educational implications

We discuss here some pedagogical implications of language in relation to the educational experiences of young learners, since language and literacy skills are generally acquired in childhood.

Language in the home

The home is important in providing a rich linguistic environment that promotes the development of speech. 'Motherese' – the exaggerated and repetitive language in which mothers speak to babies – has an important role in directing the child's attention and in concept formation (Snow and Ferguson 1977). The frequency with which parents speak to children up to the age of 2 has major consequences for their language use throughout life. Children understand more than they can say, so adults should not confine their language to structures or vocabulary that children are able to use in response. Children can appropriate language as a tool even when they have not acquired the cognitive maturity to utilize it fully. Parents can foster this anticipation of adult social life by explicitness in explaining and demonstrating the social roles that children take on in play (Bodrova and Leong 2003: 156–75).

Parents can also influence their children's communicative strategies by using an expanded language code that helps the child appreciate the listener's point of view and communicate more abstract concepts.

In order to help language development, parents should:

- talk and read to infants from the earliest age;
- have books at home and bring children with them to libraries and bookshops;
- choose stories and rhymes to encourage repetition and recognition;
- use movement in conjunction with stories and rhyme;

- give a full explanation of their actions and encourage children to do the same;
- restrict children's passive TV watching;
- provide opportunities for different types of play activity.

The language of the classroom

If the purpose of instruction is to transmit pre-existing knowledge, then classroom language will be concerned with subject content and assessment will require the production of 'right' answers through talk or written language. If the purpose of instruction is meaning construction, then communication will be more interactive and exploratory, and assessment less concerned with right answers (Barnes 1971: 27–38). However, even when teachers advocate a more constructivist role, they still emphasize correct answers (Edwards and Mercer 1987). The practical constraints of large classes and crowded curricula make the Vygotskian classroom of social interaction, scaffolding and shared construction of meaning, an aspiration rather than a reality in many cases (Bliss et al. 1996: 37–6).

Classroom spoken language can be explored under six headings:

- exposition, where the teacher describes, informs or explains;
- question and answer exchanges;
- discussion and peer talk involving the whole class or small groups;
- listening where pupils listen to the teacher or to each other;
- reading;
- writing.

(Cohen et al. 2004: 233–46)

Exposition

In typical classroom situations, two-thirds of the time is spent talking, the majority of which is carried out by the teacher (Flanders 1970). Some purposes of exposition are:

- introducing lessons;
- outlining the outcomes for the session;
- giving learners new information;
- using technical language and subject discourse;
- linking new material to previous knowledge;
- using metaphors or analogies to present concepts;
- laying out a sequence of activities;
- indicating assessment procedures.

(Cohen et al. 2004: 233)

Question and answer exchanges

Much interest has focused on 'teacherese' or the way in which teachers talk to pupils in school. These exchanges are dominated by a model known as IRE:

I   Initiate   - the teacher initiates the questioning

R   Respond   - the pupil responds

E   Evaluate   - the teacher evaluates the response

(Bruning et al. 2004: 233–46)

When this type of questioning seeks a 'correct' response it may produce guessing, rather than an explanation of pupils' thinking.

In order to use questioning effectively, teachers should:

- be clear about the purpose of questioning and the type of answer sought;
- ask open-ended questions that invite elaborated answers;
- state the name of the desired respondent immediately after the question;
- invite responses from small groups as well as individuals;
- use buzz-groups for whole group questioning: the class is divided into groups, generating answers;
- acknowledge occasionally what pupils say; without further questioning;
- acknowledge what pupils say, and repeat or write their words as validation;
- encourage and reward pupils who answer by providing feedback on answers;

With incorrect answers, teachers should:

- not simply say that answers are wrong;
- seek other responses to avoid loss of the pupil's self-esteem;
- ask pupils to explain their reasoning;
- offer clues to re-focus thinking;

In general, teachers should avoid:

- leading questions that contain the answer;
- question that require 'guessing what teacher wants to hear';
- asking so many questions that learners disengage.

Discussion and peer talk

Cognitive collaboration Children's talk about tasks can foster the joint construction of meaning through agreement. More knowledgeable or able peers can, through the ZPD, support their less knowledgeable peers by providing explanations that lead to changes in reasoning, or offer scaffolding or support in the development of theories

(Vygotsky 1978: 90). Moreover, collaboration can encourage problem-solving as friends or children in groups support each other's thinking as a form of social interaction.

Cognitive conflict In a different way to Vygotsky, Piaget identified peer talk as important in helping children progress in the active construction of understanding (Piaget 1926). A teacher's view is naturally dominant, but disagreements between peers can suggest alternatives to the child's own viewpoint that can be considered on more equal terms. The conflicts have to be resolved in order to maintain their social relationships so they seek solutions that take account of both views.

Three types of talk have been identified in pupil's discourse in classrooms:

- *disputational talk* – disagreements and individual decision-making;
- *cumulative talk* – uncritical comment, repetition, agreement and elaboration of original points;
- *exploratory talk* – constructive criticism of other people's ideas, with justifications for challenges and the proposal of solutions or new ideas.

Of these, exploratory talk should be encouraged most because it makes thinking visible in talk (Mercer 1995).

Listening to the teacher and each other

If it is to be an effective learning tool, classroom discussion needs to be structured. The role of the teacher is to:

- agree with pupils the norms and guidelines for participating in discussion
- make tolerance a rule of discussion – not interrupting weighing up opposing views
- demonstrate the difference between personal opinions, beliefs, and claims made on the basis of evidence
- show what type of evidence counts in the evaluation of a claim
- set or negotiate an agenda for discussion
- state the desired outcomes of the discussion
- link content and skill-based knowledge
- require pupils to reflect on the learning process and what they have achieved
- ask pupils to reflect on specific areas of success and difficulty
- offer other perspectives and insights to complete the picture.

(Bruning et al. 2004: 204–6)

Reading

There is an ongoing debate whether reading should be taught by a phonic method which identifies and combines sounds, or by a whole-word method which argues that they should learn whole words or sentences in context. Table 13.5 presents some of the arguments involved.

Table 13.5 Phonic and whole-word method of reading

Phonics method	Whole-word method
Behaviourist and cognitive	Constructivist
Pupils decode words and meaning by sound	The meaning of texts is emphasized over the sounds of letters
Advantages:	*Advantages*:
There is a clear methodical approach Having mastered the basics, pupils have a strategy for tackling new words and can read a wide variety of texts	It draws on the pupils' prior knowledge of words and on their linguistic and general experience It moves from the known (experiences and things) to the unknown (words)
Disadvantages:	*Disadvantages*:
Phonics can be technical and uninteresting at first There are many exceptions to phonic rules Pupils may sound out words without understanding them. Differing dialects have different pronunciations	Lack of a clear structure and methodology Reliance on having encountered the word before Necessity to learn each word anew without a strategy Reliance on the teacher for every new word

The phonics method is now being preferred in many countries, over the whole-word and language approach previously popular in the UK and the US. In addition to the phonics method, whole language meaningful approaches may still have a role in attracting the interest of some reluctant readers by reflecting their particular interests and culture.

Writing

Reading and writing are tools of thinking, since they encourage self-regulation, reflection and the drawing on memory and past experience. Writing is a more advanced tool that allows learners to distance themselves even further from immediate experience. Writing also requires the adoption and consideration of other perspectives in order to satisfy the communicative demands of readers.

In order to improve writing skills, teachers should:

- ensure that pupils write frequently and for different purposes;
- create a supportive atmosphere for writing;
- emphasize pre-writing strategies like brainstorming, visualization or storytelling;
- emphasize the stages of writing, e.g. brainstorming, structuring ideas, editing ideas;
- stress 'knowledge transforming', not 'knowledge-telling';

● take advantage of computers for structuring materials.

(Bruning et al. 2004: 307–10)

Second language learning

Up to the age of 12, children demonstrate an ability to acquire a second or even third language, especially if they are immersed in these language environments. On the whole, children never achieve the same level of fluency in a second and third language. 'We develop our first language and we learn others' (Winston 2003: 199). Methods of second language teaching have changed; from instruction in syntactical and formal grammatical structures to the recorded presentation of elements of communication which requires a response. More recently, the trend in second language teaching is towards explicit instruction, coupled with a more naturalistic 'immersion' through time spent with native speakers, or in the country of the second language.

Key ideas

● Language shapes understanding and meaning.
● Language has a relationship to power.
● There is a dynamic relationship between language and reasoning.
● Language is not learnt by imitation but is an inbuilt inherited human characteristic.
● Language confers an educational advantage on some social groups.
● The purposes and procedures of classroom communication can be made explicit.

Conclusions

It is clear from this chapter, that language plays an important role in formal and informal education. As well as its role in structuring thinking, language has social implications – for example, codes of language may operate to the advantage of some groups of learners and can act as a mechanism to indicate membership of different learning communities.

Teachers may find a knowledge of constructivist and socio-cultural implications of language useful in considering how they or other pupils may develop learning by supporting concept acquisition or by provoking disequilibrium.

Although the nature/nurture and evolutionary debates about language are interesting, they are highly complex, and their implications for education are difficult to gauge. Of most practical relevance to teachers is the conclusion that elaborated, explicit and comprehensive language usage modelled by parents and teachers is important in supporting effective learning.

References

Barnes, D. (1971) Language and learning in the classroom, *Journal of Curriculum Studies*, 3(1): 27–38.

Bernstein, B. (1977) Class and pedagogies – visible and invisible, in B. Bernstein *Class Codes and Control*, Vol. 3. London: Routledge and Kegan Paul.

Bliss, J., Askew, M. and Macrae, S. (1996) Effective teaching and learning: scaffolding revisited, *Oxford Review of Education*, 22: 37–61.

Bodrova, E. and Leong, D.J. (2003) Learning and development of preschool children from the Vygotskian perspective, in A. Kozulin, B. Gindis, V.S. Ageyev, S.M. Miller (eds) *Vygotsky's Educational Theory in Cultural Context*. Cambridge: Cambridge University Press, 156–74.

Bourdieu, P. (1977) Cultural reproduction and educational reproduction, in J. Karabel and A.H. Halsey (eds) *Power and Ideology in Education*. London: Oxford University Press, 487–511.

Bruning, R.H. Schraw, G.J., Norby, M.M. and Ronning, R.R. (2004) *Cognitive Psychology and Instruction* (4th end.). New Jersey: Pearson Prentice Hall.

Child, D. (1997) *Psychology and the Teacher* (6th edn). London: Cassell Education.

Chomsky, N. (1972) *Language and Mind*. New York: Harcourt Brace.

Cohen, L. Manion, L. and Morrison, K. (2004). *A Guide to Teaching Practice* (5th edn). London: Routledge Falmer.

Edwards, D. and Mercer, N. (1987) *Common Knowledge: The Development of Understanding in Classrooms*. London: Methuen.

Flanders, N.A. (1970) *Analysing Teacher Behaviour*. Reading, MA: Addison-Wesley.

Freire, P. (1982) *Pedagogy of the Oppressed*. Harmondsworth: Penguin.

Hoskin, K. (1990) Foucault under examination: the crypto-educationalist unmasked, in S.J. Ball (ed.) *Foucault and Education, Disciplines and Knowledge*. London: Routledge, 29–53.

Lave, J. and Wenger, E. (1991) *Situated Learning: Legitimate Peripheral Participation*. Cambridge: Cambridge University Press.

Mercer, N. (1995) *The Guided Construction of Knowledge*. Clevedon: Multilingual Matters.

Morrison, K. (2001) Jürgen Habermas 1929, in J.A. Palmer *Fifty Modern Thinkers on Education* From Praget to the Present. London: Routledge, 215–23.

Murphy, M. and Fleming, T. (2000) Between common and college knowledge: exploring the boundaries between adult and higher education, *Studies in Continuing Education*, 22(1): 77–93.

Peters, M. (2001) Michel Foucault 1926–84, in J.A. Palmer *Fifty Modern Thinkers on Education: From Piaget to the Present.* London: Routledge, 170–4.

Piaget, J. (1926) *The Language and Thought of the Child.* London: Routledge.

Piaget, J. and Inhelder, B. (1969) *The Psychology of the Child.* London: Routledge and Kegan Paul.

Pinker, S. (1994) *The Language Instinct.* New York: HarperCollins.

Quinn, P.C. and Oates, J. (2004) Early category representations and concepts, in J. Oates and A. Grayson, *Cognitive and Language Development in Children.* Milton Keynes: OU/Blackwell Publishing.

Rose, S. (2005) *The 21st Century Brain : Explaining, Mending and Manipulating the Mind.* London: Jonathan Cape.

Samovar, L.A. and Porter, R.E. (2004) *Communication Between Cultures* (5th edn). Belmont, CA: Wadsworth-Thomson Learning.

Skinner, B.S. (1957) *Verbal Behavior.* New York: Appleton Century Crofts.

Snow, C. and Ferguson, C. (eds) (1977) *Talking to Children: Language Input and Acquisition.* Cambridge: Cambridge University Press.

Vygotsky, L.S. (1962) *Thought and Language* (trans. E. Haufmann and C. Vakar). Cambridge, MA: MIT Press.

Vygotsky, L.S. (1978) *Mind in Society: The Development of Higher Psychological Processes.* Cambridge, MA: Harvard University Press.

Winston, R. (2003) *The Human Mind and How to Make the Most of It.* London: Bantam Press.

Whorf, B.L. (1956) Science and linguistics, in J.B. Carroll (ed.) *Language Thought and Reality: Selected Writings of Benjamin Lee Whorf.* Cambridge, MA: MIT Press.

Wood, D. (1988) *How Children Think and Learn: The Social Contexts of Cognitive Development.* Oxford: Blackwell Publishers.

Wood, D., Bruner, J. and Ross, G. (1976) The role of tutoring in problem solving, *The Journal of Child Psychology and Psychiatry,* 17: 89–100.

Wood, C., Littleton, K. and Sheehy, K. (2006) *Developmental Psychology in Action.* Milton Keynes: Open University/Blackwell Publishing.

Chapter 14 Experiential and competency-based learning

Introduction

If experiential learning is the best form of learning, readers should put this book down and instead experience reality. The question however then follows – 'What will be learnt from that experience?' In this chapter we examine the theories of experiential learning and the associated skills and competencies and their implications for education, since theory is a synthesis of the experience of others.

Experiential learning

Experience

'Experience is a weasel word. Its slipperiness is evident in an inconsistency characteristic of many thinkers' (Dewey 1925: 1). For example 'experiential learning' is not the same as 'experience of learning'. The former relates to experience and the latter to learning. Experience is difficult to define because it combines:

- an external or internal event or action;
- the associated sensation and perception;
- the resulting interpretation.

External events are first experienced through the senses but experience cannot be limited to sensation. Consciously experiencing an event allows interpretation. From a constructivist perspective, it is clear that meaning-making is involved. An event is experienced in the light of previous events and in terms of existing mental constructs. Take, for example, a football match: supporters of different teams experience that match in very different ways.

Action and interpretation are linked. Interpretation does not happen only after the event is completed; interpretation happens during the event and actions depend on that interpretation. For example, a teacher constantly interprets students' responses and acts accordingly. The students' behaviour is influenced in turn. Experience is an 'active engagement with the environment, of which the learner is an important part' (Boud et al. 1997: 6).

Learning

Learning occurs as a result of experience. The experience may be our prior experience or the experience of others, and it may be structured or unstructured, formal or informal, inside or outside a classroom. When student teachers construct lesson plans, they may learn in the classroom that the plans need to be adapted. Table 14.1 shows how several contemporary definitions of learning give a central place to experience.

Table 14.1 The importance of experience in definitions of learning

Theorist	Definition of learning
Kolb (1984: 38)	The process whereby knowledge is created through the transformation of experience.
Mezirow (2000: 5)	The process of using a prior interpretation to construe a new or revised interpretation of the meaning of one's experience as a guide for future action.
Wilson (2005: 7)	A relatively permanent change of knowledge, attitude or behaviour occurring as a result of formal education or training, or as a result of informal experience.
Beard and Wilson (2006: 19)	The sense-making process of active engagement between the inner world of the person and the outer world of the environment.

Source: Based on Beard and Wilson (2006: 19).

Boud, Cohen and Walker (1997: 8–16) offer five propositions on the nature of learning and experience.

1 Experience is the foundation of, and the stimulus for, learning.
2 Learners actively construct their experience.
3 Learning is a holistic process.
4 Learning is socially and culturally constructed.
5 Learning is influenced by the socio-emotional context in which it occurs.

These propositions strongly support the idea that experience and learning are inseparable: perhaps the expression 'experiential learning' may even be tautological (Beard and Wilson 2006: 19).

Theories of experiential learning

Many well-known educational theorists have touched on the relationship between experience and learning although that relationship has not necessarily been their central concern. Table 14.2 shows the way experience appears in their theories.

Table 14.2 Theorists and experiential elements

Theorist	Experiential element
Vygotsky (1962)	Social and cultural experience
Piaget (1969)	Experience of action on the world
Lave and Wenger (1991)	Experience of community
Bruner (1996)	Cognitive, social and cultural experience
Bandura (1977)	Vicarious experience

In this chapter, we are interested in theorists who have considered experience from an educational perspective, analysing the way in which people interact with experience so as to learn from it. In this interaction, reflection is one of the most important activities. Reflection can be defined as the activity of critically analysing our actions and ideas with the goal of improving performance. Here we will be considering the ideas of Dewey, Schön, Kolb and Mezirow – all of whom have treated reflection as a tool for transforming experience into learning.

Rational experiential learning

John Dewey claimed that reflection is a rational process that begins with the experience of a problem, which is then given serious and systematic consideration 'in the light of the grounds that support it and the further conclusions to which it tends' (Dewey 1933: 3, 9). Dewey emphasizes conscious reflection as an important part of experiential learning. His insights are limited, however, by his failure to recognize that, in reality, many experiences do not lead to or include problems and may not be amenable to systematic scientific analysis. Indeed, 'experiences and responses are often "messy", unpredictable and inchoate' (Carlile and Jordan 2007: 26).

Reflective experiential learning

According to Donald Schön, a leading modern thinker on reflection, professionals are characterized by their ability to respond to unpredictable experience with artistry and intelligence, using it as the basis for what he calls a 'world-making activity' (1987: 36). Schön points out that the knowledge possessed by professionals and experts is often tacit – that is, the expert's skills and knowledge are seamlessly integrated into the performance of their expert action. Schön suggests that reflection is critical to uncovering this tacit knowledge and proposes a methodology for doing so. He divides reflection into two types:

- *Reflection-in–action*: occurs at the same time as action, making tacit assumptions explicit so that they are demystified. The learning that occurs from this reflection – that is, the recognition of previously implicit skills and knowledge – can be passed on to the novices in the field.

• *Reflection-on-action*: involves a retrospective examination of events. The expert can use this reflection to clarify and learn from the experience for future improvement.

Cyclical experiential learning

David Kolb's well-known 'learning cycle' (Kolb 1984; Kolb and Fry 1975) represents a method for reflecting on experience that is non-linear and can begin at any point in the cycle (see Figure 14.1). Experiential learning can take 'concrete experience' as an effective starting point. This is observed in a reflective manner, which leads the formulation of abstract concepts and general rules for future experience, which are then tested by means of experimentation. This leads to modifications of the next experiential cycle.

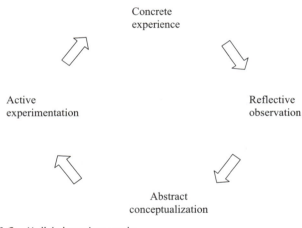

Figure 14.1 Kolb's learning cycle.
Source: Kolb (1984).

Schön and Kolb present reflection as an important means of improving future practice. 'Reflection therefore can be *on* practice, *in* practice and *for* practice' (Carlile and Jordan 2007: 30).

Transformative experiential learning

The American educationalist Jack Mezirow focuses on the reflective processes that occur when adults change their 'meaning schemes'. Meaning schemes are made up of sets of beliefs, attitudes and emotional reactions which comprise experience (Taylor 1998). For Mezirow, experience is interpreted in a constructivist way on the basis of previous experience and 'clusters of meaning schemes' (Mezirow 2000: 18). When the meaning schemes are changed and new perspectives attained, then transformative learning has occurred (Jarvis et al. 2003: 40).

Competence-based learning

Experiential learning occurs when certain activities are carried out and a range of skills and competencies are further developed. A discourse of education and training uses terms such as 'skill', 'competency' and 'competence'. Although these terms are often used loosely and interchangeably, the following is an attempt to differentiate between them.

Skill
is the ability to carry out a particular activity consistently. This ability may depend on physical or mental competence or attitude. A teacher might possess a skill in questioning, for example.

Competency
is the ability to carry out a complex task that requires the integration of knowledge, skills and attitudes – for example, if a teacher has subject knowledge, the skill of questioning and knows when and to whom it is appropriate to ask questions, then the teacher has a competency in eliciting student responses. Competencies enable people to perform effectively in a particular environment.

Competence
is the ability to perform a role effectively within a context. It requires a range of competencies. For example, teaching competence requires competencies in curriculum planning, classroom management and the assessment of learners. 'Incompetence' is the state of not being competent within a role.

Figure 14.2 shows how sets of consistent skills combine to become complex competencies necessary for competence in a contextual role.

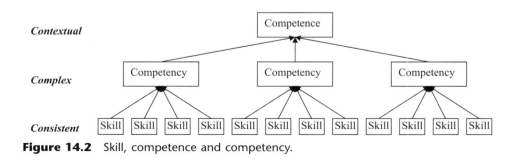

Figure 14.2 Skill, competence and competency.

The development of competence in a role is not a simple accretion of skills and competencies, however. Attitudes and values are very important in a teacher. For instance, an incompetent science teacher may have very good subject knowledge and laboratory skills and even possess competency in curricular planning but may lack a vital personal quality so that there is an ethical failure where students are not valued and respected. Although it may manifest itself in technical failure such as discipline breakdown, personal failure may be at the root of teacher incompetence (Carlile 2005: 14).

Competence in a teaching role requires a complex coordination and integration of knowledge, skills, competencies and values. This is illustrated in Figure 14.3. Skill involves the performance of a particular action. The coordination of a set of skills with knowledge produces a particular competency which is necessary to perform a particular task. The integration of a set of required competencies with attitudes and values in context leads to competence in the performance of a role.

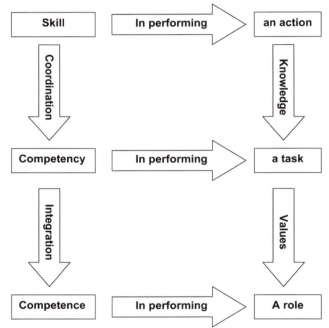

Figure 14.3 Role competence model.

Learning domains

Another way of looking at how competence develops can be found in the taxonomies of learning proposed by Bloom and his colleagues in 1956 and discussed in Chapter 3. Bloom, who has produced the best-known model of the psychomotor domain, categorizes learning into three different domains arranged in increasing order of complexity from lower to higher levels as shown in Table 14.3.

Table 14.3   Bloom's taxonomies of learning

Cognitive	Psychomotor	Affective
Synthesis and evaluation	Mastery	Generalization
Analysis	Conscious control	Value system
Application	Coordinated performance	Value
Comprehension	Partial performance	Response
Knowledge	Procedural task knowledge	Attention

Integration of competence model and domain model

The competence model shown in Figure 14.3 can be integrated with the taxonomic model in Table 14.3 to explain how competence develops. Learners possess a certain potential which is realized and developed through learning in the cognitive, psycho-motor and affective domains. This produces a body of knowledge and a set of cognitive, psychomotor and affective skills that coordinate to produce task competencies. At the same time a set of attitudes and values develops from the interaction of experience and inherent personality factors. The integration and coordination of these components – skills, competencies, knowledge and attitudes – leads through a process of experiential learning to competence in a role.

A trainee teacher begins with a certain potential.

1. In the cognitive domain she learns subject and theoretical knowledge.
2. In the psychomotor domain she learns presentation skills.
3. In the affective domain she acquires professional teaching and subject values.
4. She then possesses a range of teaching skills that she can perform consistently.
5. These skills are then coordinated so that they become competencies that can be performed simultaneously in a task such as the delivery of a lesson.
6. Finally, through the practice of teaching, the skills and competencies are integrated with professional and personal values to enable her to carry out the role of a teacher.

This is illustrated in Figure 14.4.

Educational implications of experiential learning

Experiential learning is typical of the shift from subject-centred curricula and teacher-centred instruction to student-centred experience and how it can be activated as part of learning. The teacher needs to create the conditions that provide learning experiences. The implications for the teacher can be deduced from the two parts of the expression 'experiential learning'.

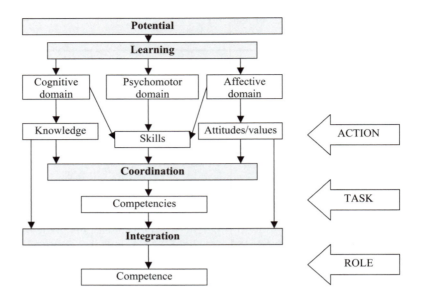

Figure 14.4 From potential to role competence.

Experiential: teachers need to provide experiences for students.

Learning: teachers need to help students to process that experi-
          ence.

Providing experience

Primary experience

In this the learner has direct multi-sensorial, fully contextualized, actual experience. Experiences can be provided that engage the senses and improve perceptual skills, discrimination, recognition and categorization while providing a rich experience of how things present themselves and an opportunity to react to them.

In order to provide primary experience, teachers should:

- engage the senses through the provision of rich environments and experiences;
- increase awareness of perception, e.g. through sensory deprivation such as blindfolding;
- provide a range of aesthetic and emotional experiences through drama, music and art;
- arrange social learning experiences through problem-based learning;
- offer practical meaningful activities such as work experience or community service;
- organize challenging lived experiences such as expeditions and outdoor activities.

Secondary experience

This involves the mediation of an actual experience through an intervening experience that offers a version that can convey some of the characteristics of the event. Historically, storytellers have been mediators of experience, and teachers are well aware of the interest that an anecdote or story can elicit from an audience. The written word too is a powerful mediator of experience and remains one of the principal means of teaching. While storytelling and books demand a response in the imagination of listeners or readers, technological advances mean that more features of experience can be presented. This can range from simple audio and video materials to computer simulation and virtual reality with practically full immersion through a range of headsets with 3-D goggles and motion-sensors. Virtual reality has the intriguing potential to go beyond the replication of real experience and permit learners, for example, to see, hear and feel what it is like to fly or to travel in miniature form through the interior of a plant or to experience, at least partially, what it is like to be a bat.

Processing experience

From the point of view of the teacher, providing students with various experiences as described above is only the first step. The student may or may not learn anything from the experience. The steps that can be taken to ensure that learning takes place will vary with the age and stage of development of the learner. The teacher should promote cognitively-provoking experiences that cause the child to think and adapt ideas. The desired learning may sometimes be the engagement with the experience and will not need to be reflected upon. The desire to have students reflect on experience can be seen as a belief that thinking is superior to acting and that ideas are superior to things.

Inquiry-based learning

An example of a methodology that includes experience and associated learning in its design is inquiry-based learning in which:

- learning is driven by the need to solve a problem or make sense of a situation;
- a problem is presented along with the information and tools to solve it;
- learners are required to draw on past experience;
- learners need engage in new experiences, such as research.

For example, primary school pupils may be given information about the way their school is heated and be required to use the World Wide Web and their own experience of the school environment to suggest environmentally-friendly, energy-saving ways to approach the issue.

Problem-Based Learning

Problem-Based Learning (PBL) is a more advanced and systematic form of inquiry-based learning. The PBL process makes students responsible for exploring the problem, identifying learning issues, researching materials, and presenting solutions. The following sequence is typical.

- The teacher considers the course design and its learning outcomes.
- The teacher designs complex and realistic problems based on learning outcomes.
- Students work in groups to consider the problem by:
  - brainstorming ideas and sharing prior knowledge;
  - identifying knowledge gaps;
  - considering research and learning needed to bridge gaps;
  - agreeing roles and sharing tasks.
- Group members undertake research and other tasks.
- They meet to discuss progress and formulate solutions.
- They present their solution and discuss its merits.
- They discuss the learning that has taken place.

Although students may initially feel abandoned, this is not the case. An important feature of PBL is that the teacher monitors all of these phases and, if necessary, steps in with supplementary problems or adaptations of the problem to ensure that the desired learning outcomes are achieved.

Reflection on experience

Reflection is a way of processing experience in order to learn from it and improve future action. Particularly in higher education, it is important that learners engage in a process of reflection. Theorists such as Dewey, Schön, Kolb and Mezirow, discussed earlier in this chapter, offer some avenues for the teacher. Dewey encourages the teacher to present problems to engage learner reflection. Schön asks that practice be made explicit so that it can be analysed, reflected upon and shared; Kolb encourages an ongoing cycle of experimentation and reflection; and Mezirow asks learners to consider the transformation that is occurring.

However, the teacher needs to suggest practical methods for carrying out the advice of these theorists. A particularly useful tool is reflective writing. The act of writing encourages the examination and organization of unstructured thoughts and ideas about experience.

In order to encourage students to reflect, teachers need to:

- explain the importance and usefulness of reflection to learners as a means of benefiting and learning from experience;
- explore the theory underlying reflective practice as proposed by Dewey, Schön, Kolb, Mezirow and others;

- encourage students to overcome reflectors' block by suggesting particular topics such as:
  - o expectations, fears and hopes for learning being undertaken;
  - o a critical incident or learning moment;
  - o an unresolved issue or problem;
- offer techniques for reflective writing such as those described in Figure 14.5;
- explain how reflective writing can be deepened and contextualized by means of description, personal view, alternative perspective, broader context;
- build in assessment with clear criteria as described in Table 14.4.

Table 14.4 Criteria for assessing reflective writing

Product		Process	
Quantity	Quality	Relevance	Depth
Length	Quality of	Understanding	Critical thinking
Presentation	expression	Application to course	Honesty
Regularity	Clarity	Relationship to	Cognitive skill
	Thoroughness	purpose	Generalizing
		Evidence of progress	experience
			Synthesis, analysis,
			evaluation

Source: Carlile and Jordan (2007: 35).

Educational implications of competency-based learning

Competency-based methods of training in industry were very successful in the US after the Second World War. Workers developed competencies in the performance of specific measurable tasks. This competency-based approach was then applied to education. It became popular in the United States in the 1970s and subsequently spread to Europe and other parts of the world. It is associated with, or has influenced, a number of educational developments:

- the learning outcomes movement;
- the standardization of education;
- initiatives in the vocational and business sectors;
- the emergence of the concept of 'transferable skills'.

The learning outcomes movement

This is a movement in education that developed in tandem with the competency-based movement. It had its genesis in:

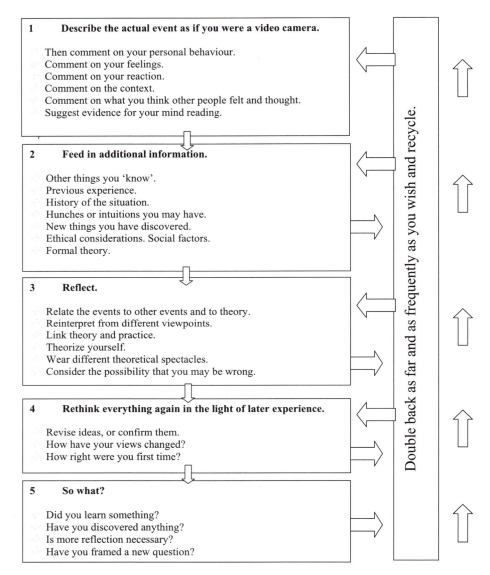

Figure 14.5 How to reflect.
Source: Based on Royce (1970).

- the unsatisfactory and vague use of aims and objectives in curriculum design;
- the popularity of the training and competency methods in industry;
- the rise in importance of the learner and the response to their needs;
- customization of education as a marketable commodity requiring product description.

Learning outcome statements

A learning outcome is an explicit statement of competency. Learning outcome statements specify:

1   a precise behavioural verb describing performance of a task;
2   the context and conditions of performance;
3   the threshold of acceptable performance.

For example:

On successful completion of this programme, participants will be able to produce a correctly proportioned life drawing from a model under studio conditions using a range of media.

Learning outcomes are the starting point for course and curriculum design. They can be used to select learning and teaching activities that are appropriate to the development of particular skills and competencies, and to develop select forms of assessment to measure their achievement.

Recognition of prior learning (RPL)

Learning outcomes are not dependent upon the method by which they are achieved. All that is important is the competencies that they describe. Educational institutions are increasingly setting up systems and procedures that recognize prior experiential learning. If an applicant can demonstrate that they have already met at least half the learning outcomes for a particular module, then credits, exemptions or advanced standing can be obtained (Whitaker 1989).

Constructive alignment

Constructive alignment, a popular approach to course and curriculum development particularly in higher education, is underpinned by the use of learning outcomes. 'Constructive alignment' has two aspects: The 'constructive' aspect refers to the idea that students *construct meaning* through relevant learning activities. The 'alignment' aspect refers to what the teacher does, which is to set up a learning environment that supports the learning activities appropriate to achieving the desired learning outcomes. The key is that the components in the teaching system, especially the teaching methods used and the assessment tasks, are aligned with the learning activities assumed in the intended outcomes.

For example, if a learning outcome in a science course nominates competence in carrying out a particular experimental procedure, the learning activities should involve practical laboratory work, and the assessment should require the student to carry out that scientific procedure according to criteria that specify levels of performance. Table 14.5 considers again the example of learning to drive. It shows some of the competencies required for driving and the way that constructive alignment would relate learning outcomes, assessment tasks and learning and teaching activities.

Table 14.5 A constructively aligned approach to learning to drive

Learning outcomes	Assessment	Teaching method
On successful completion of the module, the learner will be able to:		
Answer a range of questions on the Highway Code	Multiple choice test Viva	Guided reading Observation Video presentation Computer simulation
Demonstrate safe driving practices	Driving test (formative or summative)	Instructed driving lessons
Drive a car on the open road responding to a variety of circumstances	Driving test (formative or summative)	Instructed driving lessons

Vocational education and business sectors

Many countries have competency-based qualification systems. Such systems are attractive to the vocational and business sectors because they are, or can be:

- personalized – they can provide unique descriptions of personal achievement;
- accountable – competencies can be associated with particular people;
- transparent – they can provide clear descriptions of what is involved in carrying out a task;
- measurable – because they are clearly described, they offer clear metrics.

Governments use competencies as a tool for creating a competitive workforce and, in industry, the ease of measurement offered by competency-based systems facilitates management monitoring in line with the maxim: 'If you can measure it then you can manage it'.

Competency-based systems are particularly useful when the skills involved are psychomotor and easily measured. The transfer to complex and integrated competence is more problematic.

Transferable skills

Of particular interest to the business sector is the idea of transferable skills. In formal educational contexts, students acquire not only subject-based knowledge but also a range of skills and competencies that can be transferred to other contexts, such as the workplace. Students will continue to use these transferable skills and competencies in work and in lifelong learning. These skills or competences can be categorized as personal (soft) and professional (hard), as shown in Table 14.6.

Table 14.6 Hard and soft transferable skills

Personal (Soft)		Professional (Hard)		
Career competencies	**Self competencies**	**Work competencies**	**Communication competencies**	**Learning competencies**
Interview skills	Stress	Decision-	Report writing	Multi-tasking
Self-presentation	management	making	Presentations	Research skills
	Motivation	Team work	Listening	Reflective
	Time	Change	Understanding of	learning
	management	adaptation	diversity	Memory skills
	Emotional	Project	Conflict	Speed reading
	intelligence	management	management	Learning skills
		Problem-	Meeting skills	
		solving		
		Leadership		

Key ideas

Experience

- Experience cannot be limited to sensation.
- Experience combines the external or internal event, the associated perception and the resulting interpretation.
- The interpretation of experience is influenced by previous experience.
- Experience may be primary (first-hand) or secondary (mediated).

Learning

- Learning involves a transformation of experience.
- Learning can be categorized into cognitive, affective and psychomotor domains.

Skills, competency and competence

- Skill is the ability to carry out an activity consistently.
- Competency is the ability to carry out a task effectively.
- Competence is the ability to perform a role effectively.

Conclusions

Experiential learning is part of a student-centred movement, and stresses the direct experience of the student. This offers the teacher a range of strategies for engaging students in the learning process and provides a range of techniques such as problem-based learning that demands active involvement in learning.

However, if not done very well, experiential learning may be an inefficient way of proceeding. The knowledge built up over centuries can be appropriated by learners without the need for reinvention (Leont'ev 1981). The teacher is still very important in guiding students and helping them to appropriate the tools of thinking and techniques of the various educational disciplines. Experiential learning must not focus on learning to the neglect of teaching.

Competence-based learning focuses attention on what students will be able to do on completion of a particular class or programme. Learning outcomes specify precisely what is to be achieved and remove the ambiguity and the lack of clarity of old curricular design systems.

Although learning outcomes offer clarity on what learners are expected to be able to do as a result of learning, they are more suited to the learning of skills. They are less suited to the higher levels of the cognitive domain and to superior students who may produce creative work that learning outcomes have not specified.

It is important therefore that any approach to experiential and competence-based learning allows room for the roles of both teacher and student in any field of knowledge to engage in a shared and creative exploration of meaning.

References

Bandura, A. (1977) *Social Learning Theory*. New York: General Learning Press.

Beard, C. and Wilson, P. (2006) *Experiential Learning: A Best Practice Handbook for Educators and Trainers* (2nd edn). London and Philadelphia: Kogan Page.

Biggs, J. (2003) *Aligning Teaching for Constructing Learning*. York: The Higher Education Academy. http://www.heacademy.ac.uk/assets/York/documents/resources/resource database/id477_aligning_teaching_for_constructing_learning.pdf (accessed September 2006).

Boud, D., Cohen, R. and Walker, D. (1997) *Using Experience for Learning*. Buckingham: Society for Research into Higher Education and Open University Press.

Bruner, J. (1996) *The Culture of Education*. Cambridge, MA: Harvard University Press.

Carlile, O. (2005) The weakest links: defining and describing teacher incompetence, in M. Misztal and M. Trawinski (eds) *Studies in Teacher Education: Psychopedagogy*. Krakow: Wydownictwo Naukowa Academii, 9–15.

Carlile, O. and Jordan, A. (2007) Reflective writing: principles and practice, in C. O'Farrell (ed.) *Teaching Portfolio Practice in Ireland: A Handbook*. Dublin: All Ireland Society for Higher Education, 24–37.

Dewey, J. (1925) *Experience and Nature*. Chicago: Open Court Publishing Company.

Dewey, J. (1933) *How We Think: A Restatement of the Relation of Reflective Thinking in the Education Process*. New York: D.C. Heath.

Jarvis, P., Holford, J. and Griffin, C. (2003) *The Theory and Practice of Learning* (2nd edn). London: Kogan Page.

Jordan, A. and Carlile, O. (2005) Learning societies: global trends towards national qualification frameworks, *Comparisons of Modernization Development in the East and West: A Collection of Papers in International Symposium*. Liuzhu, Guanxi, China, 282–94.

Kolb, D. (1984) *Experiential Learning*. Englewood Cliffs, NJ: Prentice Hall.

Kolb, D. and Fry, R. (1975) Towards an applied theory of experiential learning, in C. Cooper (ed.) *Theories of Group Processes*. London: John Wiley and Sons.

Lave, J. and Wenger, E. (1991) *Situated Learning: Legitimate Peripheral Participation*. Cambridge: Cambridge University Press.

Leont'ev A.N. (1981) *Problems in the Development of Mind*. Moscow: Progress.

Mezirow, J. (2000) Learning to think like an adult, in J. Mezirow and associates (eds) *Learning as Transformation*. San Francisco, CA: Jossey Bass, 3–33.

Piaget, J. (1969) *Mechanisms of Perception* (trans. G.N. Seagrim). New York: Basic Books.

Schön, D. (1987) *Educating the Reflective Practitioner*. San Francisco, CA: Jossey Bass.

Taylor, E.W. (1998) *The Theory and Practice of Transformative Learning: A Critical Review. Information Series no. 374*. Columbus: ERIC Clearinghouse on Adult, Career, and Vocational Education, Center on Education and Training for Employment, College of Education: Ohio State University.

Vygotsky, L.S. (1962) *Thought and Language* (trans E. Haufmann and C. Vakar). Cambridge, MA: MIT Press.

Whitaker, U. (1989) *Assessing Learning: Standards, Principles and Procedures*. Pennsylvania: Council for Adult and Experiential Learning.

Wilson, J.P. (ed.) (2005) *Human Resource Development: Learning and Training for Individuals and Organisations*. London: Kogan Page.

Chapter 15   Inclusivity

Introduction

We are more similar to each other than we are different. Nevertheless, we have a range of characteristics that distinguish us. Physically, we differ in height, weight, shape, size, skin, hair, eye colour. Psychologically, we have different personality characteristics and traits, along with varying attitudes and ways of perceiving and interpreting events and experiences. We also differ in our learning and intellectual abilities.

This chapter is framed around a discourse of inclusivity in education. This means that teachers need to acknowledge and accommodate individual differences to ensure that all individuals can reach their potential, leading to their full participation in a democratic society (Dyson 2000: 36–53). There are many reasons why some members of society do not participate in education – for example disaffection, lifestyle, age or other barriers. However this chapter will confine itself to disability, which we will approach from the point of view of education. From this perspective, disabilities can be categorized either as physical, cognitive or a combination of both (see Table 15.1).

Table 15.1 Simplified typology of disabilities

Physical	Hearing, vision and speech disorders
	Psychomotor and motor-skill deficits
	Chronic medical conditions
Cognitive	Attention-deficit disorders
	Perceptual disorders
	Memory and encoding disorders
	Emotional and conduct disorders
	Low IQ
Combination	Genetic disorders
	Congenital conditions
	Developmental disorders

Historical constructs of disability

Perceptions of disability have varied throughout history. In the Middle Ages, disability was viewed as a reflection of God's will or as punishment for sin. The disabled were hidden away, used as object lessons, mocked, or occasionally set apart as 'holy fools'. Their lives were ones of poverty and deprivation. Persons with a disability were generally dependent on the care of others – often members of religious communities.

In the nineteenth century, the 'medicalization' of many mental and physical conditions led to the professional view that persons with a disability required special treatment (Foucault 1963). Where education was considered appropriate, it generally meant segregated provision. The educational segregation of children and adults with severe forms of disability persists to the present time.

Modern views about the treatment of people with disabilities are now more political, with disability perceived as a human rights issue. Disability groups and their advocates highlight many discriminatory practices in the treatment of disabled people. These include a lack of educational and employment opportunities, and the denial of personal rights leading to a lack of autonomy and to social isolation.

Labelling and language

'Labelling theory' claims that the consistent labelling of individuals who are different in behaviour or appearance leads to their negative categorization, which is then used to justify and legitimize their unequal treatment. Labelling theory is most often used to explain perceptions of deviancy (Becker 1963), but is also relevant to categorizations of disability (Gustavsson 2000: 94). Expressions such as 'idiot' or 'feeble-minded' to refer to those with an intellectual disability, or 'cripple' to refer to those who have a physical disability, leads to their stereotyping and to discriminatory treatment.

However, as the societal view of individuals with disabilities has changed, so has the language. Derogatory or dismissive epithets such as 'insane' or 'moron' are no longer acceptable. Changes in language reflect changing discourses and models of disability. The two major discourses reflect deficit and inclusivity models.

Discourses of disability: deficit model

The 'deficit' or 'medical model' represents a dominant discourse of disability. This model considers disability as a 'deficit' or 'lack' of some intellectual or physical quality that requires remediation. Diagnoses of deficiencies are made by medical professionals and officials with the power to define the deficit and prescribe its treatment (Green et al. 2005). The disabled are perceived as vulnerable, dependent and in need of special protection. The deficit model ascribes their low social and economic status to their deficiencies, rather than to the barriers that society constructs.

However, our understandings of disability are socially constructed. Professionals hold powerful positions in relation to people with disabilities, but may not always act justly. For example, a disproportionate number of ethnic minority learners in the US were categorized as having an intellectual disability because of unfair methods of identification and cultural biases in assessing intelligence (Dunn 1968).

A consequence of the deficit model is the need for remediation. In education, this has led to 'special education'.

Special educational provision

The deficit model frames the education of learners with severe disabilities, leading to segregated provision. In most advanced societies, there are schools and sheltered workshops for the deaf, the blind, the intellectually impaired and those with multiple disabilities. Advocates of special educational provision claim that its major benefit is in protecting and sheltering vulnerable learners and giving them the education or training best suited to their disabilities. The Camphill Schools provide such a non-threatening environment for severely disabled learners, using Rudolf Steiner's principles of holistic teaching and learning (Bock 2004).

Advantages

Segregated provision is claimed to be effective for a number of reasons. Segregation often results in smaller class sizes, so that learners receive additional support and one-to-one tuition. The pitch and pace of the lessons can reflect the learning needs of the group, and the curriculum can be tailored to the individual's learning needs. For example, in a school for the deaf, teachers can use sign language consistently and develop high levels of 'signing' skills in learners.

Segregation may also be less threatening to learners with specialized needs because they do not have to compare their academic ability, pace of learning and attainment to that of students without such needs (Watson et al. 1999; Jenkinson 1997). The social needs of such individuals may also be better addressed because segregated settings prevent isolation and ridicule. Therefore the settings may be more supportive of individual differences than mainstream schools where the class teacher is expected to meet the diverse needs of all learners.

From an institutional viewpoint, segregated provision concentrates the resources where they are most needed, and makes economic sense. Schools for the blind possess specialized resources and use assistive technologies such as text-recognition devices that would be difficult to justify in a mainstream school. Segregated education offers the possibility of specially trained teachers and adequate support staff.

Disadvantages

Segregated education can be criticized on several grounds. Education reproduces the inequalities of society (Bourdieu and Passeron 1970) and segregated education may marginalize those it claims to help, while increasing the advantage of higher status groups. Segregation acts to preserve the resources and academic standards of the mainstream schools. The segregation of children with attention deficit disorders may be as much for the benefit of their classmates as it is for themselves.

'Special education' also provides mechanisms that advantaged families can utilize on behalf of their children. Diagnoses of 'acceptable' conditions like dyslexia can be procured, gaining for such children more teacher attention, computers and extra time allocations in examinations (Dyson 2000: 39–40). A special school for those with disabilities in the US is popular with parents of non-disabled children, not only for the lessons in equality it offers, but because the teacher–student ratio is 1:2 (Loh 2004).

Segregated educational provision can also justify the labelling of people with disabilities as 'abnormal,' ignoring society's part in the construction of abnormality. Labelling removes any imperative for changes in social structures (Dyson 2000: 39–41). Learners and teachers may also engage in such labelling. Learners may label themselves in terms of their disabilities, and teachers may label learners with disabilities as low achievers.

Segregation is not always effective in advancing the learning of everyone who possesses a disability (Galloway and Goodwin 1987). A UK study found that curriculum choices in segregated schools are limited. Pupils cannot access a broad range of subjects, nor can they develop the skills needed for successful social integration and employment in such artificial conditions. When individuals from segregated educational settings eventually leave school they are disadvantaged in having to learn social and life skills from scratch (Burgess 2003). Segregation also creates artificial barriers that persist in later life, since opportunities for mixing with others is limited. Moreover, people's lack of familiarity with disability reinforces negative social perceptions.

Discourses of disability: inclusion

Nowadays, people with a disability do not wish to be labelled or categorized in terms of their condition: they are not 'impaired' but 'have a disability' or are 'differently-abled'. Deaf people would rather be categorized as 'deaf' or 'hard of hearing' than 'hearing-impaired.' The term 'special educational needs' has been replaced by references to 'barriers to learning and participation' in a recent document on inclusive education distributed to all English schools (Barton 2003: 11). These changes in terminology illustrate a growing rejection of the language of exclusion and a desire for inclusion by this group.

Inclusion

Although the central tenet of inclusion that everyone should be included in every aspect of social and civil life is simple, the arguments for it are more complex. These include:

- *human rights arguments* which stress the entitlement of all citizens to participate fully in society; and
- *equity arguments* which stress the obligations of the state to ensure justice for everyone in the distribution of social goods like education or employment.

Rights and justice arguments combine to form a discourse of inclusivity. This can provide a framework through which disabled people can analyse their experiences, identifying instances of 'discrimination' and 'inequality' as oppressive or unjust. Challenges to vested interests can be made which go beyond claims for the removal of discrimination to recommend positive discriminatory measures which can allow participation in civil society on equal terms with other citizens.

The demand by disabled groups for equal participation in society follows the same trajectory as other equal rights movements. It includes:

- a similar struggle for access to social institutions as those of the early twentieth-century feminist and civil rights movements;
- an identification of the causes of oppression;
- theorizing and counter-arguments as justifications for equality;
- integration and societal accommodation.

The disability movement is still in the first phase of its campaign for members to have access to a full range of educational opportunities.

Inclusive education

Inclusive education is concerned with the rationale, practicalities and consequences of educating all learners together (Barton 2003: 10). It has been the subject of many policy declarations such as the United Nation's *Rules on the Equalization of Opportunities for Persons with Disabilities*, which contains the following statement.

We believe and proclaim that:

- every child has a fundamental right to education and must be given an opportunity to achieve and maintain an acceptable level of learning;
- every child has unique characteristics, interests, abilities and learning needs;
- educational systems should be designed, and educational programmes implemented, to take into account the wide diversity of these characteristics and needs;
- those with special educational needs must have access to regular schools which should accommodate them within a child-centred pedagogy capable of meeting these needs;
- regular schools with this inclusive orientation are the most effective means of combating discriminatory attitudes, creating welcoming communities, building an inclusive society, and achieving education for all; moreover, they provide an effective education to the majority of children, and improve the efficiency and, ultimately, the cost effectiveness of the entire educational system.

(UNESCO 1994 par. 2)

Governments and advocates of disability rights face the challenge of implementing these principles. Inclusive education is not simply about placing learners with a disability within a mainstream institution, but in enabling full participation.

Inclusive educational provision

Advocates of inclusive education point out that integrating learners with disabilities into mainstream schools is not the same as including them (Barton 2003: 9).

Integration	sees the learner as 'brought in' from outside.
	assumes that the learner will need to adapt to a pre-existing system.
Inclusion	sees the learner as a community member with rights and expectations.
	assumes that the community should satisfy the learner's needs.

Advantages of inclusive education

The main advantage of inclusive education is that it acknowledges the desire and the rights of those who are disabled to be educated in the same way as everyone else.

Inclusion in mainstream education prevents marginalization, counteracting the labelling or categorization of people with disabilities as 'abnormal' or 'special'. The curriculum will be broader than in the special school, and there will be more choices available. By undertaking the same school curriculum as their peers, pupils with a disability are more likely to have the same type of experiences and gain similar skills. Because of their interactions with the general school population, they are more prepared for life after school. These pupils also have the opportunity to compare themselves with the general school population, and develop a realistic view of their abilities and potential.

Including pupils with disabilities may also benefit their classmates, teachers and the school as a whole. Classmates are more likely to be tolerant and accepting of disability, and to understand it. Teachers can develop additional skills and sensitivities and the institution is better equipped to cope with diversity as a result of more inclusive policies, practices and supports.

Disadvantages

However, the rhetoric of policy declarations as stated in the UN Declaration frequently differs from the practice. Some types of multiple or severe disability require such intensive care that pupils require the fully-supported environment of the special school. There is a danger within the mainstream school that inclusion may be construed merely as 'placement,' where pupils with a disability have to adapt to the standard school organization (Barton 2003: 10). Pupils with a disability may still be excluded from the full range of activities because physical access to locations is difficult or all activities are intended for the able-bodied. However, pupils with a physical disability are more easily accommodated in mainstream education than those with cognitive disabilities. Physical disability may only require adjustments to the environment and attention to the curriculum, but cognitive disabilities such as ADHD may be too disruptive for teachers and other pupils. If teachers and classmates are unaware or unaccepting of cognitive disability, for example, then pupils with such disability may suffer a loss of self-esteem. They may also be in danger of isolation or ridicule if their disability is not recognized.

Research shows that many teachers are still uncertain about the benefits of inclusion. They do not feel confident about managing pupils with a disability in the mainstream classroom, and are concerned that the quality of support to all pupils may be undermined. They are also worried about limited access to suitable curricular materials and inadequate training (Tam et al. 2006).

Compromise positions

Many countries have adopted compromise positions between specialized provision and full mainstream inclusion. A Japanese solution is for less severely disabled children to be educated in semi-segregated units within a mainstream school (LeTendre and Shimizu 2000: 119). The advantage is that these children still maintain regular contact with their peers and participate in many whole-school activities.

In Singapore in 2005 new education policies require 10 per cent of teachers in elementary schoold to undergo training in special needs provision (Tam et al. 2006: 2). In England in the 1990s there was a movement away from special provision towards mainstream inclusion. Table 15.2 shows the forms that this movement took.

Table 15.2 Moving to inclusion: form of organization and reorganization

Re-placement	Moving individual children to the mainstream with varying degrees of support
Moving the school	Moving the special school – with its pupils and staff – into the mainstream
Providing resourced schools	That is, schools which are especially resourced to take a group of former special school pupils
Providing a support service	Comprising support teachers and learning support assistants, usually from former special schools
Providing an inclusion service	That is, converting a special school to a service, whereby ex-special school staff re-structure and work in neighbourhood schools

Source: Based on Thomas and Davis (2007: 69).

Threats to inclusion

One issue that arises in many western schools is that of competing agendas in education. For example, the practice of target setting and an emphasis on standards in education raises the question of whether a school can do justice to all learners, both in raising general standards and in producing good outcomes for those with a disability, especially if that disability is a cognitive one. An inclusivity agenda is more difficult in view of global educational forces such as:

- increased competition between schools;
- education as a marketable commodity;
- an increased emphasis on vocational training;
- accountability and efficiency agendas in schools.

(Barton 2003: 13).

Educational implications of inclusivity

In order to promote inclusivity policies, practices and awareness, teachers and administrators should:

- provide training in inclusivity principles and practices for managers, teachers and administrative staff;
- align school policies with international and national declarations on disability and inclusivity;
- consult with disability experts concerning building contracts and procurements;
- devise a mission statement and policy for inclusiveness in the school;
- appoint a member of staff with special responsibility for inclusivity practices;
- consider inclusivity requirements in relation to workshops and laboratory spaces;
- consider access policies and health and safety requirements;
- liaise closely with all relevant agencies;
- consult with parents and children about barriers to inclusivity;
- consider whether inclusion is possible and in the best interest of the learner;
- ensure that resources are adequate to cope with pupils with a disability;
- establish home liaisons and assessment procedures;
- set up care teams.

Curriculum designers need to consider the implications of inclusivity in subject syllabi and extra-curricular activities, including the hidden curriculum, which excludes particular cohorts of pupils. Curriculum designers should ensure that:

- the values of stakeholders in the curriculum are made explicit and that the value of inclusivity is also stressed;
- inclusivity education is incorporated in the curriculum;
- the curriculum content does not exclude particular pupils;
- assessment practices are aligned to ensure that testing practices are suitable for all pupils.

Teachers should use strategies that can support learning inclusivity. These include:

- providing one-to-one or small group tuition;
- using or providing assistive technologies where available;
- asking for specialist help in solving classroom problems;
- rewarding effort as well as achievement;
- helping pupils to identify their own strategies;
- consulting pupils about their needs;
- expecting as much from pupils with disabilities as from others;
- not allowing pupils to use their disability to set limits to their achievement;
- modelling tolerance and respect for all pupils and providing explicit rules;
- making available additional teaching resources such as audio CDs, literacy books and so forth;
- promoting peer-to-peer tutoring and peer learning scenarios;
- allocating extra time for class practical exercises;
- analysing the layout of the classroom in terms of its suitability;
- devising inclusive activities in which everyone participates;
- avoiding patronising pupils with disabilities;
- modelling appropriate language and behaviour to all pupils;
- consulting pupils with a disability on how they would like to be treated.

Key ideas

- Inclusivity is concerned with enabling all individuals to reach their potential.
- Inclusivity recognizes the unique characteristics, interests, abilities and learning needs of all learners.
- The traditional discourse of inclusivity viewed disability as some sort of defect or impairment.
- Inclusivity considers special education as a means of recognizing disability and looking at best practices in accommodating the individual's needs.
- Inclusivity calls for all learners to be educated in mainstream education – this has the potential of breaking down barriers and curbing negative stereotyping among all individuals.
- Inclusivity places responsibility on the community to support all learner needs.

Conclusions

The theories in this chapter show that, like other radical equality movements, the inclusivity agenda with regard to disability will continue to be pursued, in spite of conflicts with other dominant national and international agendas.

However, it is necessary to differentiate 'inclusivity' in education from 'assimilation', 'integration', and 'placement'. In terms of policies, it is important that inclusivity in education is not simply presented as a reconstituted branch of 'special education' (Barton 2003: 9). The construct of inclusivity has more dynamic and political connotations, requiring a transformation of structural barriers and changed curricular and classroom values which recognize the rights and demands of the major stakeholder in disability, the disabled person. However, the embodied and felt experiences of disability of one individual cannot be those of another so that to consider disability as a homogenous concept requiring a homogenous response is not possible.

For example, physical disabilities are increasingly addressed by advances in technology. In relation to cognitive disabilities, more sophisticated methods of brain imaging have identified more neurological disabilities, though often of a minor nature. More learners will see that they are to some extent disabled but that it does not matter too much.

However, it is also important to be realistic and for educationalists to defend their own positions on the extent to which demands for inclusion can be accommodated. The compromise solution presented earlier may offer suggestions about the extent to which co-location can promote inclusion and equality. The modern shopping mall has an identity of its own, yet manages to incorporate shops of different types and functions. Perhaps the modern educational institution can act in the same way, embodying a distinctive identity and values but incorporating parallel, even semi-autonomous streams of provision of generic and specialized services, so that no one is excluded from the services offered.

References

Barton, L. (2003) *Inclusive Education and Teacher Education*, (Professorial Lecture 3 July 2003). London: Institute for Education.

Becker, H.S. (1963) *Outsiders: Studies in the Sociology of Deviance*. Glencoe: Free Press.

Bock, F. (ed.) (2004) *The Builders of Camphill – Lives and Destinies of the Founders*. Edinburgh: Floris Books.

Bourdieu, P. and Passeron, J-C. (1970) *Reproduction in Education, Society and Culture*. London: Sage.

Burgess, E. (2003) *Are we Nearly There Yet: Do Teenage Wheelchair Users Think Integration has been Achieved in Secondary Schools in the UK?* Cardiff: Whizz-Kidz No Limits Millennium Award.

Dunn, L.M. (1968) Special education for the mildly mentally retarded: is much of it justifiable? *Exceptional Children*, 23: 5–21.

Dyson, A. (2000) Inclusion and inclusions; theories and discourses in inclusive education, in H. Daniels and P. Garner (eds) *Inclusive Education: Supporting Inclusion in Education Systems*. London: Kogan Page, 36–53.

Foucault, M. (1963) *The Birth of the Clinic*. London: Tavistock.

Galloway, D. and Goodwin, C. (1987) *The Education of Disturbing Children: Pupils with Learning and Adjustment Difficulties*. London: Longman.

Green, S., Davis, C., Karshmer, E., Marsh, P. and Straight, B. (2005) Living stigma: the impact of labeling, stereotyping, separation, status loss, and discrimination in the lives of individuals with disabilities and their families, *Sociological Enquiry*, 75(2): 197–215.

Gustavsson, A. (2000) Integration in the changing Scandinavian welfare states, in H. Daniels and P. Garner (eds) *Inclusive Education: Supporting Inclusion in Education Systems*. London: Kogan Page.

Jenkinson, J. (1997) *Mainstream or Special: Educating Students with Disabilities*. London: Routledge.

LeTendre, G. and Shimizu, H. (2000) Towards a healing society: perspectives from Japanese special education, in H. Daniels and P. Garner (eds) *Inclusive Education: Supporting Inclusion in Education Systems*. London: Kogan Page.

Loh, L. (2004) At a city school for the disabled, young children without disabilities learn life lessons too, a winning inclusion formula, *The Baltimore Sun*, 3 December.

Tam, K.B., Seevers, R., Gardner III, R. and Heng, M. (2006) Primary school teachers' concerns about the integration of students with special needs in Singapore, in *TEACHING Exceptional Children Plus*, 3.(2) Article 3. http://escholarship.bc.edu/education/tecplus/vol3/iss2/art3 (accessed November 2007).

Thomas, G. and Davies, J.D. (2007) England and Wales: competition and control – or stakeholding and inclusion, in H. Daniels and P. Garner (eds) *Inclusive Education: Supporting Inclusion in Education Systems*. London: Kogan Page.

United Nations Educational, Scientific and Cultural Organization (UNESCO) (1994) *The Salamanca Statement and Framework for Action on Special Needs Education, Adopted by the World Conference on Special Needs Education: Access and Quality*, Salamanca, Spain, 7–10 June. UNESCO Ministry of Education and Science, Spain.

Watson, N., Shakespeare, T., Cunningham-Burley, S., Barnes, C., Corker, M., Davis, J. and Priestley, M. (1999) *Life as a Disabled Child: A Qualitative Study of Young People's Experiences and Perspectives: Final Report*. Universities of Edinburgh and Leeds.

Chapter 16   Blended learning

Introduction

Teachers use a range of pedagogies – from simple exposition to computer-based methods. They also appropriate whatever tools are available – from blackboards to Bluetooth® devices. Teachers have always blended methodologies and technologies. The expression 'blended learning' is used to describe a blend of:

- a range of delivery media;
- face-to-face class-based methods (synchronous);
- distance-learning methods (both synchronous and asynchronous);
- self-directed learning.

It might better be called blended teaching and learning methodologies.

Origins

Towards the end of the twentieth century, advances in digital technologies led to many changes in business practices including the development of e-commerce and e-business in a context of global competitiveness. The expansion of possibilities created by the Internet led large multinational companies to realize that e-learning as a methodology could:

- deliver training to widely distributed staff anywhere in the world;
- train people without the necessity to leave their workplace;
- ensure the standardization of training programmes and delivery.

Some companies have even set up corporate universities as vehicles for '[...] disseminating an organization's culture and fostering the development of not only job skills, but also such core workplace skills as learning-to-learn, leadership, creative thinking, and problem solving' (Meister 1998: 38).

Following its inception in the world of training, e-learning soon spread to other areas of education. Teachers were quick to realize that it could be a way of catering for the demands of a wide variety of students – especially potential students who would find standard class-based learning inconvenient or unavailable.

In the first phase of e-learning, teachers combined e-learning from the business world and distance education from the educational world. Traditional correspondence courses and the Open University systems had showed it was possible to provide educational programmes to learners at a distance. However, the development of materials that could be effective without any teacher support was enormously complex and very expensive. Even if that problem could be overcome, the lack of embodiment and the absence of the teacher remained a weakness.

Blended learning represents a compromise, combining a face-to-face component with computer-based distance learning where teacher and learner interact dynamically (Wilson and Smilanich 2005). The computer now operates as a communication device rather than as a teaching machine. This compromise addresses the problems of embodiment and materials. The face-to-face component provides embodiment and the interaction removes the necessity for all-encompassing and highly prescriptive materials.

Approaches to blended learning

Four possible approaches have been identified:

Self-regulated approach	Learners interact autonomously with a range of technologies such as web-based audio or video clips, simulations and virtual learning environments to achieve a particular learning outcome.
Pedagogical approach	The teacher selects suitable pedagogical approaches, which may or may not involve instructional technology, in order to achieve a particular learning outcome.
Mixed approach	Face-to-face delivery is combined with any type of instructional technology in a flexible way.
Learning outcome-based approach	The learning outcomes determine the forms of delivery, and the technology and methodology are carefully aligned with them.

(Based on Driscoll 1998)

Advantages of blended learning

Some advantages of blended learning are:

Wider audience	Blended learning can be adapted to meet the needs, styles and interests of a wide variety of learners.
Knowledge construction	Learners are actively engaged in the learning process as they interact with a range of materials and technologies.
Collaboration	Communication and collaboration with peers and teachers or experts enhance and develop learning and knowledge.

Audio-visual environment	Blended learning supports a wide variety of multiple-media elements, permitting multi-modal learning.
Interactivity	Learners interact with technology and are motivated to direct their own learning.
Reflection	Email, bulletin boards and blogs focus learners' attention and encourage them to reflect on what they write.

The class-based and independent learning components of blended learning are explored elsewhere in this book, so this chapter will focus on the computer-based element.

Teachers have always appropriated technology for their purposes. However, sometimes technology has been merely another presentation method that has led to students learning *from* technology, as in watching a film-clip, whereas they need to learn *with* technology, using it more as a tool for learning (Jonassen et al. 2003: 10–12). In order to appropriate the technological tools, the teacher needs to understand the process, so the following section describes computer-based learning and the instructional design process.

Computer-based learning

Computer-based learning (CBL) makes use of computers to facilitate learning. This may range from independent learning undertaken on a personal computer, to extensive network and web-based learning management systems. Such systems offer students and their teachers online access to notes and email, bulletin boards and web conferences, as well as acting as administrative, monitoring and assessment tools (CERI 2005).

Computer-based learning implies the use of computer technology not simply as a means of presenting material, but as the principal mode of learning, without intervention from an expert or teacher.

Computer-based learning is directed by the learners who:

- decide when and where to interact and learn;
- select content related to their learning goals;
- determine the pitch of the lesson;
- interact at their own pace;
- select content according to learning preferences;
- regulate and assess their own learning through feedback;
- take responsibility for their own learning.

Instructional design (ID)

Although teachers design and plan many different instructional events, the term 'instructional design' refers to the designing of computer-based instruction. If computer-based instruction is to lead to CBL, it requires a careful instructional design that combines technical know-how with pedagogical knowledge. Rather than just conveying information, the computer can be used by the learner as a 'mind tool'. Good instructional design results in computer learning environments that provide 'appropriate combinations of challenge and guidance, empowerment and support, self-direction and structure' (Reigeluth 1999: 21).

In order for this to occur the learning material needs to be:

- designed to meet a specific audience with specific learning needs;
- adaptable to different learning styles;
- broken down into discrete modular components;
- 'chunked' into discrete sub-sections to suit short-term memory;
- structured and organized to meet specific learning outcomes;
- enriched with hypermedia (sound and pictures) to assist dual coding;
- hyperlinked extensively to allow self-directed exploratory learning;
- sequenced appropriately;
- supported by formative assessment for feedback and for self-regulated learning.

The use of blended learning approaches is related to the technological developments that make it possible and the instructional design principles that make it effective.

Technological development

Hardware

Technological developments in computing influenced the extent to which teachers were able to use CBL and blend it with other methods. In the late 1950s and early 1960s, computers began to replace the early mechanical teaching machines. Because of the limitations in screen technology, these were mainly limited to the presentation of small blocks of text, carefully sequenced to guide learning. Some technological advances allowed graphics and interactivity in computer programs but they were not applied to education (Pagliaro 1983).

The introduction of the micro-computer near the end of the 1970s brought about the rapid spread of computing in business and made possible its use in education and home entertainment. Computer-based arcade games became popular and showed how interactivity engaged attention. Computing technology continued to develop, with the addition of 2D and 3D graphics and audio and video capabilities. Modern computers are powerful multimedia devices that can offer multiple modes of experience and interactivity to hold learners' attention and suit a variety of learning styles. The computer keyboard, although still important, has been supplemented by an ever-increasing array of input devices that can recognize speech, detect movement and react to a range of human and other variables and the simple computer screen has been supplemented by headsets and other forms of technology that deliver a rich multi-sensorial virtual experience.

The development of the Internet and World Wide Web has had an obvious impact on education and is one of the main means of delivering the CBL element in a blended learning strategy. The possibility of 'streaming' audio and video means that live radio and television can be viewed over the Internet, and the resulting live communication and conferencing supports social and collaborative learning at a distance. The Open University in the UK uses blended learning and CBL to facilitate what it calls 'supported open learning' (Open University 2007).

Software

At a time of crisis in the computer software industry when programming did not appear to be meeting the needs of users, Winston Royce described a 'waterfall model' of software development which involves a sequence of set events where one flows into the next. This is illustrated in Figure 16.1. The behaviourist ideas of Skinner and Bloom were popular at the time, and there was a natural alliance between computer programming and instructional design in their systematic step-wise approach. Royce criticized this simple model and proposed that it could be improved by feedback and iteration (Royce 1970). This process would ensure that needs were established before the next phase of development which would build on them. In this way, irrelevant design could be avoided.

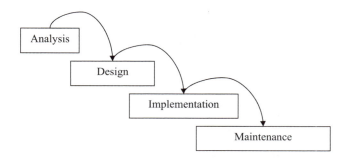

Figure 16.1 Waterfall model of software development.
Source: Based on Van Vliet (2000)

A model for instructional design

Based on constructivist learning principles, the instructional design model of Passerini and Granger is sequential like the waterfall model, but each phase is constantly revised and modified according to feedback generated from formative evaluations throughout the process. The flexible approach facilitates strategies that permit user interactivity and navigation (Passerini and Granger 2000: 8). The model is illustrated in Figure 16.2. There follows a discussion of each of the phases and their associated sub-tasks.

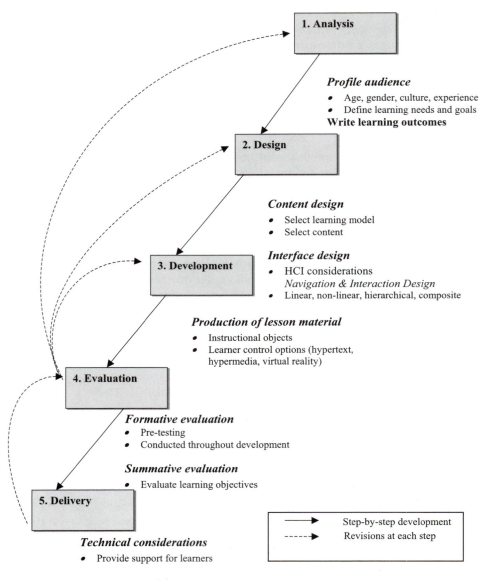

Figure 16.2 Hybrid ID model.
Source: Based on Passerini and Granger (2000)

Phase 1: Analysis

This is the most critical phase in Passerini and Granger's model. It has two important sub-tasks: developing a profile of the target audience and writing learning outcomes.

Profile target audience

Designers need to establish the characteristics of the audience that will have an effect on the level of content and how it will be presented. The audience profile will include age, gender, socio-economic background, culture, experience, physiological needs, socio-collaborative needs and learning style needs as well as their learning goals. Information-gathering techniques might include questionnaires, interviews, surveys, focus groups and observation. This research, combined with the overall aims of other stakeholders, will lead to the goals or aims of the programme.

Write learning outcomes

The aims relate to the teaching goals but the learning outcomes relate to what the learner will be able to do as a result of interaction with the material. The learning outcomes can draw on Blooms' taxonomy as described in Chapter 2 on behaviourism. As part of the process, designers should consider the following questions:

- What do you want the learners to know or to be able to do?
- How can you get them to do it?
- How can success be measured?

Phase 2: Design

In this phase, draft paper designs such as flowcharting and storyboarding are used to generate ideas for the phase's three sub-tasks: content design, interface design, and navigation and interactive design. The aims and outcomes of the programme are broken down into smaller, more manageable chunks often referred to as modules.

Content design

The next stage is the selection of actual content for the learning programme. The selection and arrangement of content may be influenced by a range of learning theories.

Behaviourist influences

The genesis of computer-based instruction was in behaviourist teaching machines and behaviourist principles are still relevant. Learning programs aligned with behaviourist learning theory should:

- take learners through a sequence of progressive instructional steps;
- contain a number of levels of increasing difficulty;
- allow learners to select a particular level;
- reward success with progression to a higher level;
- proceed from simple to more complex tasks;
- offer positive and negative learning prompts to reinforce learning.

Constructivist influences

Constructivist learning theory stresses the learner's active construction of meaning in a social context, so the content needs to be realistic and engaging for the learner.

Learning programmes aligned with constructivist learning theory should:

- encourage users to link information from one context to another;
- emphasize active participation using simulation;
- contain context-rich material with hypermedia;
- support learner meaning-making;
- require the learner to explore and interpret material using hyperlinks;
- incorporate a social dimension to learning;
- challenge the mental constructs of the learner;
- adapt to a range of learner styles;
- include realistic problems;
- incorporate authentic assessment that includes the learner's views.

Since constructivism stresses the shared social construction of meaning-making, computer-based learning management systems support a range of social interactions in synchronous and asynchronous forms as shown in Table 16.1. Asynchronous communication is more learner-focused, as it encourages reflective practice by allowing learners time to contemplate their answers prior to sending. Asynchronous communication also limits digression since responses are usually focused on a particular problem (Wang and Gearhart 2006).

Table 16.1 Synchronous and asynchronous communication tools

Synchronous	Asynchronous
• Video-conferencing systems	• Email
• Computer-conferencing systems	• Bulletin boards
• Learning management systems which support many-to-many based interactions	• Blogging
	• Web spaces such as YouTube and social networking sites
• Online chat facilities	• Learning management systems which support the posting of online resources and notes

Cognitivist influences

Cognitive learning theory suggests that material should be arranged to assist cognition. Clark and Mayer (2003: 3–5) suggest that learning programs aligned with cognitive learning theory should:

- use multimedia to stimulate the senses;
- structure related materials near to each other to assist perception and encoding;
- not overburden the visual processing channel (do not combine video clips and text);
- use separate processing channels such as visual and auditory (combine video clips and narration);
- emphasize links between materials instead of repeating them separately.

Interface design

It needs to be borne in mind that the interface between human and machine is crucial. Wonderful learning material will be of little use if the learner cannot access it or use it with ease. Interface designers need to take account of their target audience. Hix and Hartson (1993) offer some interface design guidelines:

- *audience* – conduct an analysis of user needs and levels of computer experience;
- *memory* – take account of human memory limitations, for example, prevent cognitive overload by respecting the principles outlined earlier;
- *consistency* – ensure consistency of colours, fonts, layout and placement of screen icons, for example, 'forward' and 'backward' icons/buttons should maintain the same position on all screens;
- *simple* – avoid too much clutter on screen. A good rule-of-thumb is: one-third 'air' to two-thirds 'art and copy' – one-third free space to two-thirds content;
- *errors* – anticipate human error with appropriate safeguards. For example, a dialogue box should be automatically displayed prior to deleting content;
- *feedback* – users need receive feedback on actions. For example, if a user clicks on a hyperlink – the 'egg timer' icon indicates that the computer is taking action.

Navigation and interactive design

This refers to the way a learner is permitted to move through a learning program. The navigation design may be: linear, non-linear, hierarchical or composite.

Linear navigation

This refers to a sequential structure where one thing follows the next, and learners can only move backwards or forwards one step at a time (see Figure 16.3). This kind of structure is clearly behaviourist and is used to present new concepts, principles or key ideas. It is also useful for developing practical or psychomotor skills, or for drill-and-practice scenarios

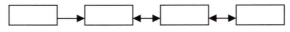

Figure 16.3 Linear navigation.

Non-linear navigation

This is characterized by extreme levels of flexibility and randomness where users interact with content to varying degrees each time (see Figure 16.4). The non-sequential access to content can support an extremely diversified audience of varying learning needs, and is clearly constructivist in its granting of autonomy to learners to explore the material in their own way. However, it does not offer much scaffolding to guide movement, so learners need to be extremely focused and self-directing or they run the risk of getting lost in the material.

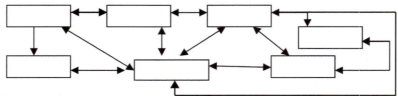

Figure 16.4 Non-linear navigation.

Hierarchical navigation

This has an initial main page (referred to as a home page) branching out into the main sub-sections. People are familiar with this from website design (see Figure 16.5). The deeper levels contain more in-depth and detailed content. In constructivist fashion the learner determines the level of detail required. However, since similar information is streamed together, it organizes the exploration to facilitate meaning-making processes.

Composite navigation

This combines linear and hierarchical structures. It is typical of the structure used in stand-alone CBL programmes (see Figure 16.6). The initial part of the design (the linear structure) provides learners with key concepts and ideas about the topic. Once they have mastered the fundamental principles – perhaps by completing a formative quiz – they advance into the main subject matter. If learners feel competent in the

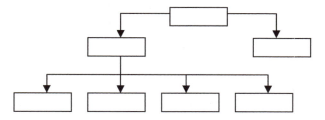

Figure 16.5 Hierarchical navigation.

fundamental principles of the topic, they may go directly to the home page at the top of the hierarchical section. This structure has the potential to support all types of learners, from novices to the more experienced.

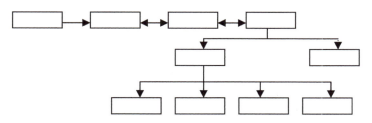

Figure 16.6 Composite navigation.

Interactivity

All of the above navigation methods relate to the way the learner interacts with the material. Interactivity is an important design sub-task because it:

- promotes self-paced learning as learners interact at their own pace;
- allows self-directed learning as learners control navigation;
- increases motivation as learners feel empowered and involved;
- aids retention as learners receive more sensory inputs from multimedia;
- adapts to individual interests as learners can select content;
- adapts to individual learning style preferences as learners can select media;
- supports less confident learners as it allows learners to revisit material;
- encourages creativity as learners can make novel connections and manipulate objects to create their own realities;
- facilitates 'just in time learning' as learners can access information they need when they need it.

Phase 3: Development

This phase is concerned with physically building each of the learning objects and binding them together into a complete, effective and organized whole. As part of the development phase of any CBL programme, sub-system components are modelled or prototyped. This means building a small representation of part of the final system. Prototyping enables users to visualize how the final system will look and how the interface will work.

Instructional objects

Learning objects represent complete instructional events designed to fulfil a particular learning goal or outcome. They are 'self-contained, reusable, high quality learning chunks that can be combined and recombined in courses, learning activities and experiences, and assessments that meet a learner's immediate needs' (Chitwood et al. 2000: 1). Learning objects are developed in accordance with sound instructional strategies and are presented in a variety of different multimedia formats, for example, as a simulation, a video clip, a piece of animation or as larger application such as a help tool.

Modern learning systems make extensive use of multimedia-enriched learning instruction and learning objects, from still images and illustrations, to more complex forms such as pieces of animation, simulation and video often combined with narration, audio clips or voice-over.

Learner control options

Multimedia-enriched learning objects and formats support user navigation and interactivity, encouraging constructivist learning approaches. Learner control options can range from simple navigation icons and hypertext to more complex hypermedia systems and virtual or simulated environments.

Hypertext:	words that take the learner to a new screen when clicked.
Hypermedia:	graphics, images and video-links that lead the learner to other information.
Adaptive hypermedia:	these store information about the learner's preferences so that when accessed at a later date the program dynamically customizes content to meet needs and preferences.
Virtual or simulated environment:	these allow users to interact with authentic learning scenarios and to manipulate them. Simulations are particularly useful in physics or chemistry applications where students can work safely with hazardous substances in a virtual mode.

Phase 4: Evaluation

This involves testing the system by implementing part of or all of the system and collecting learner feedback. By interacting with the system, learners reveal system defects and bring to light misunderstandings between learners and developers.

Formative evaluation

Throughout the entire development process, users are involved in providing designers with essential feedback. Evaluation occurs at the end of each phase. For example, once the original specification is completed at the end of the analysis phase, learners are asked to read through it to make sure that the goals of the program are correct and suited to their needs. Similarly, at the end of the design phase, when paper prototypes are completed, users are requested to assess them for potential errors. At the prototype stage, learners are asked to test the system for usability.

Summative evaluation

The final testing occurs when the completed CBL is placed into a live environment. Users interact with all parts of the system and last minute adjustments are made.

Phase 5: Delivery

This phase concerns itself with provision of technical support. Ongoing maintenance is an essential part of systems delivery and provides information to guide future upgrading.

Key ideas

- Blended learning combines a range of delivery media, class-based, distance and self-directed learning.
- It might be better termed 'blended teaching and learning'.
- Blended learning evolved from business e-learning and distance learning.
- Blended learning approaches may be self-regulated, pedagogical, mixed, or learning outcome based.
- Advantages include: wider audience, knowledge construction, collaboration, variety of environments, interactivity and reflection.
- Learners need to learn *with* technology rather than *from* it.
- Educators need to understand the CBL and instructional design processes, in order to appropriate them.
- The instructional design process has five phases: analysis, design, development, evaluation and delivery.

Conclusions

This chapter has explored blended learning from its origins in the e-learning originally used in the business and training world, and has shown how it combined distance, face-to-face and independent learning. The chapter stresses the importance of embodiment and the need for face-to-face interaction.

Blended learning may be seen as a technological solution to the problems of learners' access to education. The disadvantages of this approach relate more to values and purposes than to methodologies. If the purpose of education is to promote the just society, then blended learning may not be the answer, since access is confined to the advantaged – those in possession of the technological resources.

The human element in blended learning needs to be preserved. Even as technological advances make enhanced virtual experience possible, it is important that embodiment remains central. Virtual reality is not reality. Embodiment is important; teachers are important.

References

CERI (Centre for Educational Research and Innovation) (2005) *E-learning in Tertiary Education: Where do we Stand?* Paris: OECD Publ.

Chitwood, K., May, C., Bunnow, D., and Langan, T. (2000) Battle stories from the field: Wisconsin online resource center learning objects project, in D.A. Wiley (ed.) *The Instructional Use of Learning Objects: Online Version.* http://reusability.org/read/chapters/chitwood.doc (accessed November 2007).

Clark, R. and Mayer, R. (2003) *E-Learning and the Science of Instruction: Proven Guidelines for Consumers and Designers of Multimedia Learning.* San Francisco, CA: Wiley – Pfeiffer.

Driscoll, M. (1998) *Web-based Training: Using Technology to Design Adult Learning Experiences.* San Francisco, CA: Jossey-Bass/Pfeiffer.

Glaser, R. (1963) Instructional technology and the measurement of learning outcomes: some questions, *American Psychologist*, 18(8): 519–21.

Hix, D. and Hartson, H. (1993) *Developing User Interfaces: Ensuring Usability Through Product & Process.* New York: Wiley and Sons.

Jonassen, D.H. (1988) Integrating learning strategies into courseware to facilitate deeper processing, in D.H. Jonassen (ed.) *Instructional Design for Microcomputer Courseware.* Hillsdale, NJ, Lawrence Erlbaum, 151–81.

Jonassen, D.H., Howland, J., Moore, J. and Marra, R.M. (2002) *Learning to Solve Problems with Technology: A Constructivist Perspective* (2nd edn). Englewood Cliffs, NJ: Prentice-Hall.

McGillen, J. (2006) *How Online Learning can Enhance & Reinforce F-2-F Instruction,* White Paper for ITEC 860. http://itec.sfsu.edu/wp/860wp/F06_860_mcgillen_reinforce_f2f.pdf (accessed 14 Feb. 2008).

Meister, J. (1998) Ten steps to creating a corporate university, *Training and Development*, 52(1): 38–43.

Open University (2007) http://www.open.ac.uk/new/distance-learning.shtml (accessed November 2007).

Pagliaro, L.A. (1983) The history and development of CAI: 1926–1981, an overview, *Alberta Journal of Educational Research,* 29(1): 75–84.

Passerini, K. and Granger, M. J. (2000) A developmental model for distance learning using the Internet, *Computers and Education*, 34(1): 1–15.

Reigeluth, C.M. (1999) What is instructional design theory and how is it changing?' in C.M. Reigeluth (ed.) *Instructional Design Theories and Models: A New Paradigm of Instructional Material*. Hillsdale, NJ: Lawrence Erlbaum Associates, 5–29.

Royce, W. (1970) *Managing the Development of Large Software Systems,* Proceedings of IEEE, WESCON, 26 August: 1–9.

Wang, H. and Gearhart, D. (2006) *Designing and Developing Web-based Instruction*. Englewood Cliffs, NJ: Prentice-Hall.

Wilson, D. and Smilanich, E. (2005) *The Other Blended Learning: A Classroom-centered Approach*. San Francisco, CA: Pfeiffer/John Wiley and Sons.

Chapter 17   The future

Introduction

In the 1970s, the talk was of the leisure society and the way that the decline of work would leave people aimless and dissatisfied. Education would need to move from a concentration on the development of workplace skills to those of leisure and voluntary pastimes (Jenkins and Sherman 1979). That discourse has been replaced by a discourse of postponed retirement. It is always dangerous to make predictions.

However, present social changes have implications for future educational policy and practices, and the future depends on decisions made now. The future is not determined. An exploration of some of the issues raised by change can reveal trends which, once exposed, can be interrogated and challenged.

The nature of change

Throughout history, events have swung one way and then there has been a rebalancing, as in the swings between classical and romantic periods in the eighteenth and nineteenth centuries, or those towards collectivism and away from individualism in the latter part of the nineteenth century. But this is too simple – one movement always undercuts and interpenetrates another. For example, since the 1980s there has been a definite swing in education towards instrumentalism and the knowledge economy, but this is starting to be countered by a re-emergence of liberal values in education (Jarvis and Preece 2001: 222–3).

However, profound transformations have occurred as a result of the interactions between three emerging social phenomena; those of 'individualization', 'networks' and 'globalization'. Individuals may now have their most meaningful experiences in cyberspace, within which they can construct new forms of individual identity by means of 'avatars' (on-screen representations of themselves), engage in cyber relationships with others, and alter the 'nature' of human relationships (Ahlstrom 2007). According to the social geographer Miguel Castells, body bio-rhythms, physical activity, seasonal change and global location become irrelevant because they are not necessary to the network. A culture is created of 'real virtuality' (Castells 1996/1999).

Individualization, networks and globalization are interconnected in a dynamic relationship, each forming and being formed by the other. We explore the nature of these phenomena and, although certainty is impossible, their future has educational implications.

Individualization

According to the British sociologist, Antony Giddens, the Industrial Revolution in the eighteenth century helped develop individualism through the separation of work from private life. New institutional structures such as the workplace and schools developed outside the home, leaving it as a more private space. Within this space, private subjective feeling became possible and developed. This last phase of modernity has furthered the development of individualism, as the decline of traditional social values has created a social disembeddedness. There is now a compelling need for people to construct their own identities and find new means for its expression, rather than being thrown back on types of categorizations that no longer fit. Individuals also require the skill of reflexivity, which entails a reappraisal of the past, self-awareness in the present, and projects for the future in order to give themselves a strong sense of self-identity (Giddens 1991).

Individualization and education

Traditionally, education was seen to have a socializing function, inducting individuals into the roles expected of them by society (Durkheim 1956). But as society is no longer homogeneous, this suggests a different focus for education – that of the recognition and celebration of individualism as part of the strengthening of identity. There are many indications of the promotion of individualization as a modern aim of education. These include:

- an emphasis on self-expression in learner's writing and literature;
- the promotion of personal projects in education;
- an emphasis on the learner's individual psychology;
- an emphasis on the individual learner's strengths and styles;
- a concern for the development of self-esteem in learners;
- a promotion of learner reflection and reflexivity and the development of reflexive tools.

Not all of these emphases on individualism arise from responses to social fragmentation. The recognition and celebration of learner difference may also arise from equality and diversity agendas in a pluralist society.

The network society

The 'network' represents a new form of social organization that has emerged since the mid-1980s. There are many reasons for the growth of networks, among them a decline in state power, the spread of capitalism and the growth of digital communication systems. We talk commonly about computer, family, social, political, terrorist or media networks (Kelly 1998: 3–5). Such networks operate across distance, their structures are not obvious, and they have the power to make connections in any number of different ways, as hyperlinks do. One feature of networks is that they are inclusive in the way that information flows between members, and exclusive in ensuring that information and knowledge stays within the network. It is not surprising to find that the metaphor of the network is used as a form of knowledge representation in a number of disciplines, replacing an older computer hardware model. In cognitive science, connectionist networks are widely used to represent and explain cognitive activity (Bruning et al. 2004: 60).

The network society is underpinned by the revolution in information communication technology. This began with the rise of the personal computer and continued through the development of the Internet, the World Wide Web and increasingly sophisticated software applications for communication and information exchange. The future is likely to include the experiences of multiple realities, sentient robots or computers, and the translation of vicarious into immediate experience.

Networks and education

Educational networks have always existed, connecting groups of scholars who communicate together in scholarly activity and publication across institutions and countries. Such scholarly groups may share their research and expert knowledge without the necessity for physical contact.

Modern ideas of educational networks are shown in 'communities of practice' in which practitioners can actively create and share knowledge. In communities of practice, knowledge is always 'situated', not necessarily within a specific location, but always within a culture and a background. Knowledge is not pre-existing, but constructed from the practices of the group. The community confers identity on its members; to be excluded from the community is to be excluded from the knowledge the network constructs, and to possess no community identity. Power is dispersed or shared between the group members, rather than in a hierarchical or top-down fashion (Wenger 1998: 4).

There are many implications of seeing education as comprising communities of practice, not least for the traditional power of the teacher.

An unforeseen type of educational networking is shown by Internet sites such as 'Rate my teacher' which are constructed by school children and students to provide their own evaluations of schools and teaching. Such sites, which have sprung up in many countries, are almost impossible to control and show the effective ways in which networks can operate to subvert formal systems in the interests of the members.

The value of networks lies in their power to:

- connect groups of learners and practitioners separated by distance;
- disseminate power throughout the network to create more equal relationships between learners and teachers;
- confer identities on learners;
- create instantaneous communication-flows;
- actively construct and disseminate knowledge.

The dangers of educational networking lie in:

- the ability of the network to exclude outsiders from knowledge;
- the possibilities of illusion and deception created by virtuality;
- the difficulty of monitoring and regulating networks;
- privacy issues in relation to membership of networks.

Globalization

The other major and most obvious social phenomenon is that of globalization. The global economy, which acts as another form of network, this time at a macro-level, is self-expanding, unregulated and uncontrollable. It began as an economic network reflecting a form of advanced capitalism, but now stretches beyond economics to affect all aspects of social life (Giddens 1998: 30–1). As in other networks, power is dispersed between competing markets, often in the form of multinational corporations that operate globally, and now have more power than nation states (Beck 2000).

Globalization and education

The influx of market forces and the colonization of education by business practices are shown in many ways. Educational institutions are beginning to act more like corporations as they adopt the discourse of 'customers', 'markets' and 'efficiency'. Conversely, corporations are themselves beginning to take over educational enterprises. For example, large multinational companies like Motorola are now creating their own universities which can be used to disseminate precisely the training and knowledge that the corporation requires (Jarvis and Preece 2001: 220–1). In 2008 the MacDonalds fast-food chain gained British government approval to offer its employees awards equivalent to an A level or advanced diploma level (BBC 2008).

The characteristics of the corporate educational institution are that it:

- identifies internal and external markets:
  - *internal markets:* units or academic departments;
  - *external markets:* learners, parents, communities, government agencies;
- packages knowledge, educational programmes and services as commodities;
- distributes resources competitively;
- measures educational effectiveness by the achievement of targets;
- operates bureaucratic top-down rather than collegial management systems;
- sells a share of the educational enterprise to external investors.

The educational corporation:

- may operate virtually, on a global basis, with no physical location;

- combines work-based, professional training with education;
- cooperates with educational institutions on equal terms;
- devises its own curricula and programmes of study;
- may admit external learners as customers;
- awards certification and credits to its learners;
- blurs the boundaries between education and business.

In the future there is likely to be a further merging of corporations and educational institutions as the commodification of education continues and spreads to all sectors of education. The use of online and blended learning processes will facilitate this process.

The other aspect of globalization which has already had a marked effect on education is that of the discourse of lifelong learning. According to this discource, workers will need to upskill on a continuous basis, as knowledge is transformed, in order that companies, regions and states can maintain their competitive advantage. Lifelong learning is not simply concerned with the workplace and workplace training – it affects all educational providers and all types of provision (Kogan 2000: 341–59), though the extent to which it acts as a catchphrase to justify economic imperatives is debateable.

Knowledge itself has become the main commodity for exchange – the World Trade Organization (WTO) has recently categorized education as a tradable commodity – which has far-reaching implications for learners, or 'customers' as they are increasingly known. If education is a commodity, it must be like other products and be accountable to the shareholders who own it. Education as a commodity therefore has had to standardize its products in the interests of the market and its major shareholders, the consumers and providers. In higher education, a proliferation of private providers has led in many countries to greater student choice, but also to the potential for lowered educational standards.

The commodification of education has affected all levels of the educational system. In school systems, market forces have led to consumer choice in relation to educational provision. For example, the British school system under the 'New Right' Conservative government in the 1980s responded to the demand for parental school choice and an open educational market. This led to the need for educational transparency in the form of school league tables and the assessment of school performance on the basis of Standard Attainment Testing (SAT) of students. This publication of performance indicators meant that schools wanted to attract only the clever or the academically motivated. The net result was, 'It is not what the school can do for the child that counts, but what the child can do for the school' (Gerwirtz 2001: 176).

Implications for the teacher

The social forces involved in individualization, networking and globalization work together in a dynamic way to change the nature of social and individual life. The teacher has always been intimately involved in the life of society and of the individual learner, so the transformations that are occurring in both have many implications for the teacher.

Individualization

The traditional frames within which identity has been constructed in the past – home, school and peers – have all been weakened by the fragmentations occurring in society, and the teacher needs to be aware of these larger social processes in order to respond. Identities are now being formed in different ways, and the teacher will have no control over those identities that people wish to create. A world of multiple identities and virtuality makes the relationship between appearance and reality quite problematic. This is reminiscent of the theory of radical constructivism discussed in Chapter 4, which claims that the extent to which our knowledge reflects external reality cannot be determined (von Glaserfeld 2007).

One area where the teacher may be able to exert some influence is in helping learners develop a critical awareness of globalizing market forces. For instance, people use their bodies as 'identity projects' to express status, affiliation, and control over their lives (Giddens 1991). Body image transformations in the form of dieting, exercise, tattooing, and surgery are very common. Education should help people to see through promises of transformation, which may not be realizable. Instead, the teacher can promise a different kind of transformation – of perspectives, assumptions and of values, by showing learners how to be reflective and discriminating. Reflexivity too is an important strategy, and teachers themselves need to be reflexive in order to model this thinking skill to learners:

Reflection: thinking with a purpose;

Reflexivity: an awareness of personal involvement in meaning construction.

Networks

In the future, an extension of the individualization of learning, aided by new technologies, will probably sweep away physical classrooms. The organization of learning in large class groups makes few accommodations to personal learning styles and cognitive or cultural differences. However, the disappearance of the classroom leaves a space for communities of learning and practice which could be local, dispersed or both. Visions of a community-centred society have been articulated by the US-based 'Educational Futures Project' in which schools are replaced by an open-learning system where the community itself could be responsible for networks of learning centres of all kinds. These could be formal and informal, in which 'learning trainers', like fitness advisers, could be available to learners on demand (Meighan and Siraj-Blatchford 2003: 309).

Globalization

When we talk of community, we think of local community, but the Internet makes community global. Apart from time zone differences, the experiences of a community on an in-house computer network, and one dispersed in Newfoundland, Beijing and Siberia, is exactly the same. Bourdieu has shown that education reproduces advantage in society (Abercrombie 1984: 31), and more reproduction of advantage can be maintained on a global scale by the more economically advanced societies. Global communities are not likely to include many people in sub-Saharan Africa who lack access to the technology and the economic resources to engage in global exchanges.

Future teacher roles

Based on these trends, we can offer some suggestions as to how future teacher roles might be different to those today.

Teacher role and characteristics

In a globalized networked environment, the teacher could become a 'single point of contact' (SPOC) to mediate between the learner and a multiplicity of networks and of knowledge. Embodiment will still be important, even in a virtual environment. Teachers embody learning and knowledge through their experiences, history, expertise, immediacy and responses to learners.

If knowledge can be accessed in a multiplicity of ways, then learners will choose teachers for their ability to engage, both with the knowledge and the learning. It will require a different set of aptitudes from the teacher, requiring artistry rather than a set of technical skills.

Teachers will have a role in motivating learners through personal coaching, and in scaffolding support learners in their personal projects. Teachers will be freed from knowledge transmission or duplication, to act as critical friends and guides for learners.

Methodologies

In line with individualization teachers will help learners to construct their individual learning plans (ILPs), and to plan relevant curricula. This is undertaken to a limited extent now for special categories of learner, but needs to be extended in a process analogous to that envisaged by Vygotsky in the ZPD discussed in Chapter 4.

Knowledge transfer

It is already apparent that learners are more likely to obtain simple information through the Internet than to ask a teacher, so this role is becoming redundant. More complex knowledge transmission will be the responsibility of communities of practice that construct and share knowledge. The teacher will need to be a participant in such communities of practice, sharing expert knowledge as a valued member, rather than standing outside them. This will entail a more even and equal distribution of power relations within the network.

Cognitive organization

The organization of the classroom environment or the provision of external learning experiences will be unnecessary, since pupils will have more learning experiences outside the school than can be arranged within it. Instead, the teacher will aid in the cognitive organization of learners through modelling and illustrating the explicit communication processes which Habermas claims are vital in the construction of rationality (Habermas 1984). Teachers can help learners to become critical evaluators of knowledge claims.

Assessment

Assessment practices will not concentrate on the teacher's summative or final assessment of learner performance. This places the teacher in an invidious relationship to the learner. Since the nineteenth century, education has carried out society's work by assessing people's fitness for the workplace and for other social purposes. This was not of benefit to the majority of learners who were left with experiences of failure or of mediocre achievement. It also created role ambiguity and conflict for teachers.

Summative assessment and certification could be the responsibility of other agencies not involved directly in teaching or in supporting the learner. The role of the teacher then could be to work with the learner in the joint agreement of learning goals to be achieved, in supporting the learner in their achievement, and in providing feedback.

Key ideas

- The future directions of educational policy generally depend on decisions made in the present.
- The swing to the instrumentalism of the knowledge economy is being countered by the re-emergence of liberal values.
- Current social phenomena that have significant future implications include: individualization, networks and globalization.
- These social phenomena are shown educationally in: the emphasis on individual learner's strengths, styles and needs; the impact of communication technologies and the Internet; the commodification of education and the growth of new educational markets.

- The future role of education should lie in encouraging reflexive and critical thinkers.
- The future role of the teacher should be to embody knowledge, support learners in planning individualized curricula, and assist their cognitive development.

Conclusion

Teachers need to be aware of social and contextual developments in the world; they cannot confine themselves to the classroom or to the abstract reformulation and testing of knowledge. The world enters the classroom on two legs. Already, networks and new technologies are being used in ways that could not have been predicted when they were developed. Predictions of an increase in global market forces could be overthrown by the realities of global warming, but it is better to be prepared for both.

The embodied teacher will still be necessary in the future, in spite of further technological developments and the disappearance of schools as physical entities as we know them. If past experience has shown anything about technological advance and distance education solutions, it is that the technology on its own is always insufficient to support the learner. Somewhere, a person is needed to connect physically, experientially and emotionally to the physical experience of the learner.

Whether in the present or for the future, teachers need to develop or clarify a personal philosophy and a set of values. They may endorse some, and oppose ones imposed on them, with which they do not agree. One of the purposes of this text is to prompt educators to consider and identify their theoretical positions. Discourse with other practitioners and novices in communities of practice can lead to speech acts and the establishment of communicative rationality which can guide shared knowledge construction and rationality.

This chapter shows that the social forces which operate throughout the world are structural and outside the control of individual agency. The social changes we have identified here are creating new forms of knowledge and new ways of experiencing the world. But in the end, there will still be a teacher and a learner however they communicate.

References

Abercrombie, N. (1984) *The Penguin Dictionary of Sociology* (4th edn). London: Penguin Books.

Ahlstrom, D. (2007) Why easy-to-find e-friends cannot be counted on, *Irish Times*, 11 September, http//www.ireland.com/newspaper/frontpage/ (accessed 9 November 2007).

BBC (2008) Online News. http://news.bbc.co.uk/1/hi/education/7209276 (accessed 14 February 2008).

Beck, U. (2000) *What is Globalization?* Cambridge. Polity Press.

Castells, M. (1996) *The Rise of the Network Society*. Cambridge, MA: Blackwell.

Castells, M. (1999) An introduction to the information age, in H. Mackay and T. O'Sullivan (eds) *The Media Reader: Continuity and Transformation*. London: Sage, OU.

Durkheim, E. (1956) *Education and Sociology*. New York: Free Press.

Gewirtz, S. (2001) *The Managerial School: Post-Welfarism and Social Justice in Education*. London: Routledge.

Giddens, A. (1991) *Modernity and Self-identity: Self and Society in the Late Modern Age*. Cambridge: Polity Press.

Giddens, A. (1998) *The Third Way: The Renewal of Social Democracy*. Cambridge: Polity Press.

Habermas, J. (1984) *The Theory of Communicative Action. Volume One: Reason and the Rationalization of Society* (trans. T. McCarty) Boston, MA: Beacon Press.

Jarvis, P. and Preece, J. (2001) Future directions for the learning society, in P. Jarvis (ed.) *The Age of Learning and the Knowledge Society*. London: Kogan Page, 222–3.

Jenkins, C. and Sherman, B. (1979) *The Collapse of Work*. London: Eyre Methuen.

Kelly, K. (1998) *New Rules for the New Economy: 10 Radical Strategies for a Connected World*. New York: Penguin.

Kogan, M. (2000) Lifelong learning in the UK, *European Journal of Education*, 35(3): 341–59.

Meighan, R. and Siraj-Blatchford, I. (2003) *A Sociology of Educating* (4th edn). London: Continuum.

von Glaserfeld, E. (2007) *An Exposition of Constructivism: Why Some Like it Radical*. Italy: Associazione Oikos. http://www.oikos.org/constructivism.htm (accessed 23 August 2007).

Wenger, E. (1998) *Communities of Practice: Learning, Meaning and Identity*. Cambridge: Cambridge University Press.

Glossary

Accommodation The adaptation of existing schema in the light of new information.

Accretion The cognitive process by which repeated experience is generalized as schemata.

Activity learning Learning from action rather than transmission.

Advance organizer Ausubel's theory that meaningful learning of new knowledge builds upon existing knowledge, and that presenting an overview of that knowledge acts as a means of learning.

Affective domain Area of learning associated with feelings, beliefs and values.

Agency A concept in sociology concerned with people's freedom to act or to choose.

Andragogy A term popularized by the US educationalist Malcolm Knowles to refer to the art and science of teaching adults.

Aristotle's three laws of thought

The law of contradiction: e.g. *Socrates cannot be a man and not a man at the same time.*

The law of excluded middle: e.g. *Socrates is either alive or not alive.*

The law of identity: e.g. *Socrates is Socrates.*

Assimilation The incorporation of new information into existing schema.

Assistive technologies (**AT**) Technologies which support individuals who face major barriers to an inclusive education, e.g. Braille books, speech reading technologies, etc.

Attention The cognitive process of selectively concentrating on one thing while ignoring others.

Attribution theory The theory explains how people account for their successes or failures. People generally attribute their successes to their own abilities and their failures to uncontrollable causes such as environmental factors.

Automatic processes of attention Cognitive processes which require little attention or effort and are usually outside conscious awareness and control.

Banking model A model of education associated with Freire, which positions teachers as active and learners as passive, as though teachers deposit knowledge into students' accounts.

Baxter Magolda's epistemological development theory Theory of intellectual development claiming that there are four discrete sequential stages in the adult acquisition of knowledge.

Behaviour management The process of changing or strengthening learners' behaviour in order to develop cognitive skills.

Behaviourism A theory of learning which concentrates on behavioural changes in organisms.

Biological age Refers to the body's physical age, which is affected by chronological age, genetic factors, and personal and environmental factors such as diet, exercise and health.

Bloom's taxonomies of learning A typology devised by Benjamin Bloom which proposes three domains of learning – the cognitive, affective and psychomotor – which translate learning into overt observable behaviours.

Bottom-up processing All the information needed for perception, provided by the sensory stimuli (James Gibson 1950).

Brain plasticity The ability of brain regions to vary their usual function, either by compensation or by development.

Bronfenbrenner's ecological model of development A model which suggests that the environment influences individuals' development dynamically by means of economic, geographic, historical, social and political factors.

Bruner's representational modes According to Jerome Bruner, people acquire three major intellectual skills for representing the world: the enactive, iconic and symbolic modes.

Central executive In working memory, the system which controls what enters into STM and decides what will be transferred to LTM.

Chronological age Refers to the time since birth.

Chunking The process of combining separate items of information into chunks, for inputting to LTM.

Classical behaviourism The theory that all learning conforms to observable scientific laws governing behavioural associations and patterns; the learner responds to external stimuli in a deterministic manner.

Cognition All the mental acts or processes by which knowledge is acquired.

Cognitive apprenticeship Rogoff's theory of social learning which emphasizes the collaborative nature of cognitive development by portraying learners as 'apprentices in thinking'.

Cognitive development Piaget's theory that children's active engagement with their environment leads them to construct meaning.

Cognitive domain Area of learning associated with mental activity, like thinking and knowledge acquisition.

Cognitive map The mental coding, storing and accessing of spatial and other information.

Cognitive science The scientific study of cognition.

Cognitivism The study of mental information processing, or cognition.

Communicative rationality Habermas's claim that reason and knowledge are constructed through the social practice of communication, according to the rules of discourse.

Communities of practice Social groups set up to fulfil a particular set of aims and objectives, and with rules for membership and clear differentiation from others.

Competency The ability to carry out a complex task that requires the integration of knowledge, skills and attitudes.

Connectionist models Models which propose that knowledge is not stored as separate units but as connections between different ideas in the network.

Constructivism A broad group of theories that explain knowledge acquisition and learning. For constructivists, learning is an active process, through which learners 'construct' meaning.

Content theories Content theories concentrate on the extrinsic and intrinsic needs, factors and orientations that motivate individuals.

Continuous reinforcement A pattern in which every desirable response is followed by reinforcement.

Controlled processes of attention Processes which require intentional effort and conscious awareness.

Cooley's primary groups Family, peers and community – the three social institutions that play a vital role in shaping human behaviour and functioning, including learning.

Credit-based system A quantification of the student's effort on having achieved specified learning outcomes of a module. A credit equates to a certain number of effort hours.

Criterion-referenced assessment A system of assessment in which learner performance is judged according to criteria specified in stated learning outcomes.

Critical constructivism A category of constructivist thought which emphasizes the importance of people being self-reflective, and being able to think critically about social and cultural conditions.

Critical thinking The process of questioning, challenging and making judgements about existing assumptions and knowledge.

Crystallized intelligence Accumulated knowledge and wisdom.

Cultural awareness Awareness of the ways in which learners' cultural background informs how they construct knowledge and make sense of the world.

Cultural capital Cultural knowledge which brings status and power. According to Bourdieu there are three types of cultural capital – embodied, objectified and institutionalized.

Cultural language codes The forms of language used by different social classes.

Cultural learning A term which can mean both 'learning about a culture' and also 'learning within a culture'.

Cultural reproduction and education Education reproduces culture and habitus, sometimes very deliberately through subjects such as civics, citizenship, and personal and health education.

Cultural stereotyping The forming of inaccurate, simplistic generalizations about a group based on their cultural differences.

Culture From the Latin word 'colere', which means 'to cultivate' or 'to care for'. This means that culture is something cultivated.

Deep and surface processing model A model which proposes that incoming information is processed at different levels. Surface processing simply involves the recall of information. Deep processing involves forming associations between material already held and what is incoming.

Deep grammar Underlying structures of grammar, believed by structural linguists like Noam Chomsky to be innate, not learned.

Deep learning An approach to learning in which students try to understand material by linking it to existing concepts and principles.

Deficit model of disability Posits a category of people lacking some important intellectual or physical quality and requiring remediation.

Differentiation in learning Recognition that all learners are different and may need different forms of teaching and different learning opportunities.

Discourse Structured, coherent sequences of language on a particular topic, either written or spoken. For Foucault, the language and practices of a knowledge field.

Discovery learning A school movement of the 1960s in which children were encouraged to discover the principles of subjects such as mathematics and science through exploration.

Disequilibrium For Piaget, the destabilization of existing mental constructs, which leads to the search for new constructs, and so facilitates learning.

Drive stimuli Needs such as hunger, thirst and sleep which drive behaviour.

Durkheim's model of society Comprises three elements: system, structure and function.

Education A conscious attempt to develop personality in a preferred direction.

Empiricism The view that all knowledge is gained from the senses, brought to prominence in the seventeenth century by the English philosopher John Locke.

Enactive mode The process of learning by performing a task.

Encoding The process of transferring information from short-term to long-term memory.

Enculturation The process by which students are led to understand the needs of their culture, for example, how it is socially organized, what is considered knowledge, and what is thought to be worth learning.

Enlightenment, the An eighteenth-century literary and philosophical movement stressing the importance of reason and the critical reappraisal of existing ideas and social institutions.

Equality Refers to an equal distribution of resources for everyone, irrespective of their needs.

Equity arguments Stress the obligations of the state to ensure justice in the distribution of 'social goods' like education or employment (John Rawls).

Expectancy Individual expectations of attainment with respect to goals (motivation theory).

Experiential learning Learning from active engagement with others and with the environment.

Extinction The elimination of behaviour by removing the unconditional stimulus.

Extrinsic motivators Factors external to learners that motivate them to respond, e.g. high grades, praise or money.

Fluid intelligence Speed in cognitive processing.

Four laws of perception According to Gestalt, the laws of perception are those of proximity, similarity, continuity and closure.

Functional age A definition of people in terms of their actual abilities rather than the length of time they have been alive.

Gagné's instructional events A set of instructor behaviours and learner responses which should occur in every instructional session.

General 'g' intelligence Spearman's theory that there is an underlying general intelligence, also known as 'unitary' intelligence.

Globalization Process by which the world is said to be transformed into a single global (economic) system.

Groupthink A potential effect of group socialization, in which group consensus and conformity overrides objective analysis, in the interests of group unity.

Habit strength The frequency of association between a particular stimulus and response, which leads an organism to choose the response connected to the strongest habit.

Habitus A term used by Bourdieu to describe all manifestations of cultural diversity that are seen in daily practices and behaviours that 'go without saying'.

Hall's high-context versus low-context dimension An index for measuring the manner in which information in a culture is exchanged.

Hall's monochronic versus polychronic dimension An index for measuring the way time is perceived in a given culture.

Headstart Project A US programme of the 1960s which aimed to improve the educational and vocational opportunities for young black children through language enhancement.

Hidden curriculum Refers to values that are not articulated but may still guide the way the curriculum is experienced.

Higher-order processes Processes such as inference, deduction and knowledge of context which are necessary for perception.

Hofstede's cultural dimensions An indexing system that can be used to describe, categorize and compare cultures.

Human rights arguments These stress the entitlement of all citizens to participate fully in social life.

Iconic mode The process of learning by internalizing images that stand for an idea.

Idealism The philosophical doctrine that ideas represent reality which originated with Plato, the third-century BCE thinker.

Inclusivity Acknowledging, accommodating and drawing upon the richness of individual differences to ensure that all individuals can reach their full potential.

Individualism index (IDV) Measures the extent to which the individual is more important than the group.

Individual Learning Plans (ILPs) Plans devised by a teacher or mentor to cater for the specific needs of individual pupils.

Individualization Process whereby individuals have to forge their own identities and biographies (Giddens).

Instrumentalism The view that education should serve a purpose – usually economic.

Instructional design An approach to instruction that attempts to incorporate systematically all the events affecting learning.

Interposition The perception that closer objects obscure more distant ones.

Intrinsic motivators Factors internal to learners that are rewarding in themselves without the need for incentives, e.g. self-esteem.

Keller's ARCS motivational model A model which proposes that motivation includes attention to four categories – attention, relevance, confidence and satisfaction.

Kelly's personal construct theory A technique which enables teachers and learners to identify their own personal constructs and discover their values.

Knowledge economy The concept that knowledge can be treated as a marketable economic resource that gives a nation a competitive advantage.

Labelling The negative categorization of individuals who are different in behaviour or appearance, most often used in relation to perceptions of deviancy, but also relevant to categorizations of disability.

Language The socially shared conventions that govern communication using words, symbols or gestures.

Learned helplessness The psychological state in which individuals have learned that any behaviour they try will fail; thus, they refuse to engage in a task because they assume that they cannot succeed.

Learning A relatively permanent change in behaviour as the result of experience.

Learning outcome An explicit statement of what a learner will be able to do as a result of completing a course of study.

Learning plateau A point at which people learning new material claim to be unable to make progress. One explanation is that there is insufficient material stored in memory with which new materials can link.

Liberal education An education devoted to the study of first principles, or theoretical ideas, for their own sake.

Liberal studies A combined arts subject intended to provide students with general cultural knowledge. A descendent of 'liberal education', it generally includes the study of languages, literature, history and philosophy.

Life course The sequence of events and experiences from birth to death, and their related physical and psychological states.

Lifelong learning A philosophy based on the importance of providing learning opportunities throughout life. It is associated with the knowledge society and economic agendas.

Loci of foci A method of memory cueing supposedly invented by the ancient Greek poet Simonides, who remembered the names of those killed in a fire in a banqueting hall by memorizing where they had been sitting at dinner.

Locus of control Refers to people's beliefs about the extent to which they have control over their own situations or desires.

Long-term memory (LTM) Memory which can store very large amounts of data for a very long time. Information held in LTM is encoded in schemata.

Long-term orientation (LTO) Measures the extent to which people attach importance to a long-term future rather than to tradition or the past or present.

Masculinity index (MAS) Measures the extent to which the roles of men and women are distinct with little or no overlap.

Maslow's hierarchy of needs Maslow's theory that motivation is based on three types of basic human needs – physiological, social and cognitive/existential.

Mastery learning The statement of educational objectives and their translation into learner behaviours in order to generate criteria for assessment grades.

McGregor's X and Y Theory Two contrasting, stereotypical management styles described by McGregor, which reflect teaching styles based either on praise or reproof.

Meaning schemes Sets of beliefs, attitudes and emotional reactions which comprise experience.

Mind-body dualism Theory of the French seventeenth-century philosopher René Descartes, that the mind and body are two separate entities, with only the mind in touch with ultimate reality.

Modal Model The view that memory contains two seperate storage systems, STM (short term) and LTM (long Term).

Modularization The practice of dividing a course of study into discrete units to which credits are attached.

Moral development theory Theory associated with Kohlberg which proposes that morality is a process that develops through an individual's life stages.

Motion cues The perception that objects appear to move if the observer is moving (motion parallax).

Motivation From the Latin *movere* – 'to move'. It refers to the set of factors that 'move' people so that they respond.

Multiple intelligences (MI) Gardner's theory that there are eight separate intelligences: linguistic, logical-mathematical, spatial, bodily-kinaesthetic, musical, interpersonal, intrapersonal and naturalistic.

National Qualification Frameworks (NQF)s Systems used in most advanced countries showing the relationship between different levels of qualification, and how each level can be achieved.

Neo-behaviourism A movement in behaviourist theory which includes some attention to mental processing by considering motivation and purposive behaviour in animals and people.

Network society Term used by Castells to describe a new form of social organization created by the Internet, which bypasses space and time.

Neural network model A model which presents knowledge as a web within which memory processes operate.

Normative groups Groups in which learning is concerned with the maintenance of shared values.

Norm-referenced assessment A system of assessment in which learner performance is judged in relation to average or 'normal' group performance.

Object recognition The process by which we recognize three-dimensional objects.

Observational learning or modelling According to Bandura, a means of learning based on imitation of others.

Operant conditioning The process of shaping behaviour by following it with reinforcement that increases in frequency.

Optical flow pattern The perception that images such as the ground or sky flow as the observer approaches a point.

Ordered change framework A framework applied to human development which occurs in an ordered sequence.

Pedagogy The art and science of teaching in general, but used by Knowles to refer to the teaching of children (see Andragogy).

Peer play According to George Mead, play functions as a means for children to rehearse and act out social roles, which encourages them to cultivate a sense of identity.

Perception The process by which we interpret and make sense of the things that are presented to our senses.

Phonics Form of reading instruction in which letter/sound relationships are taught explicitly.

Phonological or articulatory loop An auditory memory store that holds a limited amount of acoustic data for a brief period of a few seconds by means of rehearsal.

Piaget's theory of cognitive development Outlines four predetermined stages of cognitive development in children; sensori-motor, pre-operational, concrete operational and formal operational.

Power distance index (**PDI**) Measures the extent to which people without power accept the unequal distribution of that power.

Praxis The practice and practical side of a field of study, as opposed to the theory.

Principle of induction The process of inferring from particular cases to general rules.

Problem of knowledge One of the most ancient problems in philosophy – that is, how do we know what we know? What is the role of the senses? Is everything we know in the mind?

Procedural knowledge Knowledge that enables an individual to perform certain activities; 'knowing how' to do something.

Process theories of motivation Focus on the cognitive, dynamic and social processes that develop, encourage and sustain motivation in individuals.

Psychological age Refers to the way people cope with and adapt to life situations. The term is also used in relation to intelligence and problem-solving abilities.

Psychometrics The branch of psychology concerned with the design and use of psychological tests.

Psychomotor domain Area of learning associated with mind-body coordination and physical skills.

Psychosocial development theory Theory proposed by Erikson and modified by Peck, that each stage of a person's life requires the achievement of a key psychosocial task, which itself involves the resolution of some crisis.

Radical constructivism A branch of constructivism championed by the US academic Ernst von Glasersfeld which maintains that all knowledge is a process and product of the human brain.

Real virtuality A culture where appearances do not simply communicate experience, but become the experience.

Recalling The process which enables memories to be retrieved from LTM and transferred to working memory for use or output.

Reconstruction The process by which inconsistent experience can cause old schemata to be replaced by new.

Reflexivity Refers to an individual's involvement in a 'reflexive project' – a continuous analysis of past, present and future, undertaken to build a sense of personal identity.

Reinforcement Any event that increases the probability that an associated behaviour will be repeated.

Repetition The pattern in which frequent and contiguous presentation of the stimulus and response is designed to produce an association between them.

Romanticism The literature, philosophy, music and art of the late eighteenth and early nineteenth centuries, usually opposed to classicism.

Sapir-Wharf hypothesis (**SWH**) That language does not simply reproduce, but influences the thoughts and categorizations that speakers make.

Scaffolding Selective help provided by a teacher and gradually withdrawn, which enables students to do things they could not do by themselves.

Schema A mental framework or organized pattern of thought about some aspect of the world such as class of people, events, situations or objects.

Segregated educational provision or 'special education' Specialized facilities for some groups of learners, generally offered in a segregated setting.

Selective attention The process by which we focus attention on one piece of information to the exclusion of others.

Self-efficacy Refers to people's perception and evaluation of their own ability within specific areas.

Self-esteem Refers to people's perceptions and evaluations of their own worth.

Self-talk According to Vygotsky, the internal dialogue that takes place when children begin to use language as a tool for self-regulation.

Semantic memory Individuals' memories for general concepts and principles and for the relationships among them; unlike episodic memory, semantic memory is not linked with a particular time and place.

Semesterization Division of the academic year into two equal parts.

Sensation The process through which information or stimuli from the external environment is held very briefly in sensory registers.

Sensory impairments Sight, sound and motor skill deficiencies.

Sensory memory Memory which can store very large amounts of data for a very short time.

Service learning A means of giving academic credits for work in the community.

Shaping The process of reinforcing behaviour as it becomes more like the target behaviour.

Short-term memory (**STM**) Memory which can store limited amounts of data for a short time. It is sometimes known as 'working memory' because it has several functions such as rehearsal, coding, decision-making and retrieval.

Skill The ability to carry out a particular activity consistently. This ability may depend on physical or mental competence or attitude.

Skinner box Method used by Skinner to demonstrate the effectiveness of positive and negative reinforcement in the training of rats.

Slots Units in schemata that can contain either fixed or variable values.

Social age Refers to a person's attitudes, behaviour and interests in relation to their chronological age.

Social constructivism A category of constructivist thought which emphasizes the role played by society and culture in learning.

Social or person-centred motivation According to Maslow social motivation is placed between intrinsic and extrinsic factors, and originates from people's desire for attention, recognition and acceptance.

Specific learning impairments Severe difficulties in language, reading/writing and mathematics.

Standard Attainment Testing (**SAT**) A system devised to test the aptitude of all pupils in core subjects.

Stimulus and response relationships A stimulus is any event which prompts and organism to respond in a certain way. There are conditional and unconditional forms of stimulus and response.

Surface learning An approach to learning in which students simply remember facts, which promotes neither understanding nor retention.

Symbolic mode The process of learning through abstract and reflective thinking.

Symbolic violence According to Bourdieu, any actions or expectations that privilege or reinforce the status of one class over another.

Systematic doubt The philosophic, method expounded by René Descartes in which everything in the universe was questioned, until he came to something he could not doubt.

Teleology Philosophical doctrine that emphasizes the purpose or end of development.

Texture gradient The perception that closer objects appear more textured than distant ones.

The 'technical-rational' model A curriculum model developed for the US school system by Ralph Tyler (1949), based on an analysis of the ways in which educational material could be broken down into discrete elements, and sequenced in the appropriate order for presentation to learners.

Thinking skills and philosophy for children Two associated movements in the 1980s, which attempted to incorporate critical thinking and logic into the school curriculum.

Thinking together A programme developed in the UK for primary school children, which aims to develop critical thinking through appropriate questioning by peers and teachers.

Top-down processing Contextual knowledge and reasoning processes are used to make sense of sensory output (Richard Gregory 1980).

Transformative learning Theory, developed by Jack Mezirow, to denote the process of individual self-examination, in an effort to develop a deeper understanding of personal experiences or political, social or economic structures.

Trivial constructivism A category of constructivist thought which assumes that the acquisition of knowledge is an individual process with individual outcomes, which depends on personal mental frameworks and processes.

Tuning The process by which new experience causes old schemata to be improved.

Typology of disabilities:

> *Physical* Impairments in hearing, vision, psychomotor and motor skills.
>
> *Cognitive* Perceptual, attentional, encoding and memory disorders such as attention deficit hyperactivity disorder (ADHD), sub-normal IQ.
>
> *Emotional and affective* Aspergers syndrome, autism, conduct disorders.
>
> *Sensory impairments* Sight, sound and motor skill deficiencies.
>
> *Specific learning impairments* Severe difficulties in language, reading/writing and mathematics.

Uncertainty avoidance (**UAI**) Measures the extent to which people wish to reduce anxiety by reducing uncertainty.

Unconscious perception The ability to perceive phenomena to which we are not consciously attending, such as being aware that one's name has been spoken.

University of the 3rd Age (**U3A**) A programme founded in France in the 1970s to provide an informal liberal education for older people.

Utilitarianism The doctrine that the morally correct course of action consists in the greatest good for the greatest number.

Variable reinforcement The pattern in which only some desirable responses are followed by reinforcement.

Variation The process of varying the stimuli in order to produce a more generalized response.

VARK learning style inventory A system which categorizes people as either visual, auditory, read/write or kinaesthetic learners.

Visual illusions Ambiguous images that need to be interpreted on the basis of previous experience and expectation.

Visuo-spatial scratchpad A shorter-term store in which visual images can be examined and manipulated.

Vygotsky's zone of proximal development (**ZPD**) An intellectual space where learner and teacher interact.

Workers Educational Association (**WEA**) Founded in 1898 by Albert Mansbridge, with the aim of providing a liberal education for working-class adults (now the UK National Institute of Adult Continuing Education, NIACE).

Workplace groups Groups based in the workplace which take responsibility for professional and vocational learning.

Young Men's Christian Association (**YMCA**) A movement which was founded in London in the 1840s to serve the minds, bodies and spirits of young working men.

Index

Locators shown in *italics* refer to figures and tables.

ABA (Applied Behaviour Analysis), 33
Abelson, R., 43
Abercrombie, N., 72–3
access and participation, as element in understanding of adult education, 133–4
acquisition and development, language
child stages and process of, 189–91, *189–90*
significance for evidence of cognitive activity, 37
administration, curriculum
as reflection of values within education, 150–51
see also planning, curriculum
adult education
definitions, 128–9, *129*
educational implications of theories of, 136–9
history of, 129–31
influence of community movements on, 134–5
theoretical and practical concerns surrounding capacity of, 133–6
theories supporting development of, 131–3
adults and adulthood
educational implications of theories of development during, 124–5, *125*
theories of development during, 120–21
see also old age
advantage, educational
impact of social class on, 73–4
structure vs. agency as element of, 72–3
'affective domain' (Bloom), *28*
age and ageing
as element of lifecourse development, 115–16
theories of, 118–23, *119, 120, 121–2*
see also old age
agency vs. structure, as element of educational advantage, 72–3
America (United States)

evolution of adult education within, 130–31
analysis, as element in instructional design, *232*, 233
andragogy
educational implications for adult education, 137
theory of as influence on adult education, 131–2
Animating Principles (Aristotle), *16*
Applied Behaviour Analysis (ABA), 33
'apprenticeship in thinking' (Rogoff), 60
ARCS model of motivation, 162, 164–5
Aristotle, 11, 15–17, 143
assessment, student
as reflection of values within education, 150
future teacher roles, 249
influence of behaviourist theory, 31–2, *32*
associate network models of memory retrieval, 47–8, *48*
Atkinson, R., 36, 45
attention
characteristics as cognition process and principle, 40–41, *42*
educational implications of, 49–50
attribution theory of motivation, 161–62
audiences, size and scope as advantage of blended learning, 228
awareness, cultural
educational implications, 87–8, *88*
awareness, self
relationship with body, 172–6, *173, 174*
Ayer, A., 12
Baddeley, A., 36, 46–7, *46*
Bandura, A., 60, *75*, 161
Bartlett, F., 36
Barton, L., 223
Baxter, Magolda, M., 120–21, *124*, 145–6
behaviourism
comparison with cognitivism and constructivism, *55–6*
educational implications, 27–33, *28, 29, 32*

evolution and characteristics, 21–6, *22, 24, 25, 26*
influence on design of instructional models, 233–4
Bernstein, B., 72, 186–7
Binet, A., 97, 100–101, *101*, 102–3, 116
Binet-Simon test for intelligence, 100–101, *101*
biology
as element in understanding of motivation, 155
educational salience in definition of humans, 170
impact on old age and ageing, 115, *121–2*
blended learning
advantages, 228–9
characteristics and history, 227–8
educational approaches to, 228
see also influences eg design, technological
Bloom, B., 13–14, 27–9, *28, 29*, 176–7, *176*, 204–5, *205*
body, human
definitions, 170–72
relationship with mind, 172–6, *173, 174*
salience in education tradition, 169–70
see also personhood
Boud, D., 200
Bourdieu, P., 72, 86–7
brain, structure, function and development, 173–6, *173, 174*, 180, *180*
Broadbent, D., 41
Bronfenbrenner, U., 82, 114, *115*
Brookfield, S., 132–3, 138
Brophy, J., 166
Brown, S., 159
Bruner, J., 57–8, *58*, 63–4, 88, 178
Bruning, R., 194, 196
Brunning, B., 75
businesses, implications of interest in competence-based learning, 212
Camphill Schools, 218
capital, cultural (Bourdieu), 86–7
Carroll, J., *104*
case study, value of educational policies and practice, 48, *48*
Castells, M., 242
Cattell, R., *104*
CBL (computer-based learning), 229
change, social

implications for educational policies, 242–7
implications for teacher roles and practices, 247–9
Child, D., 157, 160, 189
children and childhood
stages of language development, 189–90, *189–90*
theories of development during, 118–23, *119, 120*
Chomsky, N., 13, 37, 190
chronological age and ageing , 115
citizenship, as reflection of values within education, 149
Clark, R., 235
class, social
and educational advantage, 73–4
see also type eg working classes
classrooms
educational implications of language usage within, 192–6, *195*
teachers role within, 30, *30*
Cleary, L., 90
Coady, M., 130–31
codes, cultural language, 186–7
cognition
educational implications of culture on, 89–90
impact in old age, *121–2*
influence on and function in language usage, 186, 188–91, *189–90*
in relation to motivation theories, 155, 160–62
processes involved, 37–46, *37, 39, 40, 42, 44, 45*
theories of, 118–20, *119*
see also development, cognitive and psychosocial; intelligence
'cognitive domain' (Bloom), *28*
Cognitive Taxonomy of Learning (Bloom), 13–14
cognitivism
characteristics and developmental influences, 36–7, *37*
comparison with behaviourism and constructivism, *55–6*
educational implications, 48–51
Cohen, L., 160, 192
Cohen, R., 200
Colby, A, 118
collaboration, as advantage of blended learning, 228
communication

salience in Habermas's theoretical
investigations, 62
communities, learning
function and influence on learning
experiences, 77
communities, rural
evolution of Scandinavian adult
education within, 130
competence-based learning
definition and characteristics, 203–5,
203, 204, 205, 206
educational implications, 209–13, *120,
212, 213*
competition vs. cooperation
as cognitive style, 90
computer-based learning (CBL), 229
'computers'
use of term to explain cognition, 37,
37
conditioning, classical and operant
characteristics and educational
implications, 21–6, *22, 24, 25*
conflict, cognitive
and ideas of Piaget, 57
constructive alignment approach to
competence-based learning, 211–12,
212
constructivism
comparison with cognitivism and
behaviourism, *55–6*
educational implications, 62–5
influence on design of instructional
design models, 234–5, *234*
types and characteristics, 56–62, *58*
content theories of motivation, 155–60,
156, 158, 159
continuing professional development
(CPD), 135–6
control, learner
as element in instructional design
models, 238
Cooley, C., 69–72, *70*
Cooper, M., 134
cooperation vs. competition
as cognitive style, 90
CPD (continuing professional
development), 135–6
Craik, F., 47
Crick Report (1998), 149
critical constructivism, 60–62
crystallized intelligence, 122–3
'cultural dimensions' ((Hofstede and
Hall), 84–5
cultural learning

educational implications, 87–92
theories shaping, 82–7, *83*
culture
definition and characteristics, 83, *83*
impact on ethnicity, 92
impact on motivation, 90–91
impact on stereotypes and
stereotyping, 91–2
implications of cognition and
knowledge upon, 88–90
influence on learning, 82–7, *83*
see also values
see also outputs illustrating *eg* language
Culture of Education (Bruner), 58
curricula
implications of intelligence theories,
107–8, *107–8*
see also administration, curriculum;
planning, curriculum
cyclical experiential learning, 202, *202*
Darwin, C., 155
Davey, G., 101
Davis, J., 222
Deci, E., 158–9
deep and surface processing model of
memory retrieval, 47
deficit model of disability, 217–19
delivery, as element in instructional
design models, *232*, 239
Descartes, R., 8, 10, 11, 155
design, curriculum
implications of teleology upon, 17
design, instructional (ID)
characteristics and scope, 230
models of, 231–9, *232, 234, 236, 237*
design, technological
usefulness in blended learning,
230–31, *231*
determinism, reciprocal, 74–5, *75*
development
as element in instructional design,
232, 237–8
characteristics and theorists of
philosophy of, 15–17
human lifecourse *see* lifecourse, the
development, cognitive and psychosocial
Erikson's theories, 116–17, *117*
Peck's theories, 117–18, *117–1*
Piaget's theories, 57
see also intelligence
Dewey, J., 130, 144, 201
dimensions, cultural (Hofstede and Hall),
84–5
disability

history of perceptions of, 216–17
models and typologies of, *216,* 217–19
see also discourses eg inclusivity and
    inclusion, social
see also influences upon perceptions eg
    labels and labelling; language
Discipline and Punish (Foucault), 61, 171
discussion, student-teacher
    educational implications of, 193–4
distance education, 179
diversity, cultural
    suggestions for teacher
      implementation, 92–4
domains, learning and behavioural
    (Bloom), 27–9, *28, 29*
'drives'
    characteristics as element of classical
      conditioning, 23–4, *24*
dualism, as element in understanding of
    motivation, 155
Durkheim, E., 68–9
Dweck, C., 162
Ebbinghaus, H., 36
economics, as determinant of value of
    learning, 144–5
education
    implications of values within, 149–51
    meaning and purpose, 142–6
    salience of concept of human body,
      169–70
    see also learning; philosophy,
      education
    see also influences upon eg awareness,
      cultural; class, social; families;
      motivation; peers
see also types eg adult education; distance
    education; guided education; inclusive
    education; liberal education; social
    education; special education
efficacy, self
    influence on motivation, 161
Emile et Sophie on les Solitaires (Rousseau),
    14
empiricism, characteristics and
    educational implications, 12–14
encoding
    characteristic as cognition process and
      principle, 41–3, *44*
enculturation, educational implications,
    88
Enquiry Concerning Human Understanding
    (Hume), 12
environments, learning

multi-media nature as advantage of,
    229
significance for successful learning,
    177–8
epistemological development, theory of
    (Baxter Magolda), 120–21, *124,* 145–6
equality and equity, educational
    influence on expectations and
      experiences, 177–8
Erikson, E., 116–17, *117*
Essay Concerning Human Understanding
    (Locke), 12
Esser, J., 71
ethnicity
    and theories of intelligence, 106
    educational implications of culture on,
      92
evaluation, as element in instructional
    design models, *232,* 238–9
evolution, human
    and acquisition of language, 190–91
exchanges, question and answer
    educational implications of
      teacher-student exchange, 193
expectancy theory of motivation, 160–61
expectations, human
    influence of educational equality,
      177–8
experience (philosophical category)
    characteristics and theorists, 11–15
experiences, human
    educational implications for learning,
      177–80, *180*
    educational implications of primary
      and secondary, 206–7
experiential learning
    definition and characteristics,
      199–200, *200*
    educational implications, 205–9, *209*
    theories of, 200–203, *201, 202*
exposition, teacher-student
    educational implications of, 192
extrinsic motivators, 157–8
families
    educational implications of language
      usage within, 191–2
    influence on learning, 69–70, 76
Feinberg, E., 159
Feinberg, W., 159
Field, J., 128, 135
field independence vs. field sensitivity
    as cognitive style, 90
fluid intelligence, 122

focus, characteristics as element of attention, 41
Foucault, M, 61, 89, 171, 187
Freire, P., 61
Freud, S., 114
friendship, influence on learning, 70–71, *70*
functional age and ageing, 116
functional theories of human development, 118–23, *119, 120, 121–2*
Gagné, R., 165
Gallimore, R., 64
Galton, F., 97
Gardner, H., 104–5, *105*
Gayne, R., *30*
gender, and theories of intelligence, 106, *106*
generalisation, characteristics as element of classical conditioning, 23
Gibson, J., 39–40
Giddens, A., 243
globalization
    implications for educational policies, 245–6
    implications for teacher practices, 248–9
goals, setting of
    salience in relation to motivation and performance, 162
Golby, M., 147
Gopher, D., 41
governments, educational policies as reflection of societal values, 146–7, 148, *148*
Granger, M., 231–9, *232, 234, 236, 237*
Gregory, R., 40, *40*
groups, community
    impact on learning, 71–2
groups, social and peer
    and educational advantage, 73–4
    impact on learning, 69–73, *70*, 76–7
groupthink, influence on learning, 71
guided education, 64–5
Habermas, J., 62, 144, 188
habitus (Bourdieu), 86
Hall, E., 84–5
hardware, computer
    development of in assisting blended learning, 230–31
Hare, R., 143
Hartson, H., 235
Headstart Project (USA), 187
Hebb, D., 100
helplessness, learned, 161

Herzberg, F., 157
'hierarchy of moral development' (Kohlberg), 145–6
'hierarchy of needs' (Maslow), 145–6, 156, *156*, 163
high-context vs. low-context dimensions (Hall), 85
Hitch, G., 36, 46–7, *46*
Hix, D., 235
Hobbes, T., 144
Hofstede, G., 84, 88
Houle, C., 131
households
    educational implications of language usage within, 191–2
    influence on learning, 69–70, 76
Hull, C., 23–4, *24*, 27
humans
    evolution and acquisition of language, 190–91
    theories of development, 57, 116–23, *117–18, 119, 120, 121–2*
    see also body, human; expectations, human; experiences, human
Hume, D., 12
'hygiene factors' (Herzberg), 157
ID (instructional design)
    characteristics and scope, 230
    models of, 231–9, *232, 234, 236, 237*
ideas and idealism (philosophical category)
    characteristics and theorists, 7–11
identity, individual and social
    impact on learning, 73–4, 78
    see also individualization, social identity
ideology, political
    as determinant of value of learning, 144
    influence on language usage, 187–8
IDV (individualism index) (Hofstede), 84
ILPs (individual learning plans), 248–9
imitation (language acquisition), 190
impediment (concept)
    salience in definition of humans, 172
inclusive education
    advantages and disadvantages of provision, 220–222, *222*
    threats to, 222–3
inclusivity and inclusion, social
    educational implications of, 223–4
    in relation to education for disabled, 219–23
individualism index (IDV) (Hofstede), 84

individuality (concept)
  salience in definition of humans,
    170–71
individualization, social identity
  implications for educational policies,
    243
  implications for teacher practices, 247,
    248–9
individual learning plans (ILPs), 248–9
information technology (IT)
  usefulness in blended learning,
    230–31, *231*
innate language, 190
input-process-output model of
  information processing, 37, *37*
inquiry-based learning, 207
inspiration, as element in understanding
  of motivation, 154
institutions, social
  impact on learning, 69–73, *70*
instruction *see* teaching
instructional design (ID)
  characteristics and scope, 229–30
  models of, 231–9, *232, 234, 236, 237*
instrumentalism
  as element in understanding of adult
    education, 135–6
  implications for adult education
    development, 139
intelligence (concept)
  debates over nature and nurture,
    98–100
  definition and evolution, 97–8, *97–8*
  implications of theories of, 107–10,
    107–8
  theories of, 104–6, *104*), *105, 106*
  see also cognition; crystallized
    intelligence; fluid intelligence
  see also test and testing, intelligence
intelligence quotient (IQ), 101–2, *102*
interactions and interactivity
  learner-technology interaction as
    advantage of blended learning, 229
  salience of parent-child interaction,
    59–60
  see also targets of interaction eg
    exposition; listening; reading and
    writing
intrinsic motivators, 157–8
IQ (intelligence quotient), 101–2, *102*
IRE model of teacher-student linguistic
  exchange, 193
IT (information technology)

usefulness in blended learning,
  230–31, *231*
Jarvis, P., 123
Kahneman, D., 41
Kandel, E., 172
Kant, I., 6, 12–13
Keddie, N., 134
Keller, J., 162, 164–5
knowledge
  construction of as advantage of
    blended learning, 228
  educational implications of culture on,
    88–9
  future teacher roles in transmission of,
    249
  salience in Vygotsky's work, 59–60
Knowles, M., 131
Kohlberg, L., 118, *118*, 145–6
Köhler, W., 26, 37
Kolb, D., 202
Kopp, T., 162, 164–5
Körner, S., 13
Kramer, D., 121
Krathnohl, D., *28*
labels and labelling, as applied to
  disability, 217
Lakoff, G., 172
language
  cognitive functions of, 188–91, *189–90*
  educational implications of culture on,
    89
  educational implications of for
    learning, 191–6, *195*
  nature of as applied to disability, 217
  socio-cultural importance and
    function, 184–8, *184, 185*
  see also acquisition and development,
    language
'learned helplessness', 161
learning
  implications of human experiences of,
    177–80, *180*
  implications of language for, 191–6,
    195
  physical enhancement of, 180, *180*
  strategies ensuring successful, 177–80,
    180
  theories of, 68–75, *70, 75*
  see also education; environments,
    learning; outcomes, learning
  see also influences eg culture; families;
    friendship; groups, community;
    groupthink; identity, individual

and social; institutions, social;
peers; play; politics
see also specific subjects eg skills,
psychomotor
see also types eg competence-based
learning; cultural learning;
experiential learning; online
learning
liberal education, characteristics as
implication of idealism theory, 11
lifecourse, the
developmental theories of, 123–5, *124,
125*
pathway of development, 113–16, *114,
115*
theories of, 116–23, *117–18, 119, 120,
121–2*
see also age and ageing
lifelong learning *see* adult education
Lindeman, E., 130
Lindoefer, J., 71
listening, teacher-student
educational implications of, 194
literacy, educational implications of,
194–6, *195*
Locke, J., 12
Lockhart, R., 47
'logical thinking'
characteristics as implication of
idealism theory, 10
long-term memory (LTM)
characteristic as cognition process and
principle, 43–6, *44, 45*
educational implications of, 51
see also retrieval, memory
long-term orientation (LTO) (Hofstede),
84
low-context vs. high-context dimensions
(Hall), 85
McGregor, D., 158–9, *158, 159*
management, behaviour
influence of behaviourist theory, 32–3
Marquand, D., 148
Marr, D, 38–9, *39*
Marton, F., 47
masculinity index (MAS) (Hofstede), 84
Maslow, A. 145–6, 156, *156*, 163
'mastery learning' (Bloom), 29
Mayer, R., 235
Mayo, E., 159
Meade, G., 70
meaning, educational implications of
culture on, 88–9
medical model of disability, 217–19

Medsker, K., *30*, 165
memory
characteristic as cognition process and
principle, 43–6, *44, 45*
see also long-term memory; retrieval,
memory; working memory
Mercer, N., 71
metaphors, educational salience in
definition of humans, 172
Mezirow, J., 202–3
MI (multiple intelligences) (Gardner),
104–5, *105*
Miller, G., 36
mind, human
relationship with body, 172–6, *173,
174*
see also memory
modal model of memory operation, 45–6,
45
models
brain information processing, 37, *37*
computer software development, *231*
disability, *216*, 217–19
educational philosophies *see name eg*
technical-rational model of
empiricism
instruction and instructional design,
29–30, 231–9, *232, 234, 236, 237*
learner behaviour *see name and element
eg* 'drives'; taxonomy of learning
memory operation and retrieval, 45–8,
45, 46
see also theories
modes, representational (Bruner), 58, *58*
monochromic (M-time) vs. polychromic
(P-time) dimensions (Hall), 85
Montessori, M., 14
morals
as determinant of value of learning,
143
Kohlberg's theories of human
development, 118, 118
Morris, P., 115
motivators and motivation
educational implications of culture on,
90–91
educational implications of theories
of, 163–6
evolution of theories of, 154–5
theories of, 155–62, 156, 158, 159
movements, community and women's
education
influence on understanding of adult
education, 134–5

movements, learning outcome
evolution and characteristics, 209–12,
212
M-Time (monochromic time) vs.
polychromic (P-time) dimensions
(Hall), 85
multiculturalism, 92
multiple intelligences (MI) (Gardner),
104–5, 105
nature vs. nurture, in relation to
intelligence development, 98–100
navigation, as element in instructional
design models, 236–7, 236, 237
Navon, D., 41
needs, individual psycho-social
relationship with motivation, 159–60
strategies for satisfying, 163–6
needs, maintenance
Herzberg's theory, 157
Neill, A., 14
networks, social
implications for educational policies,
243–5
implications for teacher practices,
247–8, 248–9
Newman, J., 11
Newman, J.H., 145
noumena (Kant), 12
Nuffield Mathematics Project, 63
nurture vs. nature, in relation to
intelligence development, 98–100
nutrition, influence on intelligence
development, 100
old age
educational implications of theories of
development during, 124–5
theories of development during,
121–3, 121–2
see also age and ageing
online learning, 179
outcomes, learning
educational movements involved in,
209–12, 212
influence of behaviourist theory, 31
parents and parenting, influence on
intelligence development, 99
participation and access, as element in
understanding of adult education,
133–4
Passerini, K., 231–9, 232, 234, 236, 237
Pavlov, I., 21–2, 22
PDI (power distance index) (Hofstede), 84
Peacock, T., 90
Peck, R., 117–18, 117–18

Pedagogy of the Oppressed (Freire), 60
peers, influence on learning, 70–71, 70,
76–7
perception (concept)
characteristics as cognition process
and principle, 38–40, 39
educational implications of, 49
perception, unconscious, 40
performance, student
influence of behaviourist theory, 31–2,
32
see also management, behaviour
see also drivers eg goals, setting of
see also factors influencing eg praise,
student; punishment, student
personhood (concept)
educational implications for learning,
177–80, 180
educational salience in definition of
humans, 170–71
Phaedrus (Socrates), 9
phenomena (Kant), 12–13
phenomenology, educational salience in
definition of humans, 171
philosophy, education
definition, 6–7, 7
value as field of study, 6
see also specific categories
eg development; experiences,
human; ideas and idealism
Piaget, J., 57, 62–3, 114, 119–20, 119, 120,
189–90, 189–90
Pinker, S., 190–91
planning, curriculum
as reflection of values within
education, 149–50
influence of behaviourism on, 29–31
Plato, 7–8, 9, 143, 144
play, influence on learning, 70
policies, educational
as reflection of societal values, 146–7
case study of, 148, 148
implications of social change on,
242–7
politics
as determinant of value of learning,
144
influence on language usage, 187–8
polychromic (P-time) vs. monochromic
(M-time) dimensions (Hall), 85
Porter, R., 89–90
power
as element in understanding of adult
education, 134–5

educational implications for adult
education, 138–9
educational salience in definition of
humans, 171
salience in Foucault's theoretical
investigations, 61
power distance index (PDI) (Hofstede), 84
practice, reflective
as advantage of blended learning, 229
educational implications of, 208–9,
209, 210
practices, teachers and teaching
as reflection of societal values, 147–8,
148
case study of, 148, 148
implications of globalisation, 248–9
implications of intelligence theories,
107–8, 107–8
implications of social networks and
identity, 247, 248–9
practices within classrooms, 30, 30
see also specific influences
eg globalization; individualization,
social identity; networks, social
see also specific practices
eg discussion; exchanges, question
and answer; exposition; listening
praise, student
as motivator, 165–6
praxis, salience in Freire's theoretical
investigations, 61
problem-based learning (PBL), 207
processes, controlled and automatic
characteristics as element of attention,
41
processing, bottom-up and top-down
characteristics as element of
perception, 39–40, 40
process theory of motivation, 160–62
psychological age, 116
psychological theories of learning, 73–5,
75
psychology, experimental
evolution and characteristics as
influence on cognitivism, 36–7, 37
'psychomotor domain' (Bloom), 29,
204–5, 205
P-time (polychromic time) vs.
monochromic (M-time) dimensions
(Hall), 85
'punishment' (Skinner), 25
punishment, student
as motivator, 165–6
Putnam, D., 149

questioning, Socratic, 9
race
and theories of intelligence, 106
educational implications of culture on,
92
rational experiential learning, 201
Rawls, J., 146–7
reading, student
educational implications of, 194–5,
195
recognition, object and pattern
characteristics as element of
perception, 38–9, 39
recognition of prior learning (RPL), 211
reflection (concept)
as advantage of blended learning, 229
educational implications of, 208–9,
209, 210
reflective experiential learning, 201–2
'reinforcement' (Skinner), 22, 25
religion, as determinant of value of
education, 143–4
reproduction, cultural
and education, 86
Republic, The (Plato), 9, 144
Resenzweig, M., 174
responses, conditional and unconditional
(Pavlov), 22
retrieval, memory
processes and principles, 46–8, 46, 48
Ribot's Law, 122
Riegel, K., 121
Rist, R., 72
Ritalin drug, 180
Rogers, C., 147, 159–60
Rogoff, B., 60
romanticism, characteristics and
educational implications, 14–15
Rousseau, J-J., 14, 69, 169
RPL (recognition of prior learning), 211
Rules on the Equalization of
Opportunities for Persons with
Disabilities (UN), 220
Ryan, R., 158–9
Säljö, R., 47
Samovar, L., 89–90
sanctions, student
as motivator, 165–6
Sapir-Wharf hypothesis (SWH), 188
'scaffolding'
educational implications of, 64–5
Scandinavia, evolution of rural adult
education within, 130
Scarr, S., 99

Schank, R., 43
schemata, characteristics as element of
  encoding, 42–3, 44
Schön, D., 201–2
schools and schooling
  educational implications of language
    usage within, 192–6, *195*
  influence on intelligence
    development, 100
  teachers role within, 30, *30*
  segregation, advantages and
    disadvantages in education for
    disabled, 218–19
self-awareness, relationship with body,
  172–6, *173, 174*
self-efficacy, influence on motivation,
  161
self-esteem,
  impact on learning, 78
  influence on motivation, 161
sensation
  characteristics as cognition process
    and principle, 38
  educational implications of, 50
service, community
  as reflection of values within
    education, 149
Shiffrin, R., 36, 45
short-term memory (STM)
  characteristic as cognition process and
    principle, 43–6, *44, 45*
  see also retrieval, memory; working
    memory
Simon, T., 100–101, *101*
'single point of contact' (SPOC), 248
skills, transferability as element of
  competence-based learning, 212–13,
  213
skills, psychomotor
  learning and development of, 13–14,
    27–9, *28, 29*, 176–7, *176*
Skinner, B., 24–5, *25*, 27, 29–30, 32–3, 37
social age and ageing , 115
social constructivism
  characteristics, 69–60
  educational implications of ideology
    of, 64–5
social education, 68–74, *70*, 75
society (concept)
  as determinant of value of learning,
    144
  impact on learning, 68–75, *70, 75*
sociological theories of learning
  characteristics, 68–73, *70*

educational implications, 75–8
educational salience in definition of
  humans, 171
influence on language usage, 184–8,
  184, 185
Socrates, 7–8, 9
software, computer
  development of in assisting blended
    learning, 230–31
Spearman, C., 104, *104*
special education, 218–19
spheres, learning (Bloom), 27–9, *28, 29*
SPOC ('single point of contact'), 248
Stanford-Binet test for intelligence, 102–4
Stanford University, 102–3
statements
  analytic and synthetic (Ayer), 12
  learning outcome, 211
Steiner, R., 14
Stern, W., 101–2
stereotypes and stereotyping
  as applied to disability, 217
  educational implications of culture on,
    91–2
STM (short-term memory)
  characteristic as cognition process and
    principle, 43–6, *44, 45*
  see also retrieval, memory; working
    memory
structure vs. agency, as element of
  educational advantage, 72–3
students
  educational implications of
    student-teacher exposition, 192–4
  educational implications of
    student-teacher listening, 194
  educational importance of reading and
    writing, 194–6, *195*
  see also assessment, student;
    performance, student
study circles, 130
Sugarman, L., *114, 117*
SWH (Sapir-Wharf hypothesis), 188
'symbolic violence' (Bourdieu and
  Berstein), 72
Tajfel, H., 73
talk, student-teacher
  educational implications of, 193–4
'taxonomy of psychomotor development'
  (Bloom), 27–9, *28, 29*, 176–7, *176*,
  204–5, *205*
teachers and teaching
  educational implications of
    teacher-student exposition, 192–4

educational values reflected by, 146–8, *148*

implications of social change upon roles and practices, 247–9

importance of presence and practice in successful learning, 178–80

models and theories of, 29–30, 58

strategies to satisfy student motivational needs, 163–6

suggestions for implementing cultural diversity, 92–4

see also curricula; practices, teachers and teaching

technical-rational model of empiricism, 13–14

technologies, usefulness of development of for blended learning, 230–31, *231*

teleology, characteristics and educational implications, 15–17, *16*

Terman, L., 102

terminology, educational evolution of changes within adult education, 128–9, *129*

tests and testing, intelligence characteristics and types, 100–103, *101, 102, 103*

theories of educational implications of, 109–10

Tharp, R., 64

theories benefits of knowledge concerning, 1

psychosocial human development, 116–18, *117–18*

see also models

see also circumstances influenced eg cultural learning; social education

see also subject eg adult education; cognition; development, cognitive and psychosocial

intelligence; lifecourse, the; motivation;

see also type eg behaviourism; cognitivism; constructivism

'theory before practice' characteristics as implication of idealism theory, 8–10

thinking, critical educational implications for adult education development, 138

theory of as influence on adult education, 132–3

thinking, logical characteristics as implication of idealism theory, 10

Thomas, G., 222

Thompson, J., 134–5

Thorndike, E., 22

Tolman, E., 26, 37

transformative learning definition and theorists, 202–3

educational implications for adult education development, 138

theory of as influence on adult education, 132

Treisman, A., 41

trial and error vs. 'watch then do' as cognitive style, 90

trivial constructivism characteristics, 56–8, *58*

educational implications of ideology of, 62–4

Tulving, E., 44

Tyler, R., 29

typologies *see* models

uncertainty avoidance (UAI) (Hofstede), 84

United States of America, evolution of adult education within, 130–31

values (concept) definitions, 142

see also culture

see also subject embracing/reflecting eg assessment, student; education; planning, curriculum; policies, educational; practices, teachers and teaching; society

Verbal Behavior (Skinner), 37

vocationalism, implications of on competence-based learning, 212

Vygotsky, L., 59–60, 64–5, 120, *120,* 186

Walker, D., 200

'watch then do' vs. trial and error as cognitive style, 90

'waterfall model' of software development (Royce), *231*

Watson, J., 23

Wechsler, D., 122

Wechsler Intelligence Scale for Children (WISC), 103, *103,* 109

Weinberg, R., 99

Wilcox, K., 72

Wood, C., 103, 119

Workers Educational Association, 129

working classes, evolution of educational development, 129–30

'working memory' (Baddely and Hitch), 46–7, *46,* 50–51

writing, student educational implications of, 195–6

X and Y theory of motivation
(McGregor), 158–9, *158, 159*
Yao, E., 90

Yeaxlee, B., 129–30
zone of proximal development (ZPD)
(Vygotsky), 59–60

MASTER'S LEVEL STUDY IN EDUCATION

A Guide to Success for PGCE Students

Neil Denby, Helen Swift, Robert Butroyd, Jonathan Glazzard and Jayne Price

- Are you keen to study at Master's level?
- Do you need to understand what is expected from your research and written work?
- Would you like to see real examples of successful Master's level study?
- If you answered 'yes' to any of these questions, then this is the book for you.

Taking a practical approach, this book will guide you through and demystify the process of thinking, researching, writing and achieving at Master's level. It offers an insight into the knowledge, tools and skills that need to be developed for a successful outcome in an educational context.

Using detailed – and real – exemplars, the authors cover the conventions that need to be followed and consider the different elements of Master's level work. Each chapter is supported by appropriate reference to, and extracts from, the three most common types of work undertaken – traditional essay, curriculum package, and portfolio.

Now that the DCFS plans to make teaching a Master's level profession, it is vital that you can develop the confidence in making the transition from H level to M level. The book will enable you to:

- Understand how to prepare, carry out and write a literature review
- Consider the different methodologies and approaches that are inherent in Master's level work
- Understand the nature of Master's level work within education as a research/evidence based profession
- Appreciate the importance of ethical underpinning when working at this level

Master's Level Study in Education is a valuable guide not just for teacher training students but also for their mentors and for teachers in post, undertaking further Professional Development.

Contents: Foreword – Preface – Introduction – Part I: Study skills at Master's level – Writing at M Level: Good practice in essay writing – Reading at M level: Learning to use literature – Researching at M level: Focus, context and rationale – Part II: Research skills at Master's level – Methodology – Methods of evaluation – Developing a critical eye – Part III: Written outcomes at Master's level – Drawing conclusions – Presenting work; focusing on a portfolio piece – Creative approaches to assessment – Part IV: Case study material – Case Study A : Dissertation – Case Study B – Case Study C : Action research – Appendix – Suggested further reading.

2008 240pp
978–0–335–23414–1 (Paperback) 978–0–335–23413–4 (Hardback)

DOING CLASSROOM RESEARCH

A Step-by-Step Guide for Student Teachers

Sally Elton-Chalcraft, Alice Hansen and Samantha Twiselton (eds)

- Are you worried about doing your classroom-based research project?
- Do you feel daunted at the prospect of carrying out a literature review?
- Does the thought of collecting and analyzing data make you panic?

If you answer 'yes' to any of these questions, then this is the book for you!

Written in an informal style, this is the essential, practical and accessible step-by-step guide for all teacher-training students, who in addition to facing the enormous challenge of training to become a teacher, also have to conduct their own classroom-based research.

It contains three sections that mirror the process of doing classroom research. From getting started and choosing appropriate research strategies, to making your findings public, the book covers the whole range of issues to help you succeed with what can seem like a daunting task.

Each of the chapters offers gentle guidance and support at every stage of the research process. Topics covered include:

- The purpose of school-based research
- Guidance on how to carry out a literature review
- Research ethics
- The impacts of research on children's and students' learning
- Methods of data collection and analysis
- Ways of sharing research with a wider audience
- Opportunities for continued professional development

Doing Classroom Research is a must for every teacher-training student.

Contents: *List of figures and tables – Contributors – Foreword – Part I Introduction – What's in it for me? – Moving from reflective practitioner to practitioner researcher – Part II Getting started – Survival skills – Information skills for classroom research – Ethical issues – Reliability and validity – Part III Research strategies – Doing research in the classroom – Intervention, innovation and creativity in the classroom: Using findings to improve practice – Collaborative research – Analysis of data – Part IV Writing it up and making it public – Presenting research in writing – Presenting research in a range of forums – Next steps – Index.*

2008 184pp

978–0–335–22876–8 (Paperback) 978–0–335–22875–1 (Hardback)

DEVELOPING THINKING; DEVELOPING LEARNING

A Guide to Thinking Skills in Education

Debra McGregor

'This highly informative book provides a comprehensive guide to the teaching of thinking skills in primary and secondary education.'
Learning and Teaching Update

It is now recognised that thinking skills, such as problem-solving, analysis, synthesis, creativity and evaluation, can be nurtured and developed, and education professionals can play a significant role in shaping the way that children learn and think. As a result, schools are being encouraged to make greater use of thinking skills in lessons and the general emphasis on cognition has developed considerably. This book offers a comprehensive introduction to thinking skills in education and provides detailed guidance on how teachers can support cognitive development in their classrooms.

Developing Thinking; Developing Learning discusses how thinking programmes, learning activities and teachers' pedagogy in the classroom can fundamentally affect the nature of pupils' thinking, and considers the effects of the learning environment created by peers and teachers. It compares the nature, design and outcomes of established thinking programmes used in schools and also offers practical advice for teachers wishing to develop different kinds of thinking capabilities.

This is an indispensable guide to thinking skills in schools today, and is key reading for education studies students, teachers and trainee teachers, and educational psychologists.

Contents: *List of figures and tables – Acknowledgements – Introduction – What do we mean by 'thinking?' – What kind of thinking should we encourage children to do? – Thinking and learning – The nature of thinking programmes developed within a subject context – The nature of general thinking skills programmes – The nature of infusing thinking – Effectiveness of thinking programmes – Development of creative thinking – Development of critical thinking – Development of metacognition – Development of problem solving capability – Synthesising the general from the particular – Professional development to support thinking classrooms – School development to support thinking communities – References – Index.*

2007 344pp
978–0–335–21780–9 (Paperback) 978–0–335–21781–6 (Hardback)